MEANINGFUL ASSESSMENT

A Manageable and Cooperative Process

DAVID W. JOHNSON
University of Minnesota

ROGER T. JOHNSON
University of Minnesota

ALLYN AND BACON
Boston ▪ London ▪ Toronto ▪ Sydney ▪ Tokyo ▪ Singapore

Series Editor: *Arnis E. Burvikous*
Series Editorial Assistant: *Lauren Finn*
Marketing Manager: *Kathleen Morgan*
Editorial-Production Service: *Omegatype Typography, Inc.*
Composition and Prepress Buyer: *Linda Cox*
Manufacturing Buyer: *Julie McNeill*
Cover Administrator: *Kristina Mose-Libon*
Electronic Composition: *Omegatype Typography, Inc.*

Copyright © 2002 by Allyn & Bacon
A Pearson Education Company
75 Arlington Street
Boston, MA 02116

Internet: www.ablongman.com

ISBN: 0-205-32762-1

Printed in the United States of America

10   9   8   7   6   5   4   3   2   1   06   05   04   03   02   01

This book is dedicated to our wives Linda Mulholland Johnson and Anne Eaule Johnson.

CONTENTS

CHAPTER EIGHT
Observing Students   117

CHAPTER NINE
Assessing Social Skills   147

CHAPTER TEN
Assessing Student Attitudes   168

CHAPTER ELEVEN
Interviewing Students   192

CHAPTER TWELVE
Learning Logs and Journals   201

CHAPTER THIRTEEN
Total Quality Learning and Student Management Teams   214

CHAPTER FOURTEEN
Teaching Teams and Assessment   227

CHAPTER FIFTEEN
Giving Grades   243

CHAPTER SIXTEEN
Involving Students in Assessment   258

The purpose of this book is to provide you with a practical guide to (a) make your assessments more meaningful and manageable and (b) help you use cooperative learning as an inherent part of the assessment process. Read this book carefully and apply its content immediately and often in the classes you teach.

The call for increased accountability of schools has placed an emphasis on assessment. This book presents a wide range of procedures for assessment in a meaningful and practical format that makes them easy to understand. Most of the more powerful and interesting assessment procedures require considerable time and effort to implement and use. Teachers simply do not have the time and energy to use them. Cooperative learning groups provide the setting in which new assessment procedures can be integrated with instruction so that students provide the assistance teachers need. In cooperative learning you can link what is taught with what is measured. The more skillfully instruction and assessment are interwoven in cooperative learning groups, the more students can learn and the more successful the teacher can be.

This book will be most useful when read with one or more colleagues. In reading and discussing this book with colleagues, you are then in a position to help each other implement with real fidelity new assessment procedures in your classrooms. Implementing new assessment procedures, as with all teaching, is like being in love—it always goes better with two.

NATURE OF THIS BOOK AND HOW TO USE IT

This book invites you to improve the quality of your assessments. Acceptance of this invitation consists of two parts:

1. Increasing your understanding of the assessment process and assessment procedures
2. Enhancing your ability to perform assessments

This book contains resources, tools, ideas, hints, and suggestions to enable you to improve the quality of your assessments. If increasing the quality of your assessments seems, at times, overwhelming, use one procedure at a time until it becomes integrated into your instructional routines. Small successes can add up to major gains if you persevere and keep striving to improve.

The purpose of this book is to bring together the theory on assessment and the practical procedures that have proved to be useful to teachers and students. This book focuses on making classroom and school assessments more meaningful and more manageable. Each chapter in this book has a specific purpose and focuses on specific, essential assessment procedures. Assessment begins with a goal-setting conference. Once students' goals are set, students participate in the instructional program. The quality and quantity of academic learning, level of reasoning, skills and competencies, attitudes, and work habits may be assessed by standardized and teacher-made tests, compositions and presentations, individual and group projects, portfolios, questionnaires, and learning logs and journals. The assessment data is used as part of a total, quality learning procedure emphasizing continuous improvement. Teachers participate in collegial teaching teams to ensure assessments are fair and complete. Finally, periodically teachers use the assessment data to determine students' grades.

This is not a book that you can read with detachment. It is written to involve you in its content. Reading this book will enable you not only to learn the theoretical and empirical knowledge now available on assessment, but also to apply this knowledge in practical ways. As you participate in the activities, use diagnostic procedures for assessing your current practices and skills, and discuss relevant theory and research, you bridge the gap between theory and practice.

To use this book you should diagnose your present knowledge and skills in the areas that are covered, read the chapters carefully, actively participate in the activities, reflect on your experiences, and integrate the information and experiences into action theories related to assessment. You should then plan how to implement the assessment procedures and continue your skill- and knowledge-building activities after you have finished reading the book.

ACKNOWLEDGMENTS

We would like to thank Linda Johnson for developing the graphics for this book and Catherine Mulholland and Laurie Stevahn for their help in editing. Their creativity and hard work are deeply appreciated.

CHAPTER ONE

MAKING ASSESSMENT MANAGEABLE AND MEANINGFUL

WHAT IS ASSESSMENT?

Education is not filling a pail. It is lighting a fire.   — *W. B. Yeats*

Aesop tells of two travelers who were walking along the seashore. Far out they saw something riding on the waves. "Look," said one, "a great ship rides in from distant lands, bearing rich treasures!" As the object came closer, the other said, "That is not a great treasure ship. It is a fisherman's skiff, with the day's catch of savory fish!" Still nearer came the object and the waves washed it up on shore. "It's a chest of gold lost from some wreck," they cried. Both travelers rushed to the beach, but there they found nothing but a water-soaked log. The moral of the story is, *before you reach a conclusion, do a careful assessment.* ∎

ACTIVITY **1.1**

Demonstrate your understanding of the following concepts by matching the definitions with the appropriate concept. Check your answers with your partner and explain why you believe your answers are correct.

CONCEPT	DEFINITION
_____ 1. instruction	**a.** Change within a student that is brought about by instruction
_____ 2. learning	**b.** Judging the merit, value, or desirability of a measured performance
_____ 3. assessment	**c.** Structuring situations in ways that help students change, through learning
_____ 4. evaluation	**d.** Collecting information about the quality or quantity of change in a student, group, teacher, or administrator

(Answers: 1. c, 2. a, 3. d, 4. b)

Doing careful assessments is an inherent responsibility of being an educator. Instruction, learning, assessment, and evaluation are all interrelated. Teachers are responsible for instructing students to create learning, which is assessed to (a) verify learning is taking place and (b) improve the effectiveness of instruction. Periodically, assessment is used to judge the quality and quantity of learning and to award grades. Instruction, learning, assessment, and evaluation are so intertwined that it is hard to separate them. In Activity 1.1, match the definition with the appropriate concept. Compare your answers with the answers of a partner, and then explain to him or her how instruction, learning, assessment, and evaluation are interrelated.

ASSESSMENT AND EVALUATION

You can have assessment without evaluation, but you cannot have evaluation without assessment. Ideally, you assess continually whereas you evaluate only occasionally. You can use the information provided by assessments to evaluate

1. **Students.** Grades, honors (such as for National Honor Society, honor's lists, valedictorian), and graduation based on exit criteria (the knowledge and skills students need to be graduated from a program, grade, or school) can be awarded based on assessment data.
2. **Teachers.** Instructional programs can be assessed to determine whether they are effective and whether teachers deserve recognition and merit salary increases.
3. **Schools and districts.** To determine the effectiveness of schools and districts, comparisons must be made to other schools, districts, states, and countries. To make such comparisons, schools have to use the same assessment procedures.

The quality of the assessment largely determines the quality of the evaluation. If the assessment is faulty, the evaluation will be faulty. A valid judgment can only be made if an accurate and complete assessment has taken place.

Assessment, therefore, involves collecting information about the quality or quantity of a change in a student, group, class, school, teacher, or administrator. The effectiveness of an assessment depends on the use of minimal resources to

1. **Achieve the goals of the assessment.** Generally, the goals are to obtain valid and reliable information about the assessees' level of performance. **Valid assessments** actually assess what they were designed to assess, all of what they were designed to assess, and nothing but what they were designed to assess. **Reliable assessments** occur when a student's performance remains the same on repeated measurements.

2. **Maintain effective working relationships among assessors, assessees, and all other relevant stakeholders.** This is an often-neglected aspect of assessment. High-quality assessments result from collaboration among the individuals conducting the assessment, the individuals whose performances are being assessed, and the individuals who have a stake in a valid and reliable assessment taking place. If any aspect of the assessment process damages the relationships involved, the long-term effectiveness of the assessment program is decreased.

3. **Increase the motivation of all involved parties to participate in future assessments.** Ideally, the assessment experience should be such that all participants look forward to the next assessment opportunity. To conduct high-quality assessments, both the assessor and the assessee have to be motivated to ensure that the assessment has valid and reliable results. If any aspect of the assessment process decreases the willingness of the participants to engage in future assessments, the as-

sessment is ineffective. The greater the indifference or resistance to the assessment is, the lower the quality of assessment and the ease of conducting the assessment are.

The effectiveness of an assessment is decreased anytime something interferes with (a) achieving the goals of the assessment, (b) maintaining effective working relationship among assessors, assessees, and other stakeholders, and (c) motivating participation in future assessments.

ASSESSMENT ISSUES

Two central issues in conducting assessments are how to make assessments meaningful and how to make them manageable. To be *meaningful,* assessments have to

1. Be perceived by major stakeholders (such as students and teachers) as having a significant purpose. Significant purposes are tied to the motivation to have the assessment take place. The more significant the assessment seems, the more motivated the assessor and assessees will be to facilitate the assessment.
2. Consist of procedures that are clearly understood. The more clearly participants understand the procedures, criteria, and rubrics used in the assessment process, the more able and willing they will be to facilitate the assessment process and ensure that high-quality assessments take place.
3. Provide a clear direction for increasing the quality of learning and instruction. The more useful the results are expected to be in providing direction to future learning and instruction, the more motivated individuals will be to engage in the assessment.

Unless the purpose is perceived to be significant, the procedures are clearly understood, and the results are perceived to be useful and relevant, the individuals whose performances are being assessed will not do their best and will not facilitate the assessment process. Even high-stakes assessments can be resisted when they are perceived to be meaningless or unmanageable. Yet low-stakes assessments can be entered into with great enthusiasm and effort when they are perceived to be meaningful and easily manageable. (See Figure 1.1.) To be *manageable,* assessments have to provide useful information with the expenditure of minimal resources. Manageability includes whether

1. The available resources are adequate for the requirements of the assessment procedure. Each assessment procedure requires certain resources, such as time and materials. The more resources required, the harder the assessment is to manage. If the required resources are beyond the capacity of the teacher, the assessment is unmanageable unless, of course, the resources of colleagues and/or students are enlisted to help with the assessment.
2. The value of the information obtained is worth the expenditure of the resources. The value of the information resulting from the assessment must balance the resources required to obtain the information.

Manageability depends on the percentage of the available resources needed to conduct the assessment. Available resources have to be allocated to instruction, general classroom management (record keeping, relationships with parents), general school management (faculty meetings, committees), and so forth. From the total amount of resources available for assessment, the amount that each assessment procedure takes determines the likelihood that the procedure is used.

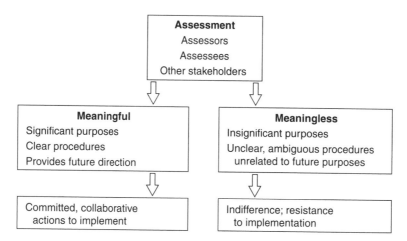

FIGURE 1.1 **Meaningful Assessment**

Power of Involvement

There are a number of reasons for involving students in assessment decisions (Johnson & F. Johnson, 2000). First, involvement tends to increase the quality of decisions by utilizing the resources of students as well as the teacher. In general, high involvement in decision making increases the use of available resources, which in turn increases the quality of the decision. The more students participate in making a decision, the more resources that are available and, consequently, the higher is the quality of the decision about assessment. Students may be interesting resources for planning, conducting, and reporting assessments because they have developed a unique perspective from many, many experiences of having been assessed and should, therefore, be especially involved in making a decision.

Second, involvement tends to increase members' commitment to implement assessment in a high-quality way. Compared with the teacher explaining the assessment procedures and having a student committee help plan the assessment, direct involvement of all students in planning the assessment results in stronger commitment to implement the procedures.

Third, involvement tends to reduce students' resistance to feedback and the need to change. To change in constructive ways, students need timely and specific feedback about their learning progress and their strengths and weaknesses. For many students, teacher-conducted assessments are threatening. Defensiveness by the students can result in resistance to the feedback and rejection of the implications. Teacher feedback can be distorted by the psychological defense mechanisms an individual uses to maintain a positive self-image. If students are involved in planning and conducting assessments, they will be less resistant to receiving and using feedback to decrease weaknesses and to increase strengths.

Fourth, involvement tends to increase student achievement. Assessing classmates' work and giving them feedback on the quality of their efforts has numerous positive effects on achievement. Participating in assessments directs students' attention toward the intended outcomes of instruction. It increases students' understanding of the criteria and rubrics being used. It requires students to learn at the levels of understanding, application, and interpretation (as opposed to just knowledge), thereby increasing their retention and transfer of what is being taught. Explaining feedback to classmates enhances students' understanding of what is being taught. Participating in assessments complements students' learning efforts and increases the likelihood that students learn, retain, and transfer what is being taught.

Fifth, involvement tends to result in greater motivation to learn and more positive attitudes toward learning and assessment. Numerous studies indicate that if you want to change people's behaviors and attitudes, you should involve them in group discussions that lead to (a) public commitment to the new behaviors and attitudes and (b) the perception that all members of the group support the new behaviors and attitudes. Involving students in planning and conducting assessments tends to result in public commitment to complete assignments at a high level of quality and the awareness that classmates are making the same commitment. The result tends to be greater motivation to learn and more positive attitudes toward learning and assessment.

Sixth, involvement tends to increase self-assessment. Assessing the work of classmates helps students gain insight into the quality of their own work, the degree of skill they have in various areas, and any misconceptions they have that need correction. Such self-assessments tend to provide students with short-term goals, to clarify the steps to be taken to complete assignments, and to provide feedback concerning their learning progress.

MEANINGFUL ASSESSMENTS

To plan, conduct, and manage meaningful assessments, you need to answer the following questions:

1. What student performances may be assessed?
2. What assessment procedures may be used?
3. What is the purpose of the assessment?
4. What is the focus of the assessment?
5. In what setting will the assessment be conducted?
6. Who are the stakeholders in the assessment?
7. What evaluation procedure should be used?

In understanding what is to be assessed, you must select the student performances that you want to assess and the procedures you will use. In doing so, you must understand the purpose of the assessment, its focus, the setting in which the assessment will take place, what is at stake, who are the relevant stakeholders, and the evaluation procedure.

Student Achievement Assessed

There is an old saying, "What gets measured gets done." What teachers assess may be the single most powerful message as to what teachers value and wish to accomplish. There are so many indices of student learning that all cannot be discussed in any one book. Given in the following list, however, are some of the most common indices of student learning:

1. **Academic learning.** What students know, understand, and retain over time
2. **Reasoning.** The quality of students' reasoning, conceptual frameworks, use of the scientific method and problem-solving, and construction of academic arguments
3. **Skills and competencies.** Examples are oral and written communication skills, teamwork skills, research skills, skills in organizing and analyzing information, technology skills, skills in coping with stress and adversity, conflict resolution skills
4. **Attitudes.** The attitudes students develop, such as a love of learning, commitment to being a responsible citizen, desire to read, liking scientific reasoning,

self-respect, liking diversity, commitment to making the world a better place, and many others
5. **Work Habits.** The work habits students develop, such as completing work on time, using time wisely, meeting responsibilities, striving for quality work, continually improving one's work, striving to add value to each job one does, and so forth

Assessment is collecting information about the quality or quantity of a change in a student, group, teacher, or administrator. **Performance assessment** is collecting information about demonstrations of achievement involving actually performing a task or set of tasks, such as conducting an experiment, giving a speech, writing a story, or operating a machine. After the intended outcomes of instruction are defined, the procedures used to determine whether they were achieved must be selected.

Assessment Procedures

After deciding which student achievements to assess, you need to decide which procedures to use to determine the extent to which students are achieving the intended learning outcomes of instruction. The procedures you can use include

Goal-setting conferences	Simulations
Standardized tests	Questionnaires
Teacher-made tests, quizzes, exams	Interviews
Written compositions	Learning logs and journals
Oral presentations	Student management teams
Projects, experiments, portfolios	Total quality learning procedures
Observations	Teacher assessment teams
Record keeping (attendance, participation, homework, extra-credit)	Student-led parent conferences

Each of the above procedures is discussed in some detail in this book. Each chapter introduces one or more tools to assess students' learning and addresses the questions:

1. What is the procedure/tool?
2. Why should you use it?
3. How should you use it?
4. How do you adapt (customize) it to your needs?

To decide which student performances are to be assessed by which procedures, you should clarify the purpose of your assessment, whether it focuses on processes or outcomes, the setting in which the assessment takes place, and whether the assessment is of high or low stakes to which stakeholders. Examples of these considerations are listed in Table 1.1.

Purpose of Assessment

To achieve your purposes, you match the student performances you can assess with the appropriate assessment method. The purposes for assessing may be to (a) diagnose students' present level of knowledge and skills, (b) monitor progress toward learning goals to help form the instructional program, and (c) provide data to judge the final level of students' learning.

TABLE 1.1   Assessment of Student Performance

PURPOSE	FOCUS	SETTING	STAKES	STAKEHOLDERS
Diagnostic	Process of learning	Artificial (classroom)	Low	Students and parents
Formative	Process of instruction	Authentic (real world)	High	Teachers
Summative	Outcomes of learning			Administrators
	Outcomes of instruction			Policymakers
				Colleges, Employers

1. **Diagnostic assessments** are conducted at the beginning of an instructional unit, course, semester, or year to determine the present level of knowledge, skill, interest, and attitudes of a student, group, or class. Diagnostic assessments are never used for assigning grades. Information about the student's entry-level characteristics enables the teacher and student to set realistic but challenging learning goals. The better the diagnosis, the more clear and specific the learning goals will be.

2. **Formative assessments** are conducted periodically throughout the instructional unit, course, semester, or year to monitor progress and provide feedback concerning progress toward learning goals. Its intention is to facilitate or form learning. Formative assessments are an integral part of the ongoing learning process for two reasons. First, they provide students with feedback concerning the progress they are making toward achieving their learning goals. On the basis of that feedback, students can plan what they need to do next to advance their learning. Second, formative assessments provide teachers with feedback concerning their progress in providing effective instruction. Teachers can then plan what to do next to help students achieve their learning goals. Formative evaluations are not used to evaluate either the student or the teacher.

3. **Summative assessments** are conducted at the end of an instructional unit or semester to judge the final quality and quantity of student achievement and/or the success of the instructional program. They sum up performance and provide the data for giving grades and determining the extent to which goals and objectives have been met and desired outcomes achieved. The judgments about student achievement are then communicated to interested audiences such as students, parents, administrators, postsecondary educational institutions, and potential employers.

It is on the basis of these assessments that schools are held accountable (see Box 1.1).

Focus of Assessment

Diagnostic, formative, and summative assessments may take place to improve the process of learning or to determine the outcomes of learning. In conducting formative assessments, you may focus on both the process of learning and the outcomes of learning. In conducting summative assessments, you focus primarily on outcomes.

1. **The processes of learning.** To improve continually the quality of students' efforts to learn, you must engineer a system whereby the processes students use to

■ ■ ■ ■ ■

BOX 1.1

ACCOUNTABILITY FOR WHAT?

Schools are under increasing accountability pressures to reexamine the outcomes they are trying to achieve.

1. **The definitions of achievement have expanded.** In addition to doing well on standardized tests, students are expected to be able to demonstrate (a) achievement-related behaviors (ability to communicate, cooperate, perform certain motor activities, and solve complex problems); (b) achievement-related products (writing themes or project reports, art products, craft products); or (c) achievement-related attitudes and dispositions (pride in work, desire to improve continually one's competencies, commitment to quality, internal locus of control, self-esteem).

2. **The organizational structure of schools is changing.** With the change to a team-based, high-performance organizational structure (that emphasizes cooperative learning in the classroom and collegial teaching teams in the building), teachers are expected to work in teams to assess (a) the quality of students' teamwork skills and (b) the quality of the instructional program.

3. **High school and college graduates often lack the competencies necessary to be citizens in our society and live a high-quality life.** Schools are being held accountable to teach successfully what students need to (a) advance educationally, (b) get and hold a job, (c) be a responsible citizen, and (d) have a high quality of life. Many graduates are unemployable, uninformed on current issues, and unmotivated to vote or participate in the political process. They fail to build and maintain stable friendships and family relationships. A fourth-grade teacher may think primarily in terms of getting students ready for the fifth grade, and a high school teacher may think primarily in terms of getting students ready for college instead of preparing students to live productive lives in society.

4. **Many schools are blind to the need to prepare students to compete with graduates of schools in other countries for jobs and promotions.** The internationalization of the economy has resulted in an internationalization of schools. It is no longer enough to be one of the best schools in a local area, in a state, or even in the nation. The quality of a school in the United States has to be compared with the quality of schools in Japan, Germany, Finland, Thailand, and every other country in the world. Schools in the United States have to be educating "world-class workers" and individuals who are able to work for and be successful in international companies that have branches and employees from all over the world.

learn are identified and assessed. Instead of only conducting summative assessments, formative assessments are conducted. The assumption is that if you continually improve the processes of learning, the quality and quantity of student learning also continually improves.

To implement total quality learning, you assign students to cooperative learning groups. Each group takes charge of the quality of the work of its members. The group (a) defines and organizes the process members are going to use to learn, (b) assesses the quality of members' engagement of each step of the process, (c) places the data on a quality chart, and (d) plans how to improve the effectiveness of the learning process.

2. The processes of instruction. To improve continually the quality of instruction, collegial teaching teams (a) define the instructional process, (b) assess the quality of members' engagement in each step of the process, (c) place the data on a quality chart, and (d) plan how to improve the effectiveness of the instructional process.

3. The outcomes of learning. To assess the quality and quantity of student learning, you need (a) an appropriate method of sampling the desired student performances and (b) a clearly articulated set of criteria to judge their quality and quantity. You can use paper-and-pencil tests or you can have students perform a procedure or skill, such as writing a composition or conducting a science experiment.

4. The outcomes of instruction. You assess the effectiveness of instruction by measuring whether the instructional program actually motivated students to strive to learn above and beyond their usual level.

Setting of Assessments

Assessments may take place in artificial situations (such as the classroom) or in authentic or "real-life" settings. **Authentic assessment** requires students to demonstrate desired skills or procedures in real-life contexts. Because it is often difficult to place students in real-life situations, you may want to have students complete simulated real-life tasks or solve simulated real-life problems. To conduct an authentic assessment in science, for example, you may assign students to research teams that work on a cure for cancer by (a) conducting an experiment, (b) writing a lab report summarizing results, (c) writing a journal article, and (d) making an oral presentation at a simulated convention. Like performance-based assessment, to conduct an authentic assessment you need procedures for (a) sampling performances and (b) developing criteria for evaluation (see Activity 1.2). You also need the imagination to find real-life situations or create simulations of them.

Stakes and Stakeholders

There are at least four audiences for the results of assessments of students' learning, instructional programs, and the effectiveness of a school: students and their parents, teachers, administrators, and policymakers. For each of these audiences, assessments can be of high or low importance (see Activity 1.3). In designing and conducting assessments, you must determine who the audiences for the assessment will be and what kind of stake they have in its results. See Table 1.2 for categories of audiences and corresponding assessments.

ACTIVITY **1.2**

List three examples of authentic assessment you have used in your classes:

1. _____

2. _____

3. _____

ACTIVITY **1.3** ■ THE STAKE YOU HAVE IN ASSESSMENTS

1. List the assessment procedures you use.

2. Divide your list into two categories: high stake and low stake.

3. Repeat Step 2 for each major stakeholder in your school.

---

1. Low-stake assessments. Formative assessments of student learning and class-room instruction tend to be low stake because they are designed and administered by teachers for the purpose of giving students feedback and guiding instructional decisions. Students are not adversely affected when they perform poorly on low-stake assessments and teachers are not penalized when a lesson does not go well.

2. High-stake assessments. Summative assessments that may partially determine students' futures or whether teachers receive merit raises tend to be high stake. College admission tests such as the SAT or the ACT are high-stake assessments for students because admission to colleges and universities is affected by these scores. Statewide assessments or some standardized tests are typically high-stake assessments for teachers, schools, or districts, but not students. In some districts, the average scores of different schools or districts within the state are published in the newspaper, which can influence real estate values and are, therefore, high stake for many interested audiences.

The danger of low-stake assessments is that students and faculty may not take them seriously. The danger of high-stake assessments is that students and faculty may be tempted to cheat in some manner.

Methods of Evaluation

Periodically, after summative assessments have been made, teachers assign value to students' work. Teachers can symbolize the value with smiley faces, written com-

TABLE 1.2 Stakeholders in Assessment

STUDENTS AND PARENTS	TEACHERS	ADMINISTRATORS	POLICYMAKERS
Determine student progress	Diagnose students' strengths and weaknesses	Monitor effectiveness of teachers	Set standards
Diagnose student's strengths and weaknesses	Give students feedback	Monitor effectiveness of instructional programs	Monitor the quality of education
Plan how to improve students' achievement	Determine students' grades	Identify program strengths and weaknesses	Formulate policies
Understand what is expected of them in school	Make grouping decisions	Designate priorities	
Make informed decisions about college and careers	Determine effectiveness of instruction and curriculum		
	Decide how to modify and improve instructional program		

TABLE 1.3   Criterion-Referenced Grading

GRADE	PERCENT CORRECT
A	95–100
B	85–94
C	75–84
D	65–74
F	Less than 64

ments, or grades. In deciding how to assign value, teachers must decide whether to make judgments based on a criterion-referenced or a norm-referenced procedure. The **criteria-referenced procedure** assigns a value or grade to a score according to a predetermined standard. Criteria-referenced evaluation is used in cooperative and individualistic learning. The **norm-referenced procedure** assigns a value or grade to a score based on a comparison to other scores. Norm-referenced evaluation is used as part of competitive learning.

Criteria-Referenced Evaluation.   Criterion-referenced or categorical judgments are made by adopting a fixed set of standards and judging the achievement of each student against these standards. Every student who can achieve up to the standard passes, and every student who cannot fails. If the criterion is for students to demonstrate ability to use propositional logic in solving a series of chemistry problems, then a teacher takes each student's answers and judges whether they have done so. A common version of criterion-referenced evaluation involves assigning letter grades on the basis of the percentage of test items answered correctly. Table 1.3 provides an example.

Criterion-referenced evaluation was first recommended as part of mastery or competency-based instruction in the 1920s and was widely used in the 1930s. Yet in the 1940s and 1950s its use declined. In the 1960s, however, a revival of interest in criterion-referenced evaluation resulted from the increased emphasis on behavioral objectives, from the sequencing and individualizing of instruction, from mastery learning, and from cooperative learning. If teachers can state their instructional objectives in measurable terms, then the teacher can determine whether a student has achieved the objectives.

Norm-Referenced Evaluation.   Norm-referenced evaluation uses the achievement of other students as a frame of reference for judging the performance of an individual. The general procedure is to administer a test to a large sample of people like those for whom the measure is designed. This group, known as the *norm group*, provides a distribution of scores against which the score of any single person can be compared. Classroom teachers usually use norm-referenced evaluation procedures by grading on a curve. (See Table 1.4). Grading on a curve was one of many proposals

TABLE 1.4   Norm-Referenced Grading

GRADING ON A CURVE	CHARACTERISTICS
15 percent receive As	Compares student performances to each other
20 percent receive Bs	Creates competition among students
30 percent receive Cs	Assumes distribution of test scores is a normal curve
20 percent receive Ds	Teacher-made tests are not designed to give normal distributions
15 percent receive Fs	Class sizes are typically too small to expect a normal distribution

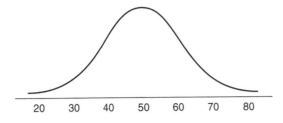

FIGURE 1.2   Normal Curve
Normal distribution with a mean of 50 and a standard deviation of 10

for educational reform in the 1930s; it represented an attempt to adopt in the classroom the same procedures used by publishers of standardized tests. To grade on a curve, teachers define the norm group as all the students in the class for which the grades are to be assigned, and assume that the distribution of test scores follows the form known as the normal curve (see Figure 1.2).

The way in which the norm group is selected is crucial to the fairness and validity of the judgments made. Although there are statistical advantages to assuming that assessment results are normally distributed, (a) teacher-made assessment measures are rarely designed to give normal distributions and (b) class sizes are typically too small to expect a normal distribution. It takes several hundred scores to have a potentially normal distribution. Terwilliger (1971) concludes that these defects are so serious and so common that it is impossible to justify the practice of grading on a curve.

There are numerous disadvantages to using norm-referenced evaluation procedures (Johnson & Johnson, 1999). Norm-referenced evaluation tends to

1. Increase student anxiety, which interferes with learning complex tasks and new information. High anxiety especially interferes with adaptive problem solving.
2. Motivate individuals to exert minimal effort. In competitions, chronic winners exert only enough effort to win and chronic losers exert little or no effort at all.
3. Create extrinsic motivation. Winning tends to become more important than learning.
4. Reduce intrinsic motivation to learn for interest in or enjoyment of an activity for its own sake.
5. Increase the frequency with which students cheat. Students tend to become more committed to winning at any cost.
6. Create a situation in which students may internalize the values of "bettering others" and "taking joy in others' mistakes." Students tend to become less committed to values of fairness and justice and more self-oriented.
7. Promote contingent self-acceptance in which the value of self and others is contingent on winning.
8. Result in overgeneralization of results to all aspects of a person's being. Winning in one arena tends to result in feeling superior in all arenas. Losing in one arena tends to result in feeling inferior in all arenas.
9. Create anger, hostility, and dislike toward those who win. Losing tends to promote depression and aggression toward winners and judges.
10. Promote a view of life as a dog-eat-dog rat race in which only the strongest survive.

MAKING ASSESSMENTS MEANINGFUL

Just because an assessment is conducted does not guarantee that it is perceived as meaningful by relevant stakeholders. Assessments have meaning when they (a) achieve a significant purpose; (b) have clear procedures, criteria, and rubrics that

ACTIVITY **1.4** ■ WHAT MAKES ASSESSMENTS MEANINGFUL?

Rank order from most important (1) to least important (10) the following ways in which assessments can be meaningful.

_____ Ensuring parents understand the assessment procedures and process and obtain a clear picture of how well their children are doing academically

_____ Ascertaining whether efforts to learn are contributing to the well-being of others and the common good as well as to self-benefit

_____ Providing direction for correcting misunderstandings, filling in gaps in learning, and advancing to the next level of knowledge and skill

_____ Having students invest their own time and energy in conducting the assessment

_____ Making assessment procedures, criteria, and rubrics easy to understand

_____ Involving students in setting their learning goals

_____ Conducting the assessment in an authentic context

_____ Establishing goals that are relevant to students' immediate lives

_____ Creating in students a sense of ownership for the assessment procedures and process

_____ Giving students and other stakeholders accurate and detailed feedback on the quality and quantity of student learning

---

are understood by all relevant stakeholders; and (c) produce results that provide clear direction for increasing the quality of learning and instruction (see Activity 1.4).

First, to be meaningful, assessment has to have a purpose that is significant. Any assessment goal may be perceived as significant if it meets one or more of four conditions: (a) students are involved in setting learning goals; (b) the goals are perceived to be interdependent with those of significant others; (c) achieving the goals requires the joint efforts of several people; and (d) the goals are perceived to be relevant to the students' current lives.

Involving students in determining their learning goals makes the goals and the assessment of the progress in accomplishing those goals more meaningful (Johnson & F. Johnson, 2000). Individuals commit energy and resources to achieve their own goals but tend to resist working to achieve goals that are imposed on them. Involvement in the goal-setting process leads to personal ownership of the goals and commitment to achieving them. The more students are involved in setting the learning goals, the more meaningful the assessment will tend to be; and the more students perceive the goals as being imposed on them, the less meaningful the assessment will tend to be.

The learning goals of students are interrelated with the goals of other stakeholders. Goals are positively interdependent when individuals perceive that they can reach their goals if and only if others in the group also reach their goals (Deutsch, 1962). Although students' goals may be interdependent with several stakeholders, the more significant the stakeholders are to the students, the more meaningful the goals are perceived to be. Stakeholders can be teachers, parents, peers, and other school personnel. Parents, for example, have goals for their children that require their children to learn to read and write at a high level of proficiency. Whenever a student demonstrates improved competence in reading and writing, the parents feel satisfaction because their goals are being achieved also. The more interdependent students' learning goals are with those of significant others, the more meaningful the students' goals are.

Goals are typically more meaningful when they are accomplished through joint efforts with others. In some classes, and in some instances, individuals work alone to achieve individual goals. In other classes, and in other instances, students work together to achieve mutual, interrelated goals. Joint efforts may be perceived as being more meaningful than individual efforts because joint efforts contribute to the well-being of others and to the common good as well as to one's own benefit (Johnson & Johnson, 1999). The greater the number of individuals who benefit from a person's efforts, the more meaningful the efforts are perceived to be.

Finally, goals are more significant when they are relevant to the student's immediate life and wants. If achieving the learning goals is perceived to improve the quality of a student's immediate life, the goals are perceived to be meaningful. Relevance is often difficult to establish because it can change from hour to hour, and what seems relevant today may seem irrelevant tomorrow.

Teachers may increase the meaningfulness of students' goals by involving students in determining what the goals should be, by highlighting the interdependence among the students' goals and the goals of significant others, by structuring the learning situation so joint efforts are required to achieve the goals, and by establishing the relevance of the goals to the student's immediate life.

Second, assessments are meaningful when all relevant stakeholders clearly understand the procedures, criteria, and rubrics being used. The more confusing and ambiguous the procedures, criteria, and rubrics seem to be, the less meaningful the assessment is. Clarity of understanding comes from the way the procedures, criteria, and rubrics are explained and from involvement in creating the procedures, criteria, and rubrics used in the assessment process. People follow the paths they have planned for themselves while deviating from and subverting the paths imposed on them by others. When students are more involved in formulating assessment procedures and creating criteria and rubrics to be used to assess the quality of their work, they have a clearer understanding of the procedures, criteria, and rubrics; they feel a greater sense of ownership for the procedures, criteria, and rubrics; and they make a more concerted commitment to carry out the assessment in ways that promote valid and reliable results. For parents, assessments tend to be meaningful when parents understand the procedures used to assess student learning and obtain a clear picture of their children's academic performance.

Third, meaningful assessments provide a direction and a road map for future efforts to learn. Assessments should provide direction by revealing (a) misunderstandings and gaps in learning that need to be remediated and (b) the next level of learning goals that need to be achieved. Assessments become more meaningful when the results are used to point toward the next steps in learning and instruction. Meaningless assessments may provide achievement scores with no implications for what the student should do to correct and advance his or her learning.

MAKING ASSESSMENT MANAGEABLE

Managing assessments includes organizing the resources needed for setting learning goals in ways that induce student commitment, for deciding on which assessment procedures to use, for collecting and analyzing the assessment data, and for recording and communicating the results of the assessments to relevant stakeholders. Each of these activities takes considerable time and effort. Planning for the assessments includes (a) setting the learning goals in a way that induces student commitment to achieve the goals, (b) selecting the procedures to be used (such as tests, compositions, portfolios, projects, observations), and (c) organizing the resources such as supplies and equipment needed to conduct the lesson and the assessment (see Figure 1.3). Collecting and analyzing the assessment data includes conducting diagnostic assessments before the lesson begins, conducting progress or formative assessments while the unit is in progress, and conducting summative assessments after the unit is completed. Recording and reporting results includes charting the results and reporting activities such as student-led conferences. New learning goals are then set that include either remediation to bring a student's performance up to the criteria for mastery or direction for the next instructional unit.

Many assessment procedures are labor intensive and may involve more than one modality, may examine diverse outcomes, may require multisources of information, may require authentic settings, and may be aimed at measuring student performance on complex procedures. It takes considerable resources to conduct such assessments. Table 1.5 lists various problems associated with managing assessments and provides a solution to each problem.

The major issue in managing assessments is teacher time. If assessment is done adequately, it is difficult for a teacher to manage the assessment system. Most teachers do not have much time to conduct assessments. Swain and Swain (1999), for example, note that in the United States almost all the official work of teachers is committed to the classroom instruction of students. Teachers in the United States devote more hours to instruction and supervision of students each week and have longer required workweeks than in any other developed, industrialized country, including the nations with 6-day weeks, such as Japan and Switzerland. Consequently, most of the assessment activities must be done in the evening or on weekends. They conclude that teachers who spend 12 minutes to plan for each class session and 9 minutes per week to assess each student's work have no choice but to work 60 hours a week or more. If teachers work 45 hours a week, they will have 6 minutes to plan for each class session and 3 minutes per week to assess each student's work. Obviously, 3 minutes a week is not enough time to conduct any sort of meaningful assessment.

Swain and Swain (1999) note that a teacher spends 15 or 20 hours outside of school to grade an essay assignment, then teachers may decide to assign fewer essays.

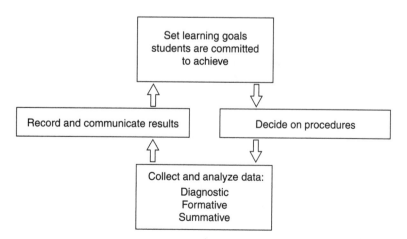

FIGURE 1.3   Process of Assessment

TABLE 1.5   Management Problems with Assessment

PROBLEM	SOLUTION
Participating in the assessment process causes students to miss learning opportunities.	Experience of conducting assessments teaches content and procedures.
The amount of time and effort required to implement the assessment process results in infrequent assessments.	Have students help manage the assessment process for classmates.
Outcomes most commonly assessed are subject matter knowledge and recognition of facts.	Student help allows more diverse outcomes to be assessed, such as critical thinking, cognitive and social skills, attitudes, and work habits.
Students are limited primarily to reading and writing as modalities.	Expand modalities by having students work in groups where they can be observed, perform cognitive and social skills, demonstrate higher-level reasoning, and so forth.
Sources of information are limited to teacher assessments.	Student help allows for self- and peer assessments as well as teacher assessments.
Assessments are biased by requiring reading and writing activities for demonstrating knowledge and skill.	Students can exchange and reveal knowledge orally and demonstrate skills to each other.
Teacher bias and expectations can affect assessment results.	Reduce possibility of teacher bias by having students assess classmates' work.
Students receive assessment results without procedures for remediation and improvement.	Classmates can provide students a support system for creating and implementing remediation and improvement plans.
Only individual outcomes can be assessed.	Students can work together so group outcomes can be assessed as well as individual outcomes.
Assessing individual students in isolation is incongruent with ideal instructional experiences.	Have students work together, assessing each other's work, to make the assessment process congruent with ideal instructional methods.

If they spend 10 hours of preparation time on the weekend to write out the materials for a new, student-directed unit, then teachers may plan fewer of these types of units. If a teacher wanted to spend 10 minutes a month talking to each student privately, the teacher would have to find about 20 hours at lunchtime or after school to do so.

Time constraints can prohibit the use of many of the most effective and helpful assessment procedures. Teachers simply do not have the time to use them without help and assistance. If the more creative and effective assessment procedures are to be used, teachers need additional sources of labor. The most natural sources of help for teachers are students and colleagues. Students are an ideal source of help because (a) they are always present in the classroom; (b) student commitment to implement the results of an assessment is greater when they collect, analyze, and interpret the data themselves; and (c) students may often learn more from conducting assessments than they do from receiving assessments. For these and many other reasons, it

ACTIVITY **1.5** ■ PROBLEMS IN CONDUCTING ASSESSMENTS

Rank the following problems in conducting good assessment from most important to you (1) to least important to you (10).

_____ Amount of time and effort required to implement the assessment process

_____ Limited primarily to reading and writing as modalities

_____ Outcomes most commonly assessed are subject matter knowledge and recognition of facts

_____ Sources of information limited to teacher observations

_____ Assessments require reading and writing as prerequisites for demonstrating knowledge and skill

_____ Learning and assessment goals are imposed on students

_____ Students do not understand the criteria and rubrics used to assess their work

_____ Assessment process is not a learning experience for most students

_____ Teacher expectations and stereotypes bias assessment procedures

_____ Many students are unable to use assessments to make improvement plans

is often advisable (and necessary) to involve students in learning the assessment rubrics and in using them to reflect on and assess their own and classmates' work. Having students help conduct assessments allows teachers to

1. Provide students with powerful learning experiences that increase their achievement. When students conduct assessments of classmates' work, they learn more thoroughly the criteria and rubrics used in assessment, thus developing internal guidelines and greater understanding of how their work should be completed. One of the paradoxes of assessment is that students typically learn more from conducting assessments than they do from receiving assessments. Assessing the accuracy, quantity, and quality of one's own and classmates' work tends to make the assessment and reporting processes important learning experiences. Having students assess classmates' work, therefore, becomes part of the instructional program. The more experience students have in using criteria and rubrics, the more thoroughly they learn the procedures, skills, and information being taught. At the very least, they will better understand how to complete the assignment at a high level of quality. In other words, involving students in the assessment process results in greater integration of assessment and instruction.

2. Conduct more frequent assessments. When the teacher is responsible for conducting all the assessments, the number of assessments that may be conducted is limited by the teacher's time. Despite a teacher's desire to have students write, if the teacher believes that he or she has to read and assess everything each student writes, the amount of writing the teacher can manage is severely restricted. Having students assess each other's work significantly increases the frequency with which assessments can be conducted as well as the amount of work that may be assigned.

3. Assess a wider variety of outcomes. Besides subject matter knowledge and expertise, student help with assessment allows teachers to assess reasoning, skills and competencies, attitudes, and work habits. Outcomes may be ignored because they are too labor intensive to assess or because they require frequent and continuous monitoring. However these outcomes can be included in an assessment plan when students are available to help. What gets measured, gets noticed and, in turn, influences what is taught. Assessment procedures that focus on higher-level reasoning, problem solving, and metacognitive thinking will be emphasized in instruction. Furthermore, when teachers observe students verbally interacting with each other, they have the opportunity to view and assess through a "window into students' minds" students' understanding of the material being studied, critical thinking, and cognitive reasoning. When students work together, covert reasoning and problem solving may be made overt so that they can be assessed and improved.

4. Use more modalities in assessing students' work. In addition to assessing each other's reading and writing, students can observe each other presenting, performing cognitive and social skills, demonstrating higher-level reasoning procedures, using visuals such as graphs and illustrations, and even acting out or role playing aspects of the content being learned.

5. Utilize more sources of information in making assessments. Student involvement makes self- and peer assessments available in addition to teacher assessments. Self-, peer, and teacher assessments can then be coordinated and integrated. Students and classmates as well as teachers can be involved in communicating the results of assessments to interested audiences.

6. Reduce the bias inherent in requiring reading and writing activities only for demonstrating knowledge or engaging in a performance. Students can learn subject matter orally and reveal their understanding of what was learned orally. They can interview each other, read to each other, and explain material to each other. Other students can read questions to a classmate who cannot read or write well, and the classmate can explain to groupmates what the answer is and how it is derived.

7. Reduce the possibility of teacher bias. Bias may be introduced into teachers' assessments in numerous ways. Even characteristics such as neatness of handwriting (Sweedler-Brown, 1992) and teachers' perceptions of students' behavior (Bennett et al., 1993; Hills, 1991) can influence a teacher's judgment of a student's achievement. The more students assess each other's work, the less potential there is for teacher bias.

8. Create classmate social support systems for remediation and enrichment activities. The restrictions on teacher time prevent teachers from monitoring each student's efforts to learn all the time. The result is that teachers are required to assess only samples of student learning. In small cooperative groups classmates can continuously monitor each other's activities. In addition, some students are more susceptible to peer influence than teacher influence. Students can keep track of each other's level of mastery, hold each other accountable for learning, and encourage remediation efforts and extending one's competencies. The involvement of students in the assessment process provides a potential support system for continuous assessment, remediation, and enrichment. Classmates provide the resources for continuous improvement.

9. Create the opportunity to assess group as well as individual outcomes. Some are scientific, dramatic, or creative projects may only be completed by groups. Without cooperative groups, such assignments cannot be given and assessed.

10. Make the assessment process congruent with ideal instructional procedures. Because cooperative learning tends to promote higher achievement, more positive interpersonal relationships, and greater psychological health than do competitive or individualistic learning (Johnson & Johnson, 1989), most teachers use it frequently.

Involving group members in assessment procedures thus increases the congruence between instruction and assessment.

Assessment has traditionally focused on individual-to-individual transfer of learning. Students worked in isolation from classmates (in either competitive or individualistic learning situations) and were given individual achievement tests to assess their achievement. Two assumptions underlie this practice. One is that individual assessment requires individual learning. This is a misconception. Group-to-individual transfer has been repeatedly demonstrated to be superior to individual-to-individual transfer (Johnson & Johnson, 1989). The purpose of cooperative learning groups is to ensure that all members learn and are, therefore, better able to perform on a subsequent individual assessment measure as a result of their group experience. The second assumption is that assessment should focus on "unassisted" student learning, which means that students should not be exposed to sources of help and assistance from classmates, parents, private tutors, educational programs on television or video, and so forth. This also is a misconception. All school learning is assisted and promoted by the instructional efforts of a wide variety of individuals within and outside of the school.

TYPES OF LEARNING GROUPS

For students to assist in the assessment process they must work together and interact. That is, they must be placed in groups. Often in the past all learning groups were assumed to be the same. There is much more to learning groups than seating students together. There is nothing magical about being in a group. Many groups are ineffective and counterproductive and take more teacher time than they are worth. At least four types of learning groups may be identified (see Activity 1.6). Pseudo and

ACTIVITY **1.6** ■ DEFINITIONS OF LEARNING GROUPS

Demonstrate your understanding of the different types of learning groups by matching the definitions with the appropriate group. Check your answers with your partner and explain why you believe your answers to be correct.

TYPE OF LEARNING GROUP

_____ 1. pseudo group

_____ 2. traditional learning group

_____ 3. cooperative learning group

_____ 4. high-performance cooperative learning group

DEFINITION

a. A group in which students work together to accomplish shared goals. Students perceive they can reach their learning goals if and only if the other group members also reach their goals.

b. A group whose members have been assigned to work together but they have no interest in doing so. The structure promotes competition at close quarters.

c. A group whose members agree to work together but see little benefit from doing so. The structure promotes individualistic work with talking.

d. A group that meets all the criteria for being a cooperative group and outperforms all reasonable expectations, given its membership.

TABLE 1.6

TYPES OF LEARNING GROUPS	COOPERATIVE GROUPS	ESSENTIAL ELEMENTS	OUTCOMES
Psuedo groups	Formal cooperative learning	Positive interdependence	Effort to achieve
Traditional groups	Informal cooperative learning	Individual accountability	Positive relationships
Cooperative groups	Cooperative base groups	Promotive interaction	Psychological health
High-performance cooperative groups		Interpersonal and small group skills	
		Group processing	

traditional learning groups, for example, provide little if any advantage over individual instruction. Assessment is only enhanced when the groups are truly cooperative. To use the new assessment procedures, students must work in cooperative learning groups. Teachers need to understand what cooperative learning is, the different types of cooperative learning groups, the essential elements of cooperation, and the outcomes resulting from cooperation among students (see Table 1.6).

UNDERSTANDING COOPERATIVE LEARNING

> Together we stand, divided we fall.   —*Watchword of the American Revolution*

Sandy Koufax was one of the greatest pitchers in the history of baseball. Although he was naturally talented, he was also unusually well trained and disciplined. He was perhaps the only major-league pitcher whose fastball could be heard to hum. Opposing batters, instead of talking and joking around in the dugout, would sit quietly and listen for Koufax's fastball to hum. When it was their turn to bat, they were already intimidated. However, the genius of Koufax could have been subverted in one simple way: by making the first author of this book his catcher. To be great, a pitcher needs an outstanding catcher (his great partner was Johnny Roseboro). David Johnson is such an unskilled catcher that Koufax would have had to throw the ball much more slowly for David to catch it. This would have deprived Koufax of his greatest weapon. Placing Roger and Edythe at key defensive positions in the infield or outfield, furthermore, would have seriously affected Koufax's success. Sandy Koufax was not a great pitcher on his own. Only as part of a team could Koufax achieve greatness. As in baseball, extraordinary achievement in the classroom takes cooperative effort, not individualistic or competitive efforts of an isolated individual.

Cooperative learning exists when students work together to accomplish shared goals. Students perceive that they can reach their learning goals if and only if the other students in the learning group also reach their goals. Thus, students seek outcomes that are beneficial to all those with whom they are cooperatively linked. Students are given two responsibilities: to complete the assignment and to ensure that all other group members complete the assignment. Students discuss material with each other, help one another understand it, and encourage each other to work hard. Individual performance is checked regularly to ensure that all students are contributing and learning. A criteria-referenced evaluation system is used. The result is that the group is more than a sum of its parts, and all students perform higher academically than they would if they worked alone.

There are three types of cooperative learning groups. A **formal cooperative learning group** lasts from one class period to several weeks. Formal cooperative learning groups ensure that students are actively involved in the intellectual work of organizing material, explaining it, summarizing it, and integrating it into existing conceptual structures. They are the heart of using cooperative learning. An **informal cooperative learning group** is an ad-hoc group that lasts from a few minutes to one class period. You use them during direct teaching (lectures, demonstrations, films, videos) to focus students' attention on the material they are to learn, set a mood conducive to learning, help set expectations as to what the lesson will cover, ensure that students cognitively process the material you are teaching, and provide closure to an instructional session. A **cooperative base group** is a long-term (lasting for at least a year), heterogeneous group with stable membership whose primary purpose is for members to give each other the support, help, encouragement, and assistance each needs to progress academically. Base groups provide students with long-term, committed relationships.

To structure instructional units so students do in fact work cooperatively with each other, you must understand the basic elements that make cooperation work. Mastering the basic elements of cooperation allows you to

1. Take your existing instructional units, curricula, and courses and structure them cooperatively.
2. Tailor cooperative learning instructional units to your unique instructional needs, circumstances, curricula, subject areas, and students.
3. Diagnose the problems some students may have in working together and intervene to increase the effectiveness of the student learning groups.

For cooperation to work well, you must structure five essential elements in each lesson (Johnson & Johnson, 1989). The first and most important element is **positive interdependence.** You must give a clear task and a group goal so that students believe they sink or swim together. You have successfully structured positive interdependence when group members perceive that they are linked with each other in a way that one cannot succeed unless everyone succeeds. The work of any member benefits all members. If one fails, all fail. Positive interdependence may be structured through common goals, joint rewards, division of resources, complementary roles, a division of labor, and a joint identity.

The second essential element of cooperative learning is individual (and group) accountability. Each member must be accountable for contributing his or her share of the work (which ensures that no one can "hitch-hike" on the work of others). **Individual accountability** exists when the performance of each individual student is assessed and the results given back to the group and the individual. The purpose of cooperative learning groups is to make each member a stronger individual in his or her right. Students learn together so that they can subsequently perform higher as individuals (see Box 1.3).

The third essential component of cooperative learning is promoting interaction, preferably face-to-face. Students need to do real work together in which they promote each other's success by orally explaining to each other how to solve problems, discussing with each other the nature of the concepts being learned, teaching their knowledge to classmates, and explaining to each other the connections between present and past learning. Cooperative learning groups are both an academic support system (every student has someone who is committed to helping him or her learn) and a personal support system (every student has someone who is committed to him or her as a person).

The fourth essential element of cooperative learning is teaching students the required interpersonal and small group skills. In cooperative learning groups students

■ ■ ■ ■ ■

BOX 1.2

THE TEACHER'S ROLE IN COOPERATIVE LEARNING

MAKE PREINSTRUCTIONAL DECISIONS

- **Specify academic and social skills objectives.** Every lesson has both (a) academic and (b) interpersonal and small group skills objectives.
- **Decide on group size.** Learning groups should be small (groups of two or three members, four at the most).
- **Decide on group composition.** Assign students to groups randomly or select groups yourself. Usually you will want to maximize the heterogeneity in each group.
- **Assign roles.** Structure student–student interaction by assigning roles such as reader, recorder, encourager of participation, and checker for understanding.
- **Arrange the room.** Group members should be "knee to knee and eye to eye" but arranged so they all can see the instructor at the front of the room.
- **Plan materials.** Arrange materials to give a "sink-or-swim together" message. Give only one paper to the group or give each member part of the material to be learned.

EXPLAIN TASK AND COOPERATIVE STRUCTURE

- **Explain the academic task.** Explain the task, the objectives of the lesson, the concepts and principles students need to know to complete the assignment, and the procedures they are to follow.
- **Explain the criteria for success.** Student work should be evaluated on a criteria-referenced basis. Make clear your criteria for evaluating students' work.
- **Structure positive interdependence.** Students must believe they sink or swim together. Always establish mutual goals (students are responsible for their own learning and the learning of all other group members). Supplement goal interdependence with celebration/reward, resource, role, and identity interdependence.
- **Structure intergroup cooperation.** Have groups check with and help other groups. Extend the benefits of cooperation to the whole class.
- **Structure individual accountability.** Each student must feel responsible for doing his or her share of the work and helping the other group members. Ways to ensure accountability are frequent oral quizzes of group members picked at random, individual tests, and assigning one member the role of checker for understanding.
- **Specify expected behaviors.** The more specific you are about the behaviors you want to see in the groups, the more likely students will do them. Social skills may be classified as forming (staying with the group, using quiet voices), functioning (contributing, encouraging others to participate), formulating (summarizing, elaborating), and fermenting (criticizing ideas, asking for justification). Regularly teach the interpersonal and small group skills you want to see used in the learning groups.

MONITOR AND INTERVENE

- **Arrange face-to-face promotive interaction.** Conduct the lesson in ways that ensure that students directly promote each other's success face to face.
- **Monitor students' behavior.** This is the fun part! While students are working, you circulate to see whether they understand the assignment and the

material, give immediate feedback and reinforcement, and praise good use of group skills. Collect observation data on each group and student.
- **Intervene to improve taskwork and teamwork.** Provide taskwork assistance (clarify, reteach) if students do not understand the assignment. Provide teamwork assistance if students are having difficulties in working together productively.

EVALUATE AND PROCESS
- **Evaluate student learning.** Assess and evaluate the quality and quantity of student learning. Involve students in the assessment process.
- **Process group functioning.** Ensure each student receives feedback, analyzes the data on group functioning, sets an improvement goal, and participates in a team celebration. Have groups routinely list three things they did well in working together and one thing they will do better tomorrow. Summarize as a whole class. Have groups celebrate their success and hard work.

are required to learn academic subject matter (taskwork) and also to learn the interpersonal and small group skills required to work together effectively (teamwork). Cooperative learning is inherently more complex than competitive or individualistic learning because students have to engage simultaneously in taskwork and teamwork. Group members must learn how to provide effective leadership, decision making, trust building, communication, and conflict management. Procedures and

BOX 1.3
COOPERATIVE LEARNING: WHOSE WORK IS IT?

When students work in cooperative groups, they provide each other with help and support. This raises the question, Whose work is it? It may be unclear what they can do individually. This same question may be asked about a student's work after a teacher has provided academic help or support. Additional complications arise when class work merges with homework. The amount of help students get from family and friends becomes an additional threat to the validity of interpretations about individual scores. Many assessment procedures put students who do not receive help from family and peers at a disadvantage. Communities in which parents are highly educated professionals, furthermore, may produce student work superior to that produced by students in districts with less educated or wealthy parents. This problem is avoided when assessment procedures lead to individual performances on demand. A student, for example, can write a series of compositions during a school year, all of which go through a peer editing process. Although these compositions reflect what the student is capable of (given the editing and feedback from classmates, parents, and teachers), it does not reflect how well the student can write on demand. The teacher, therefore, may wish to give a test in which students are given a certain amount of class time (such as 30 minutes) to write an essay. The extent to which the writing skills learned transfer to new writing demands can then be assessed.

strategies for teaching students social skills may be found in Johnson (1991, 2000) and Johnson and F. Johnson (2000).

The fifth essential component of cooperative learning is group processing. Group processing occurs when group members discuss how well they are achieving their goals and maintaining effective working relationships. Groups need to describe what member actions are helpful and unhelpful and make decisions about what behaviors to continue or change. Continuous improvement of the process of learning results from careful analysis of how members are working together and determining how group effectiveness can be enhanced.

Your use of cooperative learning becomes effective through disciplined action. The five basic elements are not just characteristics of good cooperative learning groups. They are a discipline that you have to apply rigorously (much like a diet has to be adhered to) to produce the conditions for effective cooperative action.

Over the past 100 years, hundreds of research studies have been conducted on social interdependence. Cooperation, compared with competitive and individualistic efforts, results in (Johnson & Johnson, 1989):

1. **Higher achievement.** The superiority of cooperation (over competitive and individualistic efforts) increases as the task is more complex and conceptual, requires more problem solving and creativity, entails more higher-level reasoning and critical thinking, and transfers more to the real world.

2. **More positive relationships among students and between students and faculty.** This was evidenced even when students were from different ethnic and cultural backgrounds, social classes, and language groups. It was also true for students who were and were not handicapped. Individuals tend to like others with whom they have worked cooperatively.

3. **More positive psychological well-being.** Working with classmates cooperatively has been found to promote greater self-esteem, self-efficacy, social competencies, coping skills, and general psychological health. Included in this area are also students' attitudes toward schooling and subject areas. Working cooperatively tends to result in students developing more positive attitudes toward school, learning, and subject areas and being more interested in taking advance courses and continuing one's education.

4. **A more constructive classroom and school learning environment.** The more frequently cooperative learning is used, the more students perceive the classroom climate as being both academically and personally supportive and enhancing. The more positive the attitudes toward cooperative learning are, (a) the more students report that peer and teacher encouragement helped them to exert effort to achieve, (b) the more students perceive themselves to be involved in positive and supportive personal relationships with classmates and teachers, (c) the higher students' academic self-esteem, and (d) the more fair the grading procedures are perceived to be (Johnson & Johnson, 1991a).

STANDARDS AND TESTING MOVEMENT

There are at least four levels of accountability: student, teacher, school, and parents. The high-stakes nature of these assessments raises the possibility of cheating.

Student Accountability

In Chicago students were promoted year after year regardless of schoolwork that lagged 3 or 4 years behind grade level. Then, as a result of a new policy, which drew nationwide attention, Chicago schools failed more than 40,000 students who did not pass standardized tests in the third, sixth, eighth, and ninth grades. The message sent to students, teachers, and parents was that "social promotion" was over. The students who failed were humiliated and their parents were enraged. Such high-stakes testing has many critics. In Minnesota, as in many other states, to graduate from high school students are required to pass a **basic standards test,** which measures skills in reading, writing, and math that students should have learned by a certain grade. Such standardized tests are becoming so important that in many states large portions of class time are spent specifically teaching to the test.

The modern standards movement is part of a national response to the 1983 report, entitled *A Nation at Risk,* on the condition of education in U.S. schools. This report called for the development of rigorous academic standards to ensure a high-quality education for all students. In response, national professional organizations representing content areas (such as mathematics, language arts, literacy, science, and social studies) built lists of indicators and expectations for student performance at various grade levels. These new standards tend to be set quite high and apply to a much more diverse student population than ever before. Consequently, they are both driving the curriculum, instruction, and assessment of students and becoming the criteria for successful teacher and administrator performance. New state and privately published standardized tests have been and are being developed to measure degree of attainment of the content standards, thus giving the public objective data about the performance of students, teachers, and schools. The resulting public pressure is supposed to keep schools working to improve the education of all children. Individual parents can put pressure on a school to improve the achievement of their child.

Although such accountability has obvious benefits, there are dangers. The first danger is that the tests are not valid. In Michigan, for example, suburban parents started a boycott of the state proficiency test when the school valedictorian, who enrolled at the Massachusetts Institute of Technology after getting a perfect score on his ACT test, flunked the exam. A second danger is that one group may gain control over what should be measured, to the detriment of other groups. A third danger is that this type of accountability focuses more on punishing low performers than on rewarding high performers. A fourth danger is the outcome of denying students diplomas may incite a backlash against the tests.

In the spring of 2000 a parent whose daughter was denied graduation insisted on seeing the test and found that six questions had been scored incorrectly. In addition, almost 8,000 students who actually passed the test had been told that they had failed, including 336 seniors who were incorrectly denied graduation. There has been some backpedaling. Wisconsin withdrew a test that all students had to pass to graduate. Other states have weakened planned requirements.

The fifth danger is that the criteria for passing a test may be set too high or too low. If too high, public demand will end the accountability system. If too low, the accountability system will waste time and money. After 90 percent of Arizona sophomores failed a new math test, the board of education reconsidered the test. The Virginia Board of Education planned to sanction schools in which more than 30 percent of students failed state tests, but when 93 percent of the schools had these percentages of failure, the Board relaxed the standards. Faced with holding back 50 percent of students, the Los Angeles school system has reconsidered the planned end to automatic promotions.

Teacher and Administrator Accountability

The standards and testing movement targets teachers (and administrators) as well as students. Teacher performance assessments focus on domains such as (a) organizing content knowledge for student learning, (b) creating an environment for student learning, (c) teaching for student learning, and (d) teacher professionalism in building collaborative relationships with colleagues. The most common form of teacher accountability, however, is student performance on standardized tests. In Kentucky, for example, teachers get bonuses when test scores rise and are placed on probation or face the prospect of losing their jobs when scores fall.

From Maryland to California, standardized test scores are the weapon of choice in threatening takeovers of failed schools. In New York, principals can be removed for "persistent education failure." In New Jersey, state officials can take complete control of a district for up to 5 years; board members and administrators can be dismissed. In Illinois, a district can be dissolved and realigned with another district or managed by an independent authority. At the extreme is the fresh-start or reconstitution concept; if student performance fails to improve despite normal intervention efforts, the district can close a school and start over, with teachers and administrators transferring to different schools. Many states now have laws to fight what is known as academic bankruptcy, that is, schools in which student performance is sagging.

Since 1982, William Sanders, at the University of Tennessee, has been studying Tennessee's student achievement data to devise a mathematical model to identify effective and ineffective teachers. Sander's system focuses on the academic gain a student could be expected to make in a year. He believes that small gains can add up to greater academic achievement in the long run. What surprised him was that the data indicated that the variability among teachers was much larger than the variability among schools. The students of the top teachers all make gains above expectation.

Sanders concludes that of all the influences in a student's life, the quality of teaching, not poverty, ethnicity, or family circumstance, is the most important factor. When compared to class size or ethnicity of students, or whether students are on free or reduced-price lunches, the individual classroom teacher has a much more powerful effect on student achievement. Teacher effects accumulate, so that if one third-grader gets poor teachers for 3 years and another third-grader gets excellent teachers for 3 years, by sixth grade their standardized test scores can differ by as many as 50 percentile points. Sanders wants school districts to identify ineffective teachers and provide them with mentors or involve them in team teaching. At the very least, principals should ensure that a student does not get an ineffective teacher 2 years in a row.

With the increased importance of standardized test results, more and more people are seeing students failing such tests in the eleventh grade and asking, who is responsible? Increasingly, authorities are answering, teachers! Colorado and New Mexico claim to have abolished teacher tenure, making it easier to dismiss teachers. Florida has cut in half the time it takes to dismiss a teacher. North Carolina has lengthened the teacher probation period from 3 years to 4 years. Texas uses student test scores as part of teacher evaluations. A few districts pay bonuses to teachers based on student performance. In 1994 the state of Tennessee began publishing school-by-school comparisons statewide based on gains students were making on standardized tests. Starting in 1996, second- through eighth-grade teachers have been receiving yearly reports showing how much their students progressed compared with expectations and with other students in the school system and the state. Principals also began receiving comparison reports on teachers so they could take action to help ineffective teachers.

School Accountability

Many states have decided to issue report cards for schools and often assign schools grades ranging from A to F or apply designations such as distinguished, excellent, low-performing, and unsatisfactory. An example is Colorado, which will begin printing school report cards in August 2001 and mailing them to parents. Each report card will contain a letter grade for the academic performance and improvement of the school as a whole, the grades assigned to neighboring schools, results of statewide test performance, student–teacher ratios, average levels and salaries for teacher experience, reports of disciplinary incidents, student attendance, data on the amount of money the school district receives and how that money is spent. Florida also assigns schools letter grades (based on state test scores and high school dropout rates) and allocates funds to help schools that get low grades. As a result, the number of elementary schools assigned Fs dropped from 66 in 1998 to 4 in 2000.

The Education Commission of the States reports that the majority of states issue report cards for schools and 26 states publicly categorize or rank schools. School and district assessment may increase as the political and public demand for accountability increases. In Texas, the State Education Agency publishes a pocket summary of the previous school year for each school that includes teacher and student profiles, dropout rates, a breakdown of district revenue, results of college admissions tests, and the percentage of students who passed state tests.

Parent Accountability

Throughout the United States, students and teachers are becoming more accountable every year. Perhaps the same rules should apply to parents. Some states are considering making parents accountable. In Kentucky a state dropout-prevention committee proposed that parents should pay schools for any unexcused absences of their children. In Virginia parents were fined $50 for the "willful or unreasonable failure" to sign and return a statement to the school. In 1996 the legislators dropped the fine. However, efforts to include parents in the accountability system will continue.

Cheating

The majority of high school students cheat in school, at least once in a while. In a recent survey, more than 70 percent of students admitted cheating at least once in the past year. Among high achievers, the percentage was even higher (80 percent). Many students report that they are encouraged by their teachers to cheat on standardized tests; teachers state, in turn, that they are encouraged by their administrators to have students cheat. So many teachers and administrators are encouraging cheating on standardized tests that it is becoming a national problem. Cheating, not only by students, but also by teachers and administrators, is the result of high stakes involved in students' performance on standardized tests. In the fall of 1999, for example, teachers and administrators at 32 New York City schools were reputed to have helped students cheat on standardized tests by providing them with questions in advance and even marking test forms for them. The higher the stakes of the evaluation are, and the more frequently normative procedures are used, the more cheating may occur.

SUMMARY

Assessment is the collecting of information about the quality and quantity of a change in a student or group. The *effectiveness* of an assessment depends on using minimal resources to achieve the goals of the assessment; maintaining effective working relationships among the assessor, assessees, and other interested stakeholders; and increasing motivation to participate in future assessments.

Two central issues of assessment are how to make assessments meaningful and how to make them manageable. To be *meaningful*, assessments have to a significant purpose, consist of procedures that are clearly understood, and provide a direction for future learning and instruction. To be *manageable*, assessments have to provide useful information with the application of minimal resources. Manageability includes whether the available resources are adequate for the requirements of the assessment procedure and whether the value of the information obtained is worth the expenditure of the resources.

The student performances that can be assessed are academic learning, reasoning, skills and competencies, attitudes, and work habits. The purpose of assessments may be to diagnose the level of student knowledge and skills before an instructional unit is implemented, to form the instructional program by periodically checking on its progress, and to sum up the information needed to judge the quality and quantity of student learning. The focus of assessment can be on the processes of learning and instruction or on their outcomes. The more often assessments are conducted in authentic settings, the better. The results of the assessments can be of high or low importance to students and their parents, teachers, administrators, policymakers, and colleges and employers. Evaluations of the assessment result may be based on criteria-referenced or norm-referenced procedures.

The meaning of an assessment begins with a significant purpose. Significance depends on involvement in setting goals, interdependency of goals with the goals of significant others, joint efforts being required to achieve the goals, and the relevance of the goals to the assessees' lives. Meaning also depends on the clarity of the procedures, criteria, and rubrics being used. Understanding is based on involvement. Finally, meaning depends on the assessment providing useful information about the direction of future learning efforts.

Managing assessments includes planning the assessments (setting goals that students are committed to achieving, selecting procedures, organizing resources); conducting diagnostic, formative, and summative assessments; analyzing the data and recording the results; and reporting the results to relevant stakeholders. New learning goals are then set. Each of these activities takes considerable time and effort. Teachers have very little time for assessment, perhaps 3 to 9 minutes each week on average to assess the work of each student. Teachers, therefore, do not have time to use many of the most effective and helpful assessment procedures.

If teachers are to use the more effective and helpful assessment procedures, they must involve colleagues, parents, and students in assessing students' work. Of these available resources, student assistance has the advantages of creating opportunities for powerful learning experiences that increase achievement; of allowing more frequent assessments to be conducted; of expanding the variety of outcomes to be assessed; of using more modalities, thus reducing the need for reading and writing to be prerequisites for assessment; of drawing on more sources of information for assessments; of reducing the teacher bias; of prescribing remediation and enrichment activities following the assessment; and of addressing group as well as individual outcomes to be assessed.

If students are to participate in the assessment process, they must be organized into cooperative learning groups. At least four types of learning groups can be identified: pseudo groups, traditional groups, cooperative groups, and high-performance cooperative groups. The three types of cooperative learning groups are formal, informal, and base groups. To be cooperative, five basic elements must be structured: positive interdependence, individual accountability, promotive interaction, social skills, and group processing. When implemented skillfully, cooperative learning, compared to competitive and individualistic learning, tends to result in greater efforts to learn, more positive relationships, and greater psychological health.

The accountability movement has increased the use of standardized tests for high-stakes assessments. These tests may determine whether students are promoted or graduate, whether teachers receive bonuses or sanctions, whether administrators are fired and boards of education are replaced, whether parents are fined, and whether schools are closed. The result is a clearer picture of whether schools and teachers are promoting student learning, but also of how students, teachers, and administrators are cheating.

Assessment begins with a goal-setting conference. Once students' goals are set, students participate in the instructional program. The quality and quantity of academic learning, level of reasoning, skills and competencies, attitudes, and work habits may be assessed by standardized and teacher-made tests, compositions and presentations, individual and group projects, portfolios, questionnaires, and learning logs and journals. The assessment data is used as part of a total, quality learning procedure emphasizing continuous improvement. Teachers participate in collegial teaching teams to ensure assessments are fair and complete. Finally, periodically teachers use the assessment data to determine students' grades.

ASSESSMENT PLANNING FORM

Grade Level: _____   Subject Area: _____   Date: _____

Lesson: _____

1. What are the purposes of the assessment?

a. _____

_____

b. _____

_____

c. _____

_____

d. _____

_____

2. What is the focus of the assessment?

_____ Process of learning   _____ Outcomes of learning

_____ Process of instruction   _____ Outcomes of instruction

3. In what setting will the assessment take place?

4. What area of student learning will the assessment be aimed at?

_____ Academic learning   _____ Attitudes

_____ Level of reasoning, critical thinking _____ Work habits

_____ Skills and competencies

5. What assessment procedures will be used?

_____ Standardized tests   _____ Portfolios

_____ Teacher-made tests   _____ Observation

_____ Compositions   _____ Interviews

_____ Presentations   _____ Questionnaires

_____ Individual and group projects _____ Learning logs and journals

6. Who are the stakeholders and what is the level of their stakes in the assessment?

Stakeholder	Low Stake	Medium	High Stake
_____ Students and parents			
_____ Teachers			
_____ Administrators			
_____ Policymakers			
_____ Colleges, employers			

7. How will the assessment be made more meaningful?

a. Explain how purpose is significant.

b. Explain how procedures, criteria, rubrics are made clear.

c. Explain how direction for future efforts is highlighted.

8. How will the assessment be made more manageable?

a. What resources are needed?

b. How may student assistance be utilized?

COOPERATIVE LESSON PLANNING FORM

Grade Level: _____ Subject Area: _____ Date: _____

Lesson: _____

OBJECTIVES

1. Academic _____

2. Social _____

DECISIONS

1. Group size: _____

2. Method of assigning students: _____

3. Roles: _____

_____

4. Room arrangement: _____

5. Materials: _____

   ☐ a. One copy per group _____

   ☐ b. Jigsaw _____

   ☐ c. Tournament _____

   ☐ d. One copy per person _____

   ☐ e. Other _____

EXPLAINING TASK AND GOAL STRUCTURE

1. Task: _____

_____

2. Criteria for success: _____

_____

3. Positive interdependence: _____

_____

4. Individual accountability: _____

_____

5. Intergroup cooperation: _____

_____

6. Expected behaviors: _____

_____

MONITORING AND INTERVENING

1. Observation procedure: _____ Formal   _____ Informal

2. Observation by: _____ Teacher   _____ Students   _____ Visitors

3. Intervening for task assistance: _____

_____

4. Intervening for teamwork assistance: _____

_____

5. Other: _____

_____

EVALUATING AND PROCESSING

1. Assessment of members' individual learning: _____

_____

2. Assessment of group productivity: _____

_____

3. Small group processing: _____

_____

4. Whole group processing: _____

_____

5. Charts and graphs used: _____

_____

6. Positive feedback to each student: _____

_____

7. Goal setting for improvement: _____

_____

8. Celebration: _____

_____

9. Other: _____

_____

■ ■ ■ ■ ■ ■ ■ ■ ■

CHAPTER TWO

GOAL-SETTING CONFERENCE

A FABLE WITH A SAD ENDING

Once upon a time, a young rabbit decided to go out into the world and seek his fortune. His parents gave him $300, wished him well, and he began his search. Before he had traveled very far, he met a pack rat. "Hey, little rabbit, where are you going?" asked the pack rat. "I'm seeking my fortune," replied the young rabbit. "You're in luck," said the pack rat. "I have here a fashionable suit of clothes that I will sell to you for only $100. Then you can go seeking your fortune looking quite knowledgeable and successful dressed in the latest style!" "Say, that's fantastic!" replied the young rabbit, who immediately bought the clothes, put them on, and continued to search for his fortune.

Soon he met a deer. "Hey, little rabbit, where are you going?" asked the deer. "I'm seeking my fortune," replied the young rabbit. "You're in great luck," said the deer. "For only $100, I will sell you this motorcycle so you can seek your fortune at great and exciting speeds!" "Say, that's fantastic!" replied the young rabbit, who immediately bought the motorcycle and went zooming across the countryside.

Soon he met a coyote. "Hey, little rabbit, where are you going?" asked the coyote. "I'm seeking my fortune," replied the young rabbit. "You're in great luck!" said the coyote. "For only $100, I will let you take this shortcut," said the coyote, pointing to his open mouth, "and you'll save yourself years of time!" "Say, that's fantastic!" replied the young rabbit. And paying his last $100 he put his head into the coyote's mouth, and was immediately devoured. The moral of this story is, *If you don't know where you're going, you are likely to end up somewhere you don't want to be!* ■

Specifically, the moral is that assessment practices can be the latest up-to-date fashion, conducted with great energy and speed, but if the teacher and students do not know what they are trying to accomplish, their efforts at best may be futile and at worst destructive to the quality of ongoing learning and instruction.

WHY GOALS ARE IMPORTANT

> If a man does not know to which port he is sailing, no wind is favorable.   —*Seneca*

All instruction is conducted for a purpose. Assessment begins with setting goals, progresses with progress checks, and ends with evaluating the extent to which the goals were accomplished. A **goal** is a desired state of future affairs (Johnson & Johnson, 2000). Learning to read or solve differential equations are learning goals. Goals are needed to assess the success of the student's efforts and the success of the instructional program. Goals also are important for additional reasons.

1. **Goals are guides for action.** They direct, channel, and determine what students and teachers do.
2. **Goals motivate behavior.** Goals are motivators and energizers. No goals, no motivation.
3. **Goals provide the basis for resolving conflicts.** Conflicts among students, among faculty, and among students and faculty are resolved on the basis of what students and teachers want to accomplish.
4. **Goals are a prerequisite for assessment.** Without knowing what the purpose of the activity is, no assessment can be conducted.

Even though school is not voluntary and students are in school to achieve goals that are by and large imposed on them, students and teachers are supposed to be bound together through a shared, emotional commitment to the vision of what they can accomplish if they all work together. Instruction begins with faculty inducing student commitment to what they are supposed to learn. Commitment is based on students understanding, accepting, and desiring to achieve instructional goals.

There are two aspects of ensuring student commitment to instructional goals. The first is to ensure that the instructional goals meet the START criteria (see Table 2.1).

TABLE 2.1   "START" with Learning Goals

GOAL CHARACTERISTIC	DEFINITION OF CHARACTERISTIC
S: Specific	Goals have to be specific enough so that they are clearly understood and a plan to achieve them can be developed. Specific goals indicate what needs to be done next. General and ambiguous goals do not guide action.
T: Measurable and trackable	Students and the teacher must be able to determine the extent to which students have reached their learning goals. Goals must be operationalized so that the steps to achieving the goals are clear and understandable.
A: Challenging but achievable	Students' goals must be just beyond their current competence level. Ideally, the goals will be challenging enough that the student has a 50/50 chance of achieving them. Students' must be able to achieve the learning goals if they work hard enough and utilize the support systems available to help them do so.
R: Relevant	Learning goals must be relevant to the student's interests, the parent's concerns, the instructional goals of the teacher, and the national, state, district, and school standards. Students must see the goals as meaningful and be personally committed to achieving them.
T: Transfer	Learning goals must be aimed at having students take what is learned and transfer it to real-life situations. Whatever students learn today, they should be able to use in other situations tomorrow.

To be effective, goals need to be specific (so it is clear what needs to be done next), measurable (so progress can be tracked), challenging enough to entail a moderate risk of failure, relevant to students' interests, and aimed at competencies that will be transferred to real-life situations.

The second way to ensure student commitment is to involve them in the process of forming the learning goals. Involvement leads to ownership which leads to commitment. Although indifferent to imposed goals, individuals seek out opportunities to achieve their own goals and commit considerable energy to doing so. The goal-setting conference is conducted to involve students in the goal-setting process to ensure students take ownership of the learning goals and commit themselves to achieving the goals. In the goal-setting conference students translate the instructional objectives into specific performance goals they wish to achieve. It is within the goal-setting conference that external instructional objectives and expectations become reformed and internalized as personal ambitions.

At the beginning of each day, week, instructional unit, course, semester, or year, students need to discuss thoroughly their learning goals, even when the goals are prescribed by faculty, parents, or society. During the discussion, students should reword, reorganize, and review the goals until they feel a sense of ownership toward them. Such a discussion clarifies the students' understanding of the goals and helps clear away any misunderstandings concerning the tasks necessary to reach them. Many of the more effective assessment tools, furthermore, require students to participate in setting their learning goals and conducting assessments of how well they are achieving them.

CONFERENCING WITH STUDENTS

The process of assessment involves at least three types of conferences with each individual student (see Table 2.2). First, in a **goal-setting conference,** each student sets per-

TABLE 2.2   Types of Conferences

CONFERENCE	INDIVIDUAL STUDENT	COOPERATIVE LEARNING GROUP
Goal-setting conference	Each class period, day, week, or instructional unit every student sets personal learning goals and publicly commits him- or herself to achieve them in a learning contract.	Each class period, day, week, or instructional unit all cooperative groups set group learning goals and members publicly commit themselves to achieve them in a learning contract.
Progress assessment conferences	The student's progress in achieving his or her learning goals is assessed, what the student has accomplished so far and what is yet to be done is reviewed, and the student's next steps are detailed.	The group's progress in achieving its learning goals is assessed, what the group has accomplished so far and what is yet to be done is reviewed, and the group's next steps are detailed.
Postevaluation conference	The student explains his or her level of achievement (what the student learned and failed to learn during the instructional unit) to interested parties (student's cooperative learning group, teacher(s), and parents), which naturally leads to the next goal-setting conference.	The group explains its level of achievement (what the group has accomplished and failed to accomplish during the instructional unit) to interested parties (members, teachers, and parents), which naturally leads to the next goal-setting conference.

sonal learning goals and publicly commits him- or herself to achieve them. In essence, each student makes a learning contract with him- or herself, the teacher, and a cooperative learning group that specifies what is to be learned and accomplished for either the class period, the day, the week, or the instructional unit. Second, periodic **progress assessment conferences** review the student's progress in achieving his or her goals, detailing what has been accomplished, and what is yet to be done. The student's next steps in achieving his or her learning goals are discussed.

Third, in a **postevaluation conference,** the level of student achievement is explained by the student to interested parties. The immediate interested parties may include the student and the student's cooperative learning group, teacher, and parents. Student-led conferences with parents are one example of a postevaluation conference. Each student explains what he or she learned and failed to learn during the instructional unit or assessment period. This discussion may naturally lead into the next goal-setting conference.

GOAL-SETTING CONFERENCES

Assessment begins with a goal-setting conference, which is the focus of this chapter. In a goal-setting conference, each student must formulate both personal learning goals and goals for helping others in their group and class learn. Each individual student has committed him- or herself to achieving two types of general learning goals. First, the student has academic learning goals determined by (a) what the student, parents, and teacher want the student to learn, (b) the national, state, district, and school standards and guidelines, and (c) what postsecondary educational and career organizations require.

Second, the student has community learning goals for helping and encouraging other students to learn. The classroom and school are learning communities in which each member has both a responsibility to maximize his or her own learning and a responsibility to help all other members of the community maximize their learning.

In addition to the individual learning goals of each student, cooperative learning groups have academic learning goals. Many assignments, such as completing a science experiment, performing a play, making a video, or giving a band concert, involve group goals as well as individual ones.

Individual students and cooperative learning groups develop their goals and commit themselves to achieving them in a goal-setting conference. A goal-setting conference is a meeting in which learning goals are formulated and a contract to achieve them is developed. Teachers can choose one of the following types of goal-setting conferences. (See a comparison of these types of conferences in Table 2.3.)

1. **Conducting teacher–student conferences (T/S).** The teacher can personally conduct a goal-setting conference with each individual student each day, week, semester, or year, or at the beginning of each instructional unit. This can easily lead to (a) role overload for the teacher due to the amount of time it takes to conduct a meaningful goal-setting conference and (b) a classroom focus on individual learning only, which may isolate students and create the potential for egocentrism, selfishness, alienation, and learned helplessness.
2. **Conducting teacher–cooperative learning group conferences (T/G).** The teacher personally conducts a goal-setting conference with each cooperative learning group. This cuts the time it takes to conduct the conferences considerably but may still lead to some teacher overload.

TABLE 2.3 Types of Goal-Setting Conferences

TEACHER–STUDENT (T/S)	TEACHER–GROUP (T/G)	GROUP–STUDENT (G/S)
Diagnose		
Meet with student and use evidence of expertise (previous tests, performances, and so forth) to diagnose the student's (a) current level of knowledge and expertise relevant to the instructional unit, (b) pace of learning, and (c) ability to promote and encourage classmates' learning.	Meet with group and use evidence of members' expertise (previous tests, performances, and so forth) relevant to what is to be studied to diagnose members' (a) current level of knowledge and expertise, (b) pace of learning, and (c) ability to help each other learn.	The group collects available evidence of members' expertise (previous tests, performances, and so forth) relevant to what is to be studied to diagnose members' (a) current level of knowledge and expertise, (b) pace of learning, and (c) ability to promote others' learning.
Set Goals		
Discuss with student what the student should learn (with input from parents and other interested parties) and formulate goals that meet the START criteria.	Discuss with group what each member should learn (with input from parents and other interested parties) and formulate group goals that meet the START criteria.	The group formulates learning goals for each member and the group as a whole (with input from other interested parties), making sure the goals match the START criteria.
Plan Support		
Discuss with the student the support systems and resources the student needs (such as the student's own skills and abilities, other members of the student's cooperative learning group and class, the teacher, technology, curriculum, and outside experts) and organize and structure the resources to promote the student's achievement.	Discuss with the group the support systems and resources each member and the group need (such as the members themselves, other cooperative learning groups, the teacher, technology, curriculum, and outside experts) to reach the learning goals successfully. Organize and structure these resources to promote the group's success.	The group discusses the support systems and resources each member and the group need (such as the members themselves, other cooperative learning groups, the teacher, technology, curriculum, and outside experts) to reach the learning goals successfully. The resources are structured to promote the group's success.
Make Plan		
Formulate a plan, based on the learning goals and resources committed, detailing instructional methods and a timeline specifying when and how the student's progress will be assessed. The plan is formalized into a learning contract.	Formulate a plan, based on the learning goals and committed resources, detailing instructional methods and a timeline specifying when and how the group's progress will be assessed. The plan is formalized into a learning contract.	The group makes a plan, based on the learning goals and resources committed, detailing methods to be used and a timeline specifying when and how each member's and the group's progress will be assessed. The plan is formalized into a learning contract.

3. **Engineering and supervising cooperative learning group–student conferences (G/S).** Each cooperative learning group conducts a goal-setting conference with each one of its members while the teacher monitors and supervises.
4. **Engineering and supervising cooperative learning group–cooperative learning group conferences (G/G).** Each cooperative learning group conducts a goal-setting conference with another cooperative learning group and its members while the teacher monitors and supervises.

THE THREE PHASES OF GOAL SETTING

Phase I: Preparing for the Goal-Setting Conference

The preparation for the goal-setting conference primarily involves gathering information, scheduling, planning the conference procedure, and planning how the follow-up will be conducted:

1. The information gathered includes (1) the instructional objectives, what the student wants to learn, what the parents expect the student to learn, and the relevant school, district, state, and national guidelines and (2) the data by which to diagnose students' expertise in the area to be studied.
2. Scheduling is complex if you meet with each student individually; manageable if you meet with each group; and relatively easy if you have each group conference with its members or with the members of another group.
3. Planning the conference involves making a timeline to follow and using a set of forms to document that the procedure is followed. The overall goal is to involve each student in setting his or her learning goals in a way that results in a public contract that specifies what is to be learned, when it is to be learned, and at what level.
4. Planning the follow-up includes scheduling the progress assessment and post-evaluation conferences and evaluating the assessment program to measure the achievement of the goals and the degree to which the designated resources were effectively utilized.

Phase II: The Goal-Setting Conference

You either meet with each individual student or learning group or you teach the cooperative groups how to conduct the conference and monitor their effectiveness in conducting them.

Phase III: The Follow-Up

The follow-up includes facilitating the work of each student and group, conducting the progress assessment conferences, assessing how effectively each student and group achieved their goals, and conducting the postevaluation conferences. The information is then used in the next goal-setting conference.

STEPS OF TEACHER–STUDENT GOAL-SETTING CONFERENCE

Step 1. Identify the area to be studied. You plan the instructional unit that defines the domain within which the student's learning goals will be established.

Step 2. Diagnose: You collect available evidence of the student's expertise in the subject matter to be studied. Evidence is obtained from previous tests, performances, interviews, and so forth. You use this information to diagnose the student's (a) current level of knowledge and expertise relevant to the instructional unit, (b) pace of learning, and (c) ability to promote and encourage classmates' learning.

Step 3. Set learning goals. You and the student formulate the student's learning goals by discussing what the student wishes to learn, what you expect the student to learn, the relevant aspirations of parents, and the relevant school, district, state, and national guidelines. The requirements of postsecondary educational and career organizations may also be considered. From this discussion a set of learning goals are formulated. You always *start* with learning goals formulated by the student and the interested parties to guide the student's efforts to learn and help classmates learn.

Step 4. Ensure goals meet START criteria. You ensure that the goals match the START criteria.

Step 5. Plan the process to achieve goals. You specify the process by which the goals will be achieved by listing in order each activity that must be completed to achieve the goals.

Step 6. Organize support systems and resources. You discuss with the student the support systems and resources the student needs to complete each activity required to reach the learning goals. Resources include classmates, teachers, technology, curriculum materials, and outside experts. The resources needed to complete each activity successfully need to be specified, organized into a plan to achieve the learning goals, and structured to promote the student's successful learning and achievement.

Step 7. Make a timeline. You help the student make a timeline specifying when and how each activity will be completed and how it will be assessed. The timeline is formalized into a written learning contract that both you and the student sign.

Step 8. Specify the criteria for success. You and the student agree on the criteria to use to determine whether the student has accomplished the goals successfully.

CONFERENCING WITH COOPERATIVE LEARNING GROUPS

Time is a major barrier to conducting goal-setting conferences with each student each week. In fact, very few teachers meet regularly with each student because most teachers simply do not have the time to do so. Goal-setting conferences can become more frequent when you (the teacher) meet with each cooperative learning group. The steps of the conference are the same as they are for meeting with individual students (see Table 2.4 for a summary of these steps).

Step 1. Identify the area to be studied. You plan the instructional unit that defines the domain within which learning goals will be established.

Step 2. Diagnose. You collect available evidence of the members' expertise in the subject matter to be studied. Evidence is obtained from previous tests, performances, interviews, and so forth. You use this information to diagnose members' (a) current level of knowledge and expertise relevant to the instructional unit, (b) pace of learning, and (c) ability to promote and encourage classmates' learning.

Step 3. Set learning goals. You and the group members formulate a set of learning goals by exploring all relevant expectations for each member's achievement. The discussion focuses on what group members want to learn, what you expect each member to learn, the relevant aspirations of parents, and the relevant school, district, state, and national guidelines. The requirements of postsecondary educational and career organizations may also be considered. From this discussion a set of learning goals for the group and its members are formulated to guide each member's efforts to learn and help groupmates learn.

Step 4. Ensure goals meet START criteria. You ensure the goals match the START criteria.

Step 5. Plan the process to achieve goals. You specify the process by which the goals will be achieved by listing in order each activity that must be completed to achieve the goals.

Step 6. Organize support systems and resources. You discuss with the group the support systems and resources each member and the group as a whole need to reach the learning goals successfully. The major support systems and resources include the members themselves, other cooperative learning groups, the teacher, technology, curriculum, and outside experts. You then work with the group to organize these resources and structure them to promote the group's academic success.

Step 7. Make a timeline. You and the group make a timeline specifying when and how each activity will be completed and how it will be assessed. The timeline is formalized into a written learning contract that both you and the group members sign.

Step 8. Specify the criteria for success. You and the group agree on the criteria to use to determine whether the student has accomplished the goals successfully.

COOPERATIVE LEARNING GROUPS CONFERENCING WITH THEIR MEMBERS

You save considerable time setting learning goals for each student by meeting with cooperative learning groups to do so rather than meeting with each student individually. You save even more time by having cooperative learning groups conduct the goal-setting conferences for their members. Goal-setting conferences can become a regular part of classroom life when they are primarily managed by the cooperative learning group and monitored by the teacher. While the groups are meeting, you circulate from group to group and monitor how well the groups are following the prescribed conferencing procedure. The conferencing steps are the same as they are for meeting with individual students (see Table 2.4 for a summary of these steps).

Step 1. Identify the area to be studied. You plan the instructional unit that defines the domain within which learning goals will be established.

Step 2. Diagnose. The group collects available evidence of the members' expertise in the subject matter to be studied. Evidence is obtained from previous tests, performances, interviews, and so forth. The group uses this information to diagnose mem-

TABLE 2.4   Goal-Setting Conference Steps

STEP	ACTIVITY
1	Identify area to be studied.
2	Diagnose what student already knows.
3	Set learning goals.
4	Ensure goals meet the START criteria.
5	Plan process to achieve the goals.
6	Identify resources needed for each step.
7	Make timeline with identified resources.
8	Specify the criteria for success.

bers' (a) current level of knowledge and expertise relevant to the instructional unit, (b) pace of learning, and (c) ability to promote and encourage classmates' learning.

Step 3. Set learning goals. The group formulates a set of learning goals by exploring all relevant expectations for each member's achievement and the achievement of the group as a whole. The discussion focuses on what group members want to learn, what you expect each member to learn, the relevant aspirations of parents, and the relevant school, district, state, and national guidelines. The requirements of postsecondary educational and career organizations may also be considered. From this discussion a set of learning goals for the group and its members are formulated to guide each member's efforts to learn and help groupmates learn.

Step 4. Ensure goals meet START criteria. The group ensures the goals match the START criteria.

Step 5. Plan the process to achieve goals. The group specifies the process by which the goals will be achieved by listing in order each activity that must be completed to achieve the goals.

Step 6. Organize support systems and resources. The group discusses the support systems and resources each member and the group as a whole need to reach the learning goals successfully. The major support systems and resources include the members themselves, other cooperative learning groups, the teacher, technology, curriculum, and outside experts. The group organizes and structures these resources to promote the group's success.

Step 7. Make a timeline. The group makes a timeline specifying when and how each activity will be completed and how it will be assessed. The timeline is formalized into a written learning contract that both you and the group members sign.

Step 8. Specify the criteria for success. The group members agree on the criteria to use to determine whether the student has accomplished the goals successfully.

ACTIVITY 2.1 ■ COOPERATIVE LEARNING GROUPS AND GOAL-SETTING CONFERENCES

Rank the following reasons why cooperative groups should be part of goal-setting conferences from most important (1) to least important (6). Share your ranking with your partner and listen to his or her ranking. Then come to consensus as to what the ranking should be.

_____ Makes groupmates part of the resources available to help students achieve their learning goals.

_____ Involves students in the diagnosis and goal-setting process.

_____ Saves considerable teacher time and effort.

_____ Makes it possible for goal-setting conferences to be conducted at the beginning of each instructional unit.

_____ Provides the intellectual challenge necessary for higher-level reasoning to be used in setting learning goals.

_____ Creates a system for continuous monitoring and support for each student's efforts to achieve his or her learning goals.

COOPERATIVE LEARNING GROUPS CONFERENCING WITH ANOTHER GROUP

Two cooperative groups may be paired for the goal-setting procedure. One group helps the other group (a) diagnose each member's current level of expertise, pace of learning, and ability to assist groupmates' learning, (b) formulate learning goals that meet the START criteria and take into account the expectations of the various stakeholders, (c) organize the resources each member needs to achieve the goals, and (d) formalize the plan into a learning contract. Such a group-to-group goal-setting conference increases the interdependence among groups and provides direct access to other groups as resources to help members achieve their goals. (See Activity 2.1).

SUMMARY

Assessment begins with setting goals. If there are no learning goals, there can be no assessment. Teachers may impose learning goals on students from their position of power and authority ("In this unit you will learn the causes of the Civil War!") but there are many advantages to having students and other stakeholders involved in the goal-setting process. Students are far more motivated to achieve personal goals than they are to achieve imposed instructional goals. Many of the more effective assessment tools require student participation in setting learning goals and conducting assessments.

Assessment involves three types of conferences with each student: A **goal-setting conference** to establish a contract containing the student's learning goals, **progress assessment conferences** to determine the student's progress in achieving his or her goals, and a **postevaluation conference** to explain the student's accomplishments to interested parties. Assessment begins with a goal-setting conference in which the student's learning goals and responsibilities for helping other students learn are established.

The goal-setting conference may be between the teacher and the student (T/S), the teacher and the cooperative learning group (T/G), the cooperative learning group and the student (G/S), and a cooperative learning group and another group (G/G). In all cases, the emphasis is on helping students set and take ownership for learning goals that meet the START criteria (specific, trackable, achievable, relevant, transferable). The goal-setting conference follows four steps: diagnosing current levels of expertise, setting START goals, organizing support systems and resources to help each student achieve his or her goals successfully, and constructing a plan for utilizing the resources to achieve the goals and formalizing the plan into a learning contract.

The hard truth is that most teachers do not have the time to conference with each individual student, whether it is a goal-setting conference, a progress assessment conference, or a postevaluation conference. This does not mean that such conferences cannot happen. Teachers can engineer and supervise such conferences through appropriate use of cooperative learning groups.

PREPARING FOR GOAL-SETTING CONFERENCES

Name: _____   Date: _____

Class: _____   Group: _____   Unit: _____

Source	Preliminary Goals
Student	1. _____ _____ 2. _____ _____ 3. _____ _____ 4. _____ _____ 5. _____ _____
Teacher	1. _____ _____ 2. _____ _____ 3. _____ _____ 4. _____ _____ 5. _____ _____

Group	1. _____
	_____
	2. _____
	_____
	3. _____
	_____
	4. _____
	_____
	5. _____
	_____
Parents	1. _____
	_____
	2. _____
	_____
	3. _____
	_____
	4. _____
	_____
	5. _____
	_____

DIAGNOSING MEMBERS' EXPERTISE

Student's Name: _____ Date: _____

Class: _____ Group: _____ Unit: _____

DIRECTIONS:

1. For each category, write down a list of characteristics that indicate a low, medium, or high level of aptitude and ability for this instructional unit.

2. On the basis of the member's past performances and interests, classify him or her into one of the levels for each category.

3. Discuss implications for setting learning goals for the group member.

Category	Low Expertise	Medium Expertise	High Expertise
Current Knowledge			
Pace of Learning			
Ability to Help Others' Learn			

Implications for Setting Learning Goals

1. _____

   _____

   _____

2. _____

   _____

   _____

3. _____

   _____

   _____

GOALS FOR GROUP MEMBERS

Group: _____   Unit: _____   Date: _____

DIRECTIONS:

1. Write out the learning goals for each member of your group for this instructional unit. Remember to include goals for helping and encouraging the learning of group-mates.

2. Make sure each goal meets the START criteria.

3. Have each group member sign for his or her goals. The signature indicates that the student understands the goals, agrees that they are challenging but realistic, and commits him- or herself to achieve them.

4. Set appropriate group goals for the instructional unit.

Goals	Member 1	Member 2	Member 3	Member 4
1.				
2.				
3.				
4.				
5.				
Signatures:				

Group Goals

1. _____

_____

2. _____

_____

3. _____

_____

START WITH LEARNING GOALS

Student's Name: _____   Date: _____

Class: _____   Group: _____   Unit: _____

1. Write the learning goal as specifically and precisely as you can. _____

_____

_____

_____

_____

_____

2. On what date will the goal be achieved? _____

    a. What will you finish during the first class session? _____

    _____

    b. What will you finish during the second class session? _____

    _____

    c. What will you finish during the third class session? _____

    _____

    d. List other pertinent deadlines. _____

    _____

    _____

3. Explain how the goal is challenging (beyond current competencies) but achievable with the support system. _____

_____

_____

_____

_____

_____

4. Explain how the goal is relevant to your interests, the instructional objectives, your group concerns, and your parents' concerns. _____

_____

_____

_____

_____

_____

_____

5. Explain how achieving the goal will allow you to use what is learned in other situations. _____

_____

_____

_____

_____

_____

_____

_____

_____

ORGANIZING SUPPORT SYSTEMS AND RESOURCES

Student's Name: _____ Date: _____

Class: _____ Group: _____ Unit: _____

DIRECTIONS:

To achieve each of the following goals, decide what resources you need from each source. List your goals for this instructional unit across the top of the chart. For each goal, describe the resources you need from each of the sources listed. Add other sources relevant to the unit.

Sources	Goal 1	Goal 2	Goal 3
Self			
Groupmates			
Teacher			
Curriculum			
Technology			
Outside Experts			
Field Trips			
Other:			

MY LEARNING CONTRACT

Student's Name: _____   Date: _____

Class: _____   Group: _____   Unit: _____

My Academic Goals	My Responsibilities for Helping Others Learn	My Group's Goals
1.		
2.		
3.		
4.		

The plan for achieving my learning goals, meeting my responsibilities, and helping my group is _____

_____

_____

_____

The timeline for achieving my goals:

Beginning date: _____

First road-mark: _____

Second road-mark: _____

Third road-mark: _____

Final date: _____

Resources include (a) organizational skills, (b) responsibility, (c) work ethic, (d) positive attitudes, and (e) previous achievements.

Signatures:

_____   _____

_____   _____

CHAPTER THREE

STANDARDIZED TESTS

WHAT ARE STANDARDIZED TESTS?

One of the most widespread assessment procedures used is standardized tests. Although standardized tests have many critics, and the pressure to change them is considerable, they will be part of the assessment procedures in most school districts in the foreseeable future. Teachers should be able to use the results. **Standardized tests** are prepared for nationwide use (usually commercial) to provide accurate and meaningful information on students' levels of performance relative to others at their age or grade levels. To make test scores comparable, the tests are administered and scored under carefully controlled conditions that are uniform to all students so that students all over the country (and world) have equal chances to demonstrate what they know. Standard methods are used to develop items, administer the test, score it, and report the scores to interested audiences. Such tests are usually constructed by subject matter specialists and experts on testing.

Standardized tests are typically used to provide a yardstick (which teacher-made tests cannot provide) against which to compare individuals or groups of students. The interpretation of scores on standardized tests are based on national and subnational norms (see Box 3.1 for definitions of measurement criteria). **Test norms** are records of the performances of groups of individuals who have previously taken the test. Test norms are used to determine how the score of any test taker compares with the scores of a sample of similar individuals. The test publishers provide one or more ways of comparing each student's raw score (number of correct answers) with the norming sample.

Standardized tests evolved and proliferated because of the unreliability of school assessments. The Scholastic Aptitude Test (SAT), for example, was created in 1926 as an efficient and economical way for college admission officers to select the most promising students from the pool of applicants. The SAT test scores were found to be a better predictor of grades in college than were high school grades. Since that time standardized tests have been used to (a) select and place students into classes, programs, special schools, or colleges, (b) decide whether a student should advance to the next level, (c) diagnose students' problems in learning, (d) determine honors, awards, and scholarships, (e) evaluate the effectiveness of instructional programs, (f) apply for federal funds, and (g) conduct research. Standardized test scores have become the yardstick for measuring the quality of schools, school districts, and even education within a state and the country as a whole.

There are two types of standardized tests: achievement tests and aptitude tests. **Achievement tests** focus on the knowledge and skills learned in school and may be in the form of achievement batteries, diagnostic tests, or subject-specific tests. **Aptitude tests** focus on the potential maximum achievement of students and may measure general intellectual aptitude, aptitude to do well in college or certain vocational training programs, reading aptitude, mechanical aptitude, or perceptual aptitude. Although aptitude tests and achievement tests are theoretically different, their results are so

■ ■ ■ ■ ■

BOX 3.1

CRITERIA FOR GOOD MEASUREMENT PROCEDURES

CRITERIA	DEFINITION
Reliability	**Reliability** exists when a student's performance remains the same on repeated measurements. On a norm-referenced measure, this means that when the measure is repeated and the raw scores of students are arranged in order from highest to lowest, all students will keep the same rank.
Validity	**Validity** means that the test actually measures what it was designed to measure, all of what it was designed to measure, and nothing but what it was designed to measure.
Objectivity	**Objectivity** is the agreement of (a) experts on the correct answer to a test item and (b) different scorers on what score should be assigned to a test paper or questionnaire.
Practicality	**Practicality** of a measure is determined by the cost per copy, the time it takes to administer it, the ease of scoring, and other factors teachers have to take into account before deciding to use a particular measure.
Discrimination	When a norm-referenced measure is used, each item has to **discriminate** among students as high, medium, and low on the skill or knowledge being measured.
Norm-referenced tests	**Norm-referenced tests** are designed to test a student's performance as it compares to the performances of other students.
Criteria-referenced tests	**Criteria-referenced tests** are designed to compare a student's test performance to preset criteria defining excellence on learning tasks or skills.

highly correlated that both may be considered achievement tests (see Box 3.2 for definitions of statistical interpretations of test results).

ADVANTAGES OF STANDARDIZED TESTS

1. Standardized tests are easily administered and they take little time away from instruction.
2. Standardized tests provide a standard situation in which all students are required to answer the same questions. This ensures that all students may be evaluated on the same criteria—some students will not be evaluated on different criteria than others.
3. Standardized tests provide a permanent record of behavior when they are written (some tests can be oral). A permanent record of answers allows teachers to examine the same answers several times to ensure that the evaluation is fair and unbiased.
4. Standardized test scores allow simple comparisons between students, schools, districts, states, and nations. From the global comparisons provided, an overall assessment can be made.

■ ■ ■ ■ ■

BOX 3.2
INTERPRETING STANDARDIZED TEST SCORES

STATISTIC	DEFINITION
Frequency distribution	A list of the number of people who obtain each score or fall into each range of scores on a test. This information may be expressed as a simple graph, called a histogram or bar graph, where the horizontal or x-axis indicates the number of possible scores and the vertical or y-axis indicates the number of students who attained each score.
Measures of central tendency	The **mean** is the sum of all scores in the class divided by the number of students. The **median** is the midpoint in a set of scores arranged in order, from highest to lowest. It is most useful when a few unusually high or low scores distort the mean.
Standard deviation	The average of the differences of all students' scores from the mean score. A large standard deviation indicates that students obtained a wide range of scores on the test. A small standard deviation indicates that the range of scores is low and most students scored right around the mean.
Standard score	An indication of how far each student's score is above or below the mean as measured by standard deviation units, which allows for the comparison of scores from different tests, regardless of the size of the class or the number of items on the test. To find the standard score you subtract the mean from the student's raw score and divide by the standard deviation. Three common standard scores are z-score, stanine, and the normal curve equivalent. **Z-scores** have a mean of 0 and a standard deviation of 1. **Stanine** (a combination of the words, *standard nine*) scores have a mean of 5 and a standard deviation of 2. The **normal curve equivalent** (NCE) scores range from 1 to 99 with a mean of 50 and a standard deviation of about 21.
Percentile rank	The percentage of the class with scores below that obtained by the student. Percentile rank can range from 0 to 100.
Grade-equivalent scores	The average of the scores of all students in the norming sample at that grade level. Grade-equivalent scores are generally listed as numbers, such as 11.4, 9.6, 7.2, or 3.5. The whole number expresses the grade level and the decimals stand for tenths of a year. Grade-equivalent scores are easy to interpret and understand.

5. Standardized tests are used by psychometricians and major institutions and, therefore, they carry scientific credibility and tradition.
6. Standardized tests are unparalleled for certain purposes, such as large-scale, cost-effective assessment of large numbers of students on low-level cognitive objectives.
7. Standardized tests tend to have high predictive validity. Advanced placement tests, for example, accurately predict how students will perform in college courses.

DISADVANTAGES OF STANDARDIZED TESTS

1. **The content of standardized tests is problematic.** Standardized tests measure factual or declarative information and a narrow group of verbal skills (such as word recall, fluency, and recognition vocabulary). They tend not to measure depth of understanding, integration of knowledge, and production of discourse, let alone social progress, individual worth, or school effectiveness. Abstract verbal skills, for example, do not determine excellence in writing a poem, singing a lullaby, tutoring a child, or giving an order in a factory.

2. **The range of what standardized tests can assess is limited.** Standardized tests are inadequate in assessing students' generative capabilities, such as (a) expressing themselves orally or in writing, (b) organizing and analyzing an abundance of data, (c) devising an experiment to answer an interesting question, and (d) working cooperatively with others.

3. **The ability of standardized tests to identify students with special needs is negligible.** Standardized tests are of little help in identifying students who need either support and help to succeed or challenges beyond those offered by the curriculum because they are
   a. **Not timely.** They are administered at most once per year and usually only once every several years.
   b. **Not aligned.** Assessment must be aligned with the curriculum and conducted regularly and frequently to avoid having students fall farther and farther behind and having other students endure repetition and slow pace (because they learn quickly or already know what is being taught). Any student is potentially in need of special assistance at some point. And any student is potentially eligible for additional challenge. Unless teachers have the capability frequently to assess students with regard to the curriculum, they have no way of knowing whether a challenge or special assistance is needed.

4. **Standardized tests are not helpful in assessing (a) student learning in specific courses or (b) achievement of district program goals.** A generic test for high school juniors will not yield information on the degree to which students have learned in a specific class, for example, physics, auto mechanics, or family life. Prepared program goals (what students will have learned as a result of studying social studies or language arts) typically include broad statements such as "understand major historical trends" or "communicate effectively in speaking and writing." Such goals involve higher-level outcomes not included in standardized tests.

5. **Standardized tests have limited use in assessing student exit outcomes.** Exit outcomes are statements of the knowledge and skills students will possess after completing schooling. Exit outcomes address the question, When students leave us what will they know and what can they do? Most schools use exit outcomes to guide curriculum planning and curriculum audits. Thus, if a district has an exit outcome relating to critical and creative thinking, faculty may examine the science program to ensure it does not rely solely on the memorization of facts and the performance of "cookbook" labs. In some schools, furthermore, a condition for graduation is that students demonstrate proficiency on the exit outcomes to a committee of teachers, community or business leaders, and other students. Such demonstrations may include an original garment design, a creative solution to a situation in auto mechanics, or a unique approach to a problem in trigonometry.

6. **Standardized tests are not useful in conducting external curriculum audits.** To determine the quality of a school or district curriculum, student performance must be compared with students from all over the state or nation, using the same procedures and techniques and sharing the results. Although this is

precisely the purpose of a standardized test, the tests are not capable of assessing the full range of the curriculum—all the knowledge and skills that educators and the community consider important. A curriculum audit should reflect the entire range of the curriculum deemed important by educators and the community.

7. **Standardized test results that are used for high-stake purposes create a temptation to cheat in some manner.** There are many stories about schools that exclude low-achieving students from a standardized test because including them would depress their average score and cause them to lose face (or worse) in comparison with other schools. There are also stories about teachers who unfairly coach their students on test items or provide unauthorized assistance during the actual assessment.

8. **The impact standardized tests have on instruction is problematic.** Test construction emphasizes basic skills and neglects many of the most important outcomes of schooling. When teachers "teach to the test," they emphasize basic skills at the expense of higher-order reasoning skills.

9. **Use of standardized test results is limited.** Standardized tests predict how many years of conventional education a student will attain. They do not, however, predict occupational success in fields such as medicine, engineering, teaching, scientific research, and business.

Cautions

In and of themselves, tests are incapable of harming students. It is the way test results are used that is potentially harmful to students. (See Activity 3.1 to conduct your own analysis of standardized tests.) Even the best tests can create problems if their results are misused. The issue is not whether standardized tests should exist, but rather how their results should be used. Some helpful hints follow.

1. **Make sure you are using the right tests.** Schools often devise new goals and curriculum only to assess their success with tests that are not relevant to either the goals or the new instruction or materials. Whatever the purposes of assessment, they cannot be accomplished unless the correct tests are used.

2. **Do not use the results of standardized tests to judge the success of local programs and goals.** Standardized tests cover large segments of subject matter or general abilities related to learning. They focus on general goals common to schools across the country and are not suitable for evaluating limited instruction, such as in a single learning unit or for judging how well a strictly local instructional goal is achieved.

3. **Assume that test results are fallible and not always accurate.** Low scores can be the result of (a) poor health, negative moods, and distractions; (b) lack of test-taking skills; and (c) inability to take tests well due to factors such as anxiety. Every test score contains possible error. Many students who score poorly on standardized tests excel in school, college, or occupations.

4. **Use more than a single test score to make important decisions.** Given the possibility of error that exists for every test score, a single test score is too suspect to serve as the sole criterion for any crucial decision. Supporting evidence is needed.

5. **Do not set arbitrary minimums for performance on tests.** Using arbitrary minimums to make critical decisions is inherently unfair. If the standard is arbitrarily set at 85, for example, there may be no valid reason to predict that a person who scores 86 will perform better in the future than a person who scores 84. Tests do not have sufficient validity and reliability to make such fine distinctions.

ACTIVITY **3.1** ■ ANALYZING STANDARDIZED TESTS

1. Select a standardized test that either you or your students have taken. Note the type of questions used in the test. Write sample questions that are appropriate for your students based on the types used in the test. Have your students practice answering the questions until you are sure they are familiar with how to answer each type of question.

2. Choose several of the test questions in the standardized test. Analyze and label them according to the following categories:

   a. Prior knowledge needed
   b. Higher-level reasoning needed
   c. More than one answer seems correct
   d. Ambiguous wording
   e. Recall required
   f. Culturally biased
   g. Other:

Comment on your findings:

6. **Remember that a test does not measure *all* the content, skills, or behaviors of interest.** Tests are limited to what they cover, which is usually a sample of what a student knows or can do. Another test that samples differently could get quite different results. Scores are approximations of students' knowledge and competencies.

7. **Remember, in some cases there is no alternative to standardized tests.** The SAT and GRE provide important information, as do advanced placement tests. Standardized tests have their place and if used appropriately, provide information that cannot be currently obtained any other way.

HOW TO HELP YOUR STUDENTS DO BETTER ON STANDARDIZED TESTS

Three steps can help students do better on standardized tests: (a) making students comfortable in the test-taking situation, (b) showing students how to complete tests efficiently, and (c) helping students understand that their scores on standardized tests are neither a cause for pride nor shame.

The First Step Is the Warm-Up. It involves familiarizing students with the mechanics of the testing situation. Pass out facsimiles of the answer sheet and have students practice filling in their names and other information. Rehearse the preliminary instructions, using the exact language the manual advises. Practice arranging the seats according to the seating plan suggested by the test makers. Give students proper pencils and have them practice filling in answer sheets rapidly because speed is essential on standardized tests and neatness does not help one's score. During practice, watch for students who tend to lose their place or have trouble marking the proper boxes. Having students practice reading questions on one sheet and marking answers on another sheet is especially helpful. The purpose of such warm-up procedures is to make the mechanics of test taking so familiar that students will be relaxed and competent when faced with the real thing.

The Second Step Is the Dry Run.   Use old copies of the test that contain questions no longer used to familiarize students with question format, the vocabulary of instructions, and the general appearance of the test. Have students devise their own best strategies for test taking and then share their ideas with one another. Look through the test to determine whether any special skills, such as reading graphs and charts, are needed. If so, drill students on those skills. Tell students whether they should guess or avoid guessing. Because skimming is a vital skill, have students practice reading passages both aloud and silently, stressing only key words, and reading passages with the question and answers in mind. At the end of each practice session, discuss with students the following rules for test taking:

1. As quickly as possible, complete the entire test or section. First answer only questions you are sure of and those with obvious answers. Lightly mark the questions that make you pause and return to them later.
2. Leave a minute at the end of the test to fill in any blank boxes. Guess on every question you don't know unless there is a penalty for doing so.
3. Do not get interested in the reading passages or any information contained in the test. Standardized tests are not for learning or thinking. They are for gauging how well students take tests.
4. Never argue with answers. Simply select answers the testing agency will score as correct.

The Third Step Is the Follow-Through.   This involves letting students know that what was tested was their ability to take a test and their scores are neither cause for pride nor shame. The real work completed during the school year measures achievement and ability.

SUMMARY

Standardized tests are tests prepared for nationwide use (usually commercial) to provide accurate and meaningful information on students' levels of performance relative to others at their age or grade levels. National and subnational normative data are provided for most standardized instruments so that student performance can be compared to other than local norms. Standardized test scores may be used to evaluate the effectiveness of instructional programs, to select and place students, to diagnose students' problems in learning, and to conduct research.

There are two types of standardized tests—achievement and aptitude. Standardized achievement tests may be in the form of achievement batteries, diagnostic tests, and subject-specific tests. Aptitude tests may be general intelligence tests or multifactor aptitude batteries. Standardized tests ensure that all students are evaluated by the same criteria. They yield more accurate and fairer evaluations than unsystematic observations. On the other hand, standardized achievement and aptitude tests measure a narrow group of verbal skills and primarily contain multiple-choice items that do not allow students to demonstrate complex cognitive and problem-solving skills.

To interpret standardized test scores, you need to understand frequency distributions, measures of central tendency and standard deviation, percentiles, grade equivalents, and normal curve equivalents. The criteria that standardized tests (and all other measurement procedures) have to meet are reliability, validity, objectivity, practicality, and discrimination. A measure is reliable if it is consistent and accurate. A measure is valid if it measures what it is supposed to measure. A measure has objectivity if there is agreement among (a) experts on the correct answer to a test item and (b) different scorers on what score should be assigned to a test paper or questionnaire. Practicality is determined by the cost of and ease with which a measure can be used. A measure discriminates if it differentiates among high-, medium-, and low-achieving students.

Teachers can help their students score higher on standardized tests by making students comfortable in the test-taking situation, showing students how to complete tests efficiently, and helping students understand that their scores on standardized tests are neither a cause for pride nor shame. In holding teachers accountable for student scores on standardized tests, it should be remembered that teachers can only provide an opportunity for students to learn, they cannot make students learn.

STANDARDIZED TESTS: PLANNING FORM

1. How will you drill students on the mechanics of taking standardized tests?

a. _____

_____

b. _____

_____

c. _____

_____

d. _____

2. How will you drill students on test-taking skills?

a. _____

_____

b. _____

_____

c. _____

_____

d. _____

3. How will you teach students to interpret standardized test scores?

a. _____

_____

b. _____

_____

c. _____

_____

d. _____

_____

CHAPTER FOUR

TEACHER-MADE TESTS

TESTING STUDENTS

Tests are given to assess student learning, to increase student learning, and to guide instruction. From 5 to 15 percent of all class time is used in administering written teacher-made tests. **Teacher-made tests** are written or oral assessments of student achievement that are (a) designed specifically for the teacher's students and (b) not commercially produced or standardized. They tend to be used more frequently, to cover more of the curriculum, and count more for final grades than other forms of assessment and evaluation. Ideally, teacher-made tests are used to increase learning, guide instruction, and provide insight into what students need to be taught next. Actually, they are used primarily to measure final achievement and assign grades at the end of an instructional unit. Teacher-made tests are almost always of the paper-and-pencil variety and may be classified as either objective or essay tests.

OBJECTIVE TESTS

Objective tests are frequently used for a number of reasons. They can be easily scored and analyzed (once a key is constructed); they can be given to large numbers of students; they take little time to administer and score; and they are free of bias in scoring and in requiring the use of unrelated skills, such as writing. Objective tests allow teachers to sample more fully the content of an instructional unit because many questions can be asked and students can answer them relatively quickly. Efficiency and reliability, therefore, tend to be high.

Objective tests also have a number of pitfalls. Determining what questions to ask and how to ask them is highly subjective; writing good objective questions takes considerable time and skill; assessing knowledge and skills relies on recognition and recall; and poor readers are penalized. (See Box 4.1 for a summary of the advantages and disadvantages of objective tests.)

TYPES OF OBJECTIVE TEST ITEMS

There are several types of objective test items: multiple choice, true–false, matching, short answer, and interpretive.

Multiple-Choice Items

Multiple-choice items consist of a direct question or incomplete statement (called the *stem*) followed by two or more possible answers (called *responses*), only one of

■ ■ ■ ■ ■

BOX 4.1
ADVANTAGES AND DISADVANTAGES OF OBJECTIVE TESTS

ADVANTAGES	DISADVANTAGES
Allow broad sampling of knowledge	Can be very time-consuming to construct
Assess knowledge quickly and efficiently	Represent highly subjective selection of questions
Can be easily scored and analyzed	Entail difficulty in writing unambiguous questions
Can be administered to large groups	Rely on recognition and recall for assessment
Prevent bias in scoring	Require specific, predetermined answers
Measure student knowledge without bias toward writing, grammatical, or neatness skills	Penalize poor readers

which is to be selected. Students can be instructed to choose either the correct answer or the best answer. An example of a multiple-choice item follows:

Drilling a hole with a drill that has one lip ground longer than the other will result in a hole that is

a. oversized   c. bell-mouthed

b. out-of-round   d. undersized

The advantages of multiple-choice items are that many levels of cognitive understanding can be assessed, they are easy to grade, and guessing is difficult. The disadvantages are that writing good items is difficult and time-consuming, especially if higher-level reasoning is to be tested; items test only recognition of the correct answer; and providing feedback on each item is difficult. Teachers should ensure that they write questions that require translation, interpretation, application, analysis, and evaluation. (See Box 4.2 for guidelines on writing multiple-choice items.) Too often, multiple-choice test items assess only at the knowledge level.

True–False Items

True–false items require students to identify the correctness of facts, statements, definitions, and principles. An example of a true–false item follows:

T   F   A virus is the smallest known organism.

True–false items have three advantages: they are easy and quick to construct, answer, and score. Thus, a large amount of knowledge can be sampled in a short amount of time. Their disadvantages are that students' scores can be influenced considerably by guessing and only lower-level learning can be measured. (See Box 4.3 for guidelines on how to write true–false items.)

■ ■ ■ ■ ■

BOX 4.2
GUIDELINES FOR WRITING MULTIPLE-CHOICE ITEMS

1. **Write the stem first.** The stem should present a problem, stand on its own without qualification, include most of the item, be as short as possible, and be clearly worded. Phrases or words that begin every choice should be part of the stem.
2. Avoid using negative constructions (*not*) in the stem. If used, underline *not* to alert readers' attention to it.
3. Include only one clearly correct or best response.
4. Make all alternatives grammatically consistent with the stem. Each choice should have the same grammatical form (such as a verb) at its beginning.
5. Make all alternative responses equal in length. Avoid making the correct response either the longest or the shortest. Often the longest alternative is correct because absolutely correct answers require qualification and precision.
6. Make all incorrect responses equally plausible. Do not include responses that are absurd or unbelievable.
7. Place the correct response in each possible position equally often.
8. Avoid using the expression *none of these* as an alternative because too often it reduces the possible correct choice to one or two items.
9. Never have the answer to one question depend on knowing the answer to another.
10. Avoid using (a) no-exception words such as *never, all, none,* and *always* (they signal an incorrect response) and (b) qualifying words such as *often, seldom, sometimes, typically, generally,* and *ordinarily* (they signal correct responses).

■ ■ ■ ■ ■

BOX 4.3
GUIDELINES FOR WRITING TRUE–FALSE ITEMS

1. Use statements that are clearly true or false without qualification.
2. Avoid absolute words such as *all, always,* and *never.*
3. Restrict each statement to a single idea.
4. Use an approximately equal number of true and false items.
5. Do not use the exact wording of the textbook in the questions.
6. Make all items approximately the same length.
7. Avoid trivial and general statements.
8. Have students make false statements true to encourage higher-level thinking.

Matching Items

A **matching item** consists of a list of concepts and a list of responses. Students match one of the responses to each concept, which requires them to categorize and associate. An example of a matching question follows:

Match the names of the psychologists with the concept they popularized.

_____	Benjamin Bloom	a. competency motivation
_____	Abraham Maslow	b. fully functioning person
_____	Carl Rogers	c. mastery learning
		d. self-actualization

The advantages of matching questions include the ability to cover considerable material in a small amount of space, ease of scoring, and the ability to assess discrimination among similar events or issues. The disadvantages include teachers being restricted to measuring factual information and students being able to cheat with ease. (See Box 4.4 for guidelines on writing matching items.)

Short Answers and Completion Items

In **short-answer and completion items** students are required to supply a brief answer consisting of a name, word, phrase, or symbol. An example of a short-answer question follows:

A figure that has three sides is called a _____.

Advantages of these questions are that they are easy to write, require recall of information, and guessing is not likely to be successful. Their disadvantage is that they measure only lower-level learning. (See Box 4.5 for guidelines on writing short-answer questions.)

Interpretive Items

Interpretive items are objective questions based on a graph, diagram, map, or descriptive paragraph. They require students to interpret written or pictorial material and, therefore, can measure complex learning in a more structured form than can essay items. Disadvantages of these items are that they test only at the recognition level, are difficult and time-consuming to construct, favor good readers, and measure only the ability to solve problems presented in a structured form. When writing interpretive items, teachers should ensure that the questions are at an appropriate reading level and require analysis and interpretation.

BOX 4.4
GUIDELINES FOR WRITING MATCHING ITEMS

1. Keep the lists as short as possible (six items or less).
2. Keep the lists as homogeneous as possible (do not mix names with dates).
3. List more responses than concepts to reduce guessing.
4. Arrange the lists in alphabetical or chronological order.
5. State in the directions the basis on which the matching is to be done.

BOX 4.5
GUIDELINES FOR WRITING SHORT-ANSWER QUESTIONS

1. Ensure only one answer is correct.
2. Ask a direct question.
3. Put the blank toward end of the sentence.
4. Use blanks of equal length.
5. Ensure the answer is brief and definitive.
6. Have one blank per sentence.
7. In computation problems state the degree of precision expected.
8. For completion items, put blanks in a column on the right side of the paper.

ESSAY TESTS

Essay tests consist of a few questions requiring students to write paragraphs or themes as answers. Essay items require students to recall, select, organize, and apply what they have learned and express it in their own words. Essay tests have several advantages. They can be used to assess students' recall of what was learned, understanding of concepts and principles, ability to organize material and develop arguments, and ability to apply what students know. Essay questions are especially useful in measuring higher-level reasoning processes (analysis, synthesis, and evaluation) and the ability to express oneself in writing. (See Box 4.6 for guidelines on how to write essay questions.)

Essay tests also have several disadvantages. First, only a few questions can be asked, so requests for a representative sample of the content to be tested cannot be granted. Second, nonverbal students and students who do not write well may be penalized by the exclusive use of essay tests. Third and fourth, essay tests require much more time to score than do objective tests and are difficult to score in an objective and reliable way.

Scoring essay questions is notoriously unreliable. Different teachers may award different grades for the same answers and the same teacher may arrive at different scores for the same answer at different times. Relatively poor answers have been found to receive higher grades when read after even poorer ones than when read after much better ones. Teachers have been found to assign lower grades to students whose handwriting is illegible, whose paper is untidy, or whose grammar or spelling is faulty. Although certain procedures can increase the reliability of essay test grading, they require great discipline and commitment on the part of the teacher.

Short-Essay Items

Short-essay items require students to recall, explain, and apply specific information they have learned in their own words. Students are required to write short, succinct answers in which they demonstrate how much they know. Students may write an answer as long as two or three sentences to a page. Short-essay items have the same

---

BOX 4.6
GUIDELINES FOR WRITING ESSAY QUESTIONS

1. Gear questions directly to desired outcomes of the instructional program not easily assessed by objective items (e.g., analysis, synthesis, argumentation).
2. Define assessment criteria and point values. Be sure the criteria clearly communicate how questions should be answered. Inform students which items will be weighted heavier than others and how much time they should spend on each question.
3. Make questions specific. Avoid broad and ambiguous questions (e.g., *discuss…, tell all you know about…*).
4. Allow students sufficient time to complete the questions.
5. Adopt procedures to make scoring as objective as possible:
    a. Outline model answers before scoring tests.
    b. Prepare assessment criteria in advance.
    c. Assess all answers for one question before going on to the next.
    d. Scan a random sample of the papers to begin assessing.
    e. Apply the same criteria to all papers (i.e., if one student is penalized for spelling and grammar, all students should be).
    f. Have colleagues score a number of papers using your criteria and compare their assessments with yours.

advantages and disadvantages as essay items. They can be used advantageously to elicit a wide variety of student responses from defining terms to comparing and contrasting important concepts or events. They can be used to assess higher-level reasoning in the form of analysis, synthesis, and evaluation. And guessing is minimized. Disadvantages include scoring responses reliably and the amount of time required to assess student responses.

TEST BLUEPRINTS

Whether a test consists of essay or objective questions, it needs to measure accurately and fairly the parts of the subject area covered in instruction. A blueprint of a test, or **test blueprint,** can be constructed to ensure that the test assesses a representative, accurate sample of what is covered in the learning unit. In most cases you will not have the time to test students' knowledge and performance on everything covered in class. Your tests, therefore, will only partially sample what students know and can do. The more precisely and completely learning goals are described at the beginning of a unit, the easier it will be to (a) include an adequate sample of the most significant topics on a test and (b) use the types of test items that are most appropriate for measuring the desired learning outcomes. Box 4.7 provides guidelines for creating your own tests. Activity 4.1 provides exercises that allow you to think through how you will devise your test.

■ ■ ■ ■ ■

BOX 4.7
GUIDELINES FOR TEACHER-MADE TESTS

1. Construct test items to reflect instructional objectives and desired outcomes.
2. Each student should have a neatly and accurately typed copy of the test. Teachers should avoid whenever possible writing items on the board or reading them aloud to the class. All items of the same format should be grouped together.
3. Vary the question types (true–false, multiple choice, matching, completion, short answer, essay).
4. Divide question types into separate sections.
5. Precede each set of items with clear completion instructions, and provide the total amount of credit (points) possible for each question, for example, multiple choice (3 points each).
6. Vary types of questions to cover many levels of learning: recognition, recall, processing, analysis, integrative, application.
7. Within each type of item, order the questions from simple to complex (easiest to hardest).
8. For broad, integrative, complex questions (e.g., essay and graphic organizer questions), provide students a choice of questions from which they can select to answer.
9. Administer the test in a way that cheating can be eliminated or detected.
10. Provide a criterion-referenced grading scale so students know what score represents a certain grade (e.g., A = 93–100, B = 85–92, C = 75–84, D = 65–74; F = Below 65).
11. Make sure the reading level of the test is appropriate for your students.
12. Give sufficient time for all students to finish. Inform students of time remaining.
13. Type or print the test clearly and leave space between questions and sections to facilitate easy reading and responding.
14. Include a variety of visual, oral, and kinesthetic tasks.
15. Vary the way the test is given for students with special needs.

ACTIVITY **4.1**   ■   REFLECTION ON TEACHER-MADE TESTS

1. Choose a unit you are going to teach soon.

2. Decide whether to emphasize essay or objective test items. Explain why one is more useful than the other for assessing the outcomes of this unit. Indicate what percentage of the questions will be

   _____   Essay questions

   _____   Objective questions

3. Summarize the strengths and weaknesses of each type of question and explain why you have decided on the percentages you have.

4. Of the objective questions you are going to include in the test, indicate what percentage will be of the following types:

   _____   Multiple-choice questions

   _____   True–false questions

   _____   Matching questions

   _____   Short-answer and completion questions

   _____   Interpretative questions

5. Summarize the strengths and weaknesses of each type of question and explain why you have decided on the percentages you have.

6. List five pieces of advice for teachers on constructing tests:

   a. _____

   b. _____

   c. _____

   d. _____

   e. _____

A test blueprint can also serve as a guide to students preparing for an exam. Imagine, for example, that you have been teaching a unit on mathematics that includes fractions, multiplication, division, measuring, and decimals. During the time spent on the unit, the major emphasis was placed on fractions. Thus, the test blueprint for your unit would be as shown in Figure 4.1. After you have finished constructing your test, you can use Activity 4.2 to check whether your test reflects a representative sample of topics covered and the most appropriate types of questions for assessing student learning of these topics.

COOPERATIVE LEARNING AND TEACHER-MADE TESTS

Cooperative learning can be incorporated into a testing procedure in at least four ways: group–individual–group procedure, weekly group tests with an individual final exam, group discussion tests, and academic tournaments. Involving coopera-

FIGURE 4.1   **Sample Test Blueprint**

TEST BLUEPRINT

Subject Area	Routine Computation	Taught Procedures	Total
Fractions	10	5	15
Multiplication	5	3	8
Division	5	3	8
Measuring	5	3	8
Decimals	5	3	8
Total	30	17	47

tive learning groups in administering traditional tests has two advantages (Johnson, Johnson, & Holubec, 1998a; Johnson, Johnson, & Smith, 1998). First, having students work together to prepare for the assessment can level the playing field by enabling students to compare understandings and to establish a common background knowledge.

ACTIVITY **4.2** ■ CHECKLIST FOR TESTS

_____ **1.** All items relate to the instructional objectives and desired learning outcomes.

_____ **2.** There are _____ different question types in the test.

_____ **3.** Each question type is in a separate section.

_____ **4.** The directions for the overall test and each section are clear.

_____ **5.** Questions that assess _____ different learning levels have been included.

_____ **6.** Questions are ordered from simple to complex.

_____ **7.** Students can choose among essay and graphic organizer questions.

_____ **8.** Point values are given for each section.

_____ **9.** Students have been informed of the criterion-referenced grading scale.

_____ **10.** The reading level is appropriate to your students.

_____ **11.** Each question is easy to read and respond to.

_____ **12.** The test has been adapted for students with special needs.

Second, having students work in groups immediately following the assessment (a) allows each group member to discover what he or she did and did not understand, (b) allows each group member to discover where in the course materials the information is located to answer the questions, and (c) allows the group to provide remediation to members who did not understand the course content covered in the test. In this way, involving cooperative learning groups in the administration of tests can serve both to assess and to increase student learning.

Group Preparation, Individual Test, Group Test (GIG) Procedure

The sequence of the **GIG test procedure** for using cooperative learning groups in testing is group preparation, individual test, group test. These three components of the sequence correspond to the following description: (a) students work together in cooperative learning groups to review the material to be covered in the test; (b) each student takes the test individually; and (c) students retake the test together as a cooperative learning group. (See Box 4.8 for a list a reasons and steps for using the GIG procedure.)

Group Preparation.   Students are assigned to cooperative learning groups that are heterogeneous in terms of reading and math ability. Students meet in their cooperative learning groups and are given (a) study questions and (b) class time to prepare for the examination. The task is for students to discuss each study question and come to consensus about its answer. The cooperative goal is to ensure that all group mem-

■ ■ ■ ■ ■

BOX 4.8
THE GIG PROCEDURE FOR GIVING TESTS

You should frequently give tests and quizzes to assess (a) how much each student knows and (b) what students still need to learn. Whenever you give a test, cooperative learning groups can serve as bookends by preparing members to take the test and providing a setting in which students review the test. Reasons for using the GIG procedure follow.

1. Optimizing each student's preparation for the test
2. Making each student accountable to peers for his or her performance on the test
3. Assessing how much each student knows
4. Assessing what students still need to learn
5. Providing students with immediate clarification of what they did not understand or learn
6. Providing students with immediate remediation for what they did not learn
7. Preventing arguments between you and your students over which answers are correct and why.

The steps for this procedure follow.

1. Students prepare for and review for a test in cooperative learning groups.
2. Each student takes the test individually, making two copies of his or her answers. Students submit one set of answers to you to grade and keep one set for the group discussion.
3. Students retake the test together as a group in their cooperative learning groups.

bers understand how to answer the study questions correctly. If students disagree on the answer to any study questions, they must find the page number and paragraph in the resource material explaining the relevant information or procedures. The groups study together all week. On Thursday, the groups meet to ensure that all group members know and understand the material on which they will be tested. When the study/review time is up, students give each other encouragement for doing well on the upcoming test. On Friday, the examination is given.

Individual Test. The students take the test individually, making two copies of their answers. The task (and individual goal) is to answer each test question correctly. One copy they hand in to the teacher (who then scores the answers). The students keep the second copy for group discussion. If all members of the group score above a preset criterion (such as 90 percent correct) on the individual tests, then each member receives a designated number (for example, 5) of bonus points. The bonus points are added to their individual score to determine their individual grade for the test.

Group Test. After these procedures are completed for the individual test, all members meet in their cooperative learning groups to take the test again, but this time together as a group. Their task is to answer each question correctly. The cooperative goal is for all group members to understand the material covered by the test. Members do so by (a) reaching consensus on the answer for each question and the rationale or procedure underlying the answer and (b) ensuring that all members can explain the answer and the rationale or procedure. For any answer that they disagree about or are unsure of, they are required to find the page and paragraph in the text that contains the answer. The teacher randomly observes the groups to ensure they are following the procedure correctly.

Steps for following this procedure are:

1. Students should compare their answers to the first question.
2. If there is agreement, one member explains the rationale or procedure underlying the question and the group moves on to question 2.
3. If there is disagreement, members find the page number and paragraph in the resource materials explaining the relevant information or procedures. The group is responsible for ensuring that all members understand the material they missed on the test. If necessary, group members assign review homework to each other. When all members agree on the answer and believe other members comprehend the material, the group moves on to question 2.
4. The learning groups repeat this procedure until they have covered all test questions.
5. The group members celebrate how hard members have worked in learning the material and how successful they were on the test.

Weekly Group Tests and Individual Final Exam

To maximize students' higher-level reasoning and long-term retention of knowledge, the following procedure may be followed. Assign students to cooperative learning groups of four members and have them complete their assignments together all week. The groups should be heterogeneous in terms of math and reading ability. On Friday, an examination is given.

Each cooperative group is divided into two pairs. Each pair takes the test, conferring on the answer to each question. The task is to answer each question correctly. The cooperative goal is to produce one answer for each question that both agree upon and both can explain. They cannot proceed until they agree on an answer. Once the two pairs have done so, the cooperative group of four meets and retakes the test.

Their task is to answer each question correctly. The cooperative goal is for all group members to understand the material covered by the test. Group members confer on each question. On any question to which the two pairs have different answers or members are unsure of the answer, they find the page number and paragraph in the textbook where the answer is explained.

Each group is responsible for ensuring that all members understand the material they missed on the test. If necessary, group members assign review homework to each other. The teacher randomly observes each group to ensure that they are answering the questions correctly. Each cooperative group then hands in one answer sheet with the names of all members. Each member signs the answer sheet to verify that (a) he or she understands the content and (b) all other group members understand the content covered by the test. All group members are given equal credit for successfully passing the test.

At the end of the grading period, each student takes an individual final examination. If any student scores below a preset criterion (such as 90 percent), the cooperative group meets and reviews the content with the student until the student can successfully pass the test. This rarely happens, as the group members have verified each week that they all are learning the assigned content.

Group Discussion Test

For the **group discussion test** students meet with their cooperative base group and discuss the content of the assigned readings. The purpose of the group discussion test is for students to have a thorough, intellectually stimulating, creative, fun, and practically useful discussion of the assigned texts. More specifically, the task is to demonstrate mastery and in-depth understanding of the assigned readings. This task is to be accomplished *cooperatively*.

A number of discussion questions are attached to the readings. These questions are aimed at being *integrative* in the sense that material from many different sources are relevant to answering them. The responsibilities of each group member are to

1. Choose two of the suggested discussion questions and to think carefully about the answers. The student's answers should combine information derived from the assigned texts as well as incorporate their own relevant personal experiences and background. Each student should learn the answers to his or her questions so thoroughly that they can serve as the group expert on what the readings have to say about the issue highlighted in the question.
2. Plan how to lead a group discussion on his or her questions. The discussion should entail higher-level reasoning, critical thinking, conceptual integration of a variety of material from the assigned texts, and a working knowledge of the specific relevant theories and research findings. To do so the student will need to prepare the following materials for each group member:
   a. A typed outline of his or her answers to the questions with relevant page numbers from the assigned readings
   b. Copies of relevant written information to facilitate discussion
   c. Visuals such as diagrams, charts, and cartoons to help group members who are visual rather than auditory learners, learn, think critically about, and conceptually integrate the relevant theories, research, and practical experiences
3. Come to the examination prepared to contribute to the discussion of each question and to learn, think critically about, and conceptually integrate the theory, research, and practical experiences relevant to each question discussed.

The group discussion test should cover at least one question from each member. Because each member will come prepared to lead a discussion on two questions, flip a coin to select which question will be part of the examination. Members are to generate one set of answers for the group and all members must agree with and be able to explain the answers. A list of guidelines follow.

1. Stick to the questions. It is easy to go off on tangents.
2. Cite specific theories, research, and concepts discussed in the texts. Refer to specific pages. It is easy to make overly broad generalizations and to state personal opinions that are not supported by current knowledge.
3. Refer to personal experiences. Comparing the theories and research findings against your personal and practical experiences is valuable and often allows for integration of several concepts. Do not chat about "what happened to me."
4. Set time limits for each question and stick to these limits rigidly.
5. Encourage disagreement and controversy. All viewpoints and positions should be encouraged as long as they can be supported by theory and research. Follow the rules for constructive controversy.
6. Take responsibility for both task and maintenance actions. Your group has a definite task to accomplish (e.g., demonstrating understanding of the field of social psychology), but the discussion should be enjoyable as well as a productive learning experience.
7. All members must participate actively to (a) contribute to the learning of others and (b) demonstrate overtly to the other members of the group that he or she has read the texts and mastered the content of the course.

During the group test, group members should focus on

1. Integrating relevant theory, research, and practical experiences
2. Analyzing in depth possible answers to the question to achieve insights into the issue
3. Thinking divergently
4. Critically examining each other's reasoning and engaging in constructive controversy
5. Making the examination a fun and enjoyable experience for everyone

To document that the group test did take place and that the criteria for passing were met by all group members, require each member to sign a certification form (see p. 77). Make sure that there are no "free-loaders." Do not sign off for a group member unless he or she arrived at the examination fully prepared and participated actively in the discussion of each question. If any group member was absent, the group is to determine what the member has to do to make up the test.

The group will be expected to hand in a report consisting of the certification form, a list of the questions discussed with a summary of the answers and conclusions generated by the discussion, a description of the procedures followed, and a subjective evaluation of the learning that resulted from the experience.

ACADEMIC TOURNAMENT

An alternative to the group test is an academic tournament. An **academic tournament** is an objective test (usually recognition or total recall level) conducted in a game format (Johnson, Johnson, & Hollebec, 1998b). The purpose of the tournament is to determine which cooperative learning group best learned the assigned material. The procedure, adapted from the Teams–Games–Tournament procedure (DeVries & Edwards, 1974), follows.

1. **Assign students to heterogeneous cooperative learning groups whose members are of different achievement levels.** One high-, two medium-, and one low-achieving student, for example, may be placed in one group. Group members study the

assigned material and complete the assignments together and prepare each other for the tournament.

2. Assign students to competitive triads. A class tournament is structured around a game in which each student competes as a representative of his or her team with students of equal achievement levels from other teams. When students compete, they should be placed in homogeneous groups based on previous achievement. Groups of three maximize the number of winners in the class (pairs tend to make the competition too personal). Rank the students in each cooperative learning group from highest to lowest on the basis of their previous achievement. Given that only one student from a group can be in a competitive triad, assign the three highest-achieving students in the class to table 1, the next three to table 2, and so on until all students in the class have a table assignment. This creates equal competition within each triad and makes it possible for students of all achievement levels to contribute maximally to their team scores if they do their best. Figure 4.2 illustrates the relationship between the cooperative learning groups and the competitive triads.

3. Arrange the classroom. The room should be arranged so that the triads are separated from each other and students within each triad sit close to each other.

4. Prepare instructional materials. During the tournament the students play an instructional game for 10 to 30 minutes. Make a game sheet consisting of about 30 items, a game answer sheet, and a copy of the rules. Make a set of cards numbered from 1 to 30. On each card write (a) one question from the game sheet and (b) the number of the question on the answer sheet. The questions can be either recognition or recall questions.

5. Conduct the tournament. The tournament is conducted to determine which cooperative learning group best learned the assigned material. Students receive points according to how well they mastered the material (compared with the other two members of their tournament triad). The procedure for playing the game is outlined in Activity 4.3, in the Rules of Play instruction sheet.

6. Determine winning cooperative learning group. A team score is derived by adding the scores of all the individual members. Team scores are then ranked and announced. The winning group is congratulated.

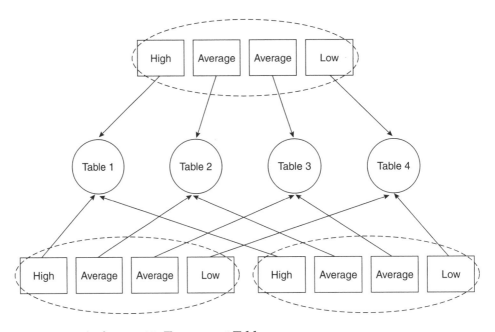

FIGURE 4.2   Assignment to Tournament Tables

ACTIVITY 4.3 ■ RULES OF PLAY

Purpose

This tournament is being conducted to determine which cooperative learning group has best learned the assigned material. You will receive points according to how well you have mastered the assigned material (compared to the other two members of your tournament triad). The points of the members of your cooperative learning group will be added together to determine a group score. The cooperative learning group with the most points wins.

Directions:

1. You have been given a deck of specially constructed cards and an answer sheet. To start the game, shuffle the cards and place them face down on the table. Play is in a clockwise rotation. Three rotating roles are assigned to players (roles are rotated in a clockwise direction after each question):

   a. **Question Reader:** Player draws a card, reads it aloud.
   b. **Answer Giver:** Player decides whether or not to give an answer.
   c. **Answer Checker:** If an answer is given, the player reads the answer to the question from the answer sheet (regardless of whether the answer is challenged).

2. To play, the Question Reader takes the top card from the deck and reads it aloud. The Question Giver has a choice of two responses:

   a. This student can say he or she does not know or is not sure of the answer. The two other students may then volunteer to answer the question. (The Question Reader has the first chance to answer the question.) If no one wants to answer, the card is placed on the bottom of the deck.
   b. This student can answer the question and ask whether anyone wants to challenge his or her answer. The player on the Answer Giver's right has the first right of challenge.

3. If there is no challenge, the Answer Checker reads the answer on the answer sheet out loud.

   a. If correct, the Answer Giver keeps the card.
   b. If incorrect, the card is placed on the bottom of the deck.

4. If there is a challenge, the challenger gives an answer.

   a. If Answer Giver is correct, he or she keeps the card and the challenger must give up one of his or her cards (which is placed on the bottom of the deck).
   b. If the Answer Giver is incorrect and the challenge is correct, the challenger keeps the card.
   c. If both the Answer Giver and the challenger are incorrect, then the card is placed on the bottom of the deck.

5. The roles are rotated after each question.

6. The game ends when all the cards have been claimed. Players count their cards and determine who has the most, second most, and least cards. The score for each ranking is represented by points.

(continued)

ACTIVITY 4.3 *Continued*

Ranking	Score
First place	6 points
Second place	4 points
Third place	2 points
Two tie for first place	5 points each
Three tie for first place	4 points each
Two tie for second place	3 points each

SUMMARY

Teacher-made tests are written or oral assessments of student achievement. They are specifically designed for an individual teacher's students, and are not commercially produced or standardized. They may be either objective or essay tests created to assess student learning, to guide student learning, and to guide instruction. Objective tests include multiple choice, true–false, matching, completion (short answer), and interpretative items. Essay tests require students to write paragraphs or themes as answers. Each has it advantages and disadvantages. Four of the ways that tests can be used as cooperative experiences are the group-individual-group procedure, weekly group tests with an individual final exam, group discussion tests, and academic tournaments.

GROUP EXAM CERTIFICATION FORM

Students' Names: _____

Class: _____ Group: _____ Unit: _____ Date: _____

We, the undersigned, certify that we have participated in the group discussion examination and have met the following criteria:

1. We understand the basic concepts, theories, and bodies of research presented in the texts and lectures.

2. We know the major theorists and researchers discussed in the texts and lectures.

3. We can apply the theories and research findings to practical situations.

4. We can conceptualize a research question and design a research study to test our hypotheses.

5. We have submitted our choice of questions and a brief summary of each answer we have formulated as a group.

NAME	SIGNATURE	DATE
_____	_____	_____
_____	_____	_____
_____	_____	_____
_____	_____	_____
_____	_____	_____

TOURNAMENT SCORING SHEET

Students' Names: _____

Tournament Triad: _____   Unit: _____   Date: _____

DIRECTIONS:

Write the names of the triad members in the top row of the table. For each question answered, place a plus (+) for each correct answer and a minus (–) for each incorrect answer. Total the number right for each member and rank the three members according to the greatest number of correct answers to the least number of correct answers.

Question			
1.			
2.			
3.			
4.			
5.			
6.			
7.			
8.			
9.			
10.			
Total			

CHAPTER FIVE

COMPOSITIONS AND PRESENTATIONS

STUDENT PERFORMANCES AND COOPERATIVE LEARNING

Aesop tells of a man who visited foreign lands and, when he returned to his home, could talk of little except his wonderful adventures during his travels and the great deeds he had done. One of his feats was an amazing leap he had made in a city called Rhodes. "My leap was so great," he said, "no other person could leap anywhere near that distance! Many people witnessed my leap and if you go to Rhodes they will tell you that what I say is true." "No need for witnesses," one of his listeners said, "Imagine this city is Rhodes. Now, show us how far you can jump!" The moral of this tale is, *actual performances count, not descriptions of what a person believes he or she can do.* ∎

It is not enough to ask students to describe their skills, students have to demonstrate what they can do in actual performances that others can view and assess. **Student performance** refers to a set of actions students engage in to demonstrate their level of skill in enacting a procedure or creating a product. These performances can include performing a music recital, presenting a play, participating in a discussion, creating a newspaper, conducting a science experiment, presenting a mock trial, engaging in a debate, giving a speech, and writing a composition.

Gaining competence and expertise in such performances requires students to engage in four activities. First, students must engage in the performances frequently. The more frequently students write, for example, the better writers they can potentially become. The more presentations students make to an audience, the better the public speakers they may potentially become. Ideally, students should write and present every day.

Second, students need to receive immediate and detailed feedback on the quality of their performance. For every composition and presentation, students should receive detailed, helpful feedback on how to improve.

Third, students must observe and analyze the performances of others. In order to learn how to play baseball, for example, one must watch others play baseball and analyze how they field and bat. In order to learn how to write well, students must study other people's writing and analyze what is good about it and what could be improved. In order to learn how to present well, students must observe others present and analyze what is effective and ineffective.

Fourth, assessing others' performances teaches students how to improve their own performances. From assessing their classmates' performances, students increase their understanding of (a) what constitutes a high-quality performance, (b) what actions are required to engage in a high-quality performance, and (c) the criteria to be used in assessing their own performances.

These four activities (a) are labor intensive and time-consuming and (b) cannot take place in competitive or individualistic situations. Performances must be observed and discussed if they are to be improved. If students write every day, someone has to read their compositions and give critical but helpful feedback. The clear fact is, teachers do not have the time to assess numerous performances daily. The labor intensive nature of performance assessment means that teachers have to engineer assessment systems that involve others. They do not have to assess each student's performances, they create a system that ensures that each student's performance is assessed. If a teacher has 30 students in a class, for example, that is 30 compositions to assess each day. If a teacher divides the class into writing pairs, however, each student has one paper to assess each day. The former is unworkable, the latter is doable.

Students can most effectively assess the quality of each other's performances within a cooperative context. In a competitive context students will be tempted to be over critical of classmates' work in order to increase their own chances for getting an A. In an individualistic context students will be unmotivated to conduct quality assessments of classmates' work because it takes away from the time they can spend on their own work. It is only within a cooperative context in which students benefit from the quality of each other's work, that the conditions facilitate high-quality assessments of classmates' performances. Teachers, for example, may assign students to writing pairs, inform students their goal is to ensure that both members of the pair write a composition that meets certain criteria, and then add that if a student's partner's composition exceeds the preset criteria for excellence, the student will receive five bonus points. This clearly communicates that each student benefits from the hard work of his or her partner and has a stake in ensuring his or her partner writes well. Cooperative learning groups provide an arena in which performances can be developed, practiced, and perfected.

In other words, if student are to learn to write and present, they must write and present frequently, receive immediate and detailed feedback on the quality of their performances, and observe, analyze, and assess the performances of others. More time is needed to assess each student's work and to provide the feedback needed than any one teacher has. Therefore, teachers may wish to involve students in observing, analyzing, and assessing each other's work. It is only within a cooperative context, however, that such peer assessments are beneficial. This chapter covers the use of cooperative learning groups in assessing two common types of student performances: compositions and presentations.

COOPERATIVE WRITING AND EDITING PAIRS

When your lesson includes students writing an essay, report, poem, story, or review of what they have read, you should use cooperative writing and editing pairs (Johnson, Johnson, & Holubec, 1998a). Using cooperative writing and editing pairs involves four aspects of student learning; accomplishing an assigned task, evaluating criteria for success, establishing a group goal, and exercising individual accountability.

Tasks. Students write a composition and edit other students' compositions.

Criteria for success. Each student produces a well-written composition. Depending on the instructional objectives, compositions may be evaluated for grammar, punctuation, organization, content, or other criteria set by the teacher.

Cooperative goal. All group members must verify that each member's composition is perfect according to the criteria set by the teacher. Students receive an individual score on the quality of their compositions. You can also give a group score based on the total number of errors made by the pair (the number of errors in their composition plus the number of errors in their partner's composition).

Individual accountability. Each student writes his or her own composition.

The procedure for organizing student learning in cooperative writing and editing pairs follows.

1. The teacher assigns students to pairs with at least one good reader in each pair.
2. Student A describes to Student B what he or she is planning to write. Student B listens carefully, probes with a set of questions, and outlines Student A's composition. The written outline is given to Student A.
3. This procedure is reversed with Student B describing what he or she is going to write and Student A listening and completing an outline of Student B's composition, which is then given to Student B.
4. The students research individually the material they need to write their compositions, keeping an eye out for material useful to their partner.
5. The two students work together to write the first paragraph of each composition to ensure that they both have a clear start on their compositions.
6. The students write their compositions individually.
7. When completed, the students proofread each other's compositions, making corrections in capitalization, punctuation, spelling, language usage, topic sentence usage, and other aspects of writing specified by the teacher. Students also give each other suggestions for revision.
8. The students revise their compositions, making all the suggested revisions.
9. The two students then reread each other's compositions and sign their names (indicating that they guarantee no errors exist in the composition).

While the students work, the teacher monitors the pairs, intervening where appropriate to help students master the needed writing and cooperative skills. When students complete their compositions, they discuss how effectively they worked together (listing the specific actions they engaged in to help each other); they plan what behaviors they are going to emphasize in the next writing pair; and they thank each other for the help and assistance received.

WRITING TOGETHER

HOW MY PARTNER AND I ARE GOING TO WRITE TWO OF THE WORLD'S GREATEST COMPOSITIONS

Step 1. Creating a partnership. Have students identify their partner, say hello, and make sure they have all the materials (pen, paper, topic) they need to complete the assignment of writing a composition. They are to work cooperatively with their partner to ensure that both write a high-quality composition. Each student will receive two scores for the composition. The first is based on the quality of his or her composition. The second is based on the total number of errors each student and his or her partner made (the number of errors in the composition plus the number of errors in the partner's composition).

Step 2. Outlining the compositions. Have students flip a coin to determine who will be Student A and who will be Student B. Student A describes to Student B what he or she is planning to write. Student B listens carefully, probes with a set of questions, and outlines Student A's composition. The written outline is given to Student A.

This procedure is then reversed, with Student B describing what he or she is going to write and Student A listening and completing an outline of Student B's composition, which is then given to Student B. Students should be instructed to teach partners how to construct an outline if their partner does not know how to do so.

Step 3. Researching the topic and collecting helpful materials. This can be done co-operatively or individually. In either case, students should search for information on their topic and keep an eye out for material useful to their partner. Students should be responsible for teaching their partner what they know about using reference materials and the library, and learn what their partner knows.

Step 4. Writing the first paragraph (or sentence). Students should work cooperatively with their partner to write the first paragraph of each composition. They should first write the starting paragraph of Partner A's composition and then of Partner B's composition. They should make sure there is a clear and coherent beginning to both compositions.

Step 5. Writing the composition individually. Working individually, each student should write the best draft of the assignment that he or she can. Each student should try to meet the criteria for the assignment set by the teacher. Any draft, however, is better than no draft. Students should write something.

Step 6. Editing a partner's composition. Students should trade compositions with their partner, carefully reading what their partner has written. Each student should make suggestions to his or her partner as to how the partner may improve his or her composition and better meet the criteria set by the teacher. Suggestions should include corrections in capitalization, punctuation, spelling, language usage, topic sentence usage, and other aspects of writing specified by the teacher. When both a student and his or her partner have finished, students need to explain suggestions to their partner and listen carefully to his or her explanations of the suggested revisions for the composition.

Step 7. Rewriting a composition (the second draft!). Things get better the second time around. Working individually, students should carefully consider the suggestions made by their partner to improve their composition, deciding which ones to use. Students should then revise their compositions to make them better and to better meet the criteria set up by the teacher.

Step 8. Reediting a partner's composition. Students should trade compositions with their partner again, carefully reading what their partner has written. Each student should consider how his or her partner may improve his or her composition, making constructive suggestions as to how his or her partner may do so. The criteria set by the teacher should be kept in mind. When the pair of students have finished editing, they should explain their suggestions to their partner and listen carefully to explanations for improving the composition. The composition should keep being revised until both partners agree that it meets all the criteria set by the teacher and is ready to be turned in.

Step 9. Signing off. When partners agree that their compositions are the best they can be under the circumstances, they sign their name as the author of the composition and their partner signs as the editor, personally guaranteeing that no errors exist in the composition and that the composition is ready to be read by the teacher.

Step 10. Discussing the quality of the partnership (How well did the students work together?). With their partner, students should discuss the effectiveness of their partnership. They can list specific actions each did that helped the other to write a good composition. They can think of how they could work together even better next time. Students thank each other for the help and assistance received, and celebrate the success of their partnership.

Many benefits can be derived from peer editing relationships. Complete Activity 5.1 to help you reflect on what aspects of the relationship benefit the editor and what aspects benefit the editee.

ACTIVITY **5.1** ■ REFLECTION ON PEER EDITING AND ASSESSMENT

Benefits to Editee	Benefits to Editor
1.	1.
2.	2.
3.	3.
4.	4.
5.	5.
6.	6.
7.	7.
8.	8.
9.	9.
10.	10.

PRESENTING TOGETHER

HOW MY PARTNER AND I ARE GOING TO GIVE TWO OF THE WORLD'S GREATEST PRESENTATIONS

Step 1. Creating a partnership. Have students identify their partner, say hello, and make sure they have all the materials (pen, paper, topic) they need to complete the assignment. The learning tasks include students (a) preparing a presentation, (b) making a presentation, and (c) assessing its effectiveness. The presentation has to include visuals and/or active participation by the audience. The cooperative goal is to ensure that all group members learn the material they study, and develop and deliver a high-quality presentation on it.

Step 2. Selecting a topic. Each person, working individually, selects a topic to present (or considers the one assigned by the teacher) and collects his or her initial thoughts about what he or she may say.

Step 3. Outlining the presentations. Have students flip a coin to see who will be Student A and who will be Student B. Student A describes to Student B what he or she is planning to present. Student B listens carefully, probes with a set of questions, and outlines Student A's presentation. The written outline is given to Student A. This procedure is then reversed, with Student B describing what he or she is going to present and Student A listening, completing an outline of Student B's presentation, and giving it to Student B. Partners should teach each other what they know about how to construct an outline and learn what each other knows.

Step 4. Researching a topic and collecting helpful materials. This can be done cooperatively or individually. In either case, the student should search for information on his or her topic and keep an eye out for material useful to his or her partner. If their partner does not know how to use reference materials and the library effectively, the partner should be taught how to do so.

Step 5. Writing the introduction. Students should work cooperatively with their partner to write the introduction for each presentation. They should first write the introduction for Partner A's presentation and then for Partner B's presentation. They should make sure there is a clear and coherent beginning to both presentations.

Step 6. Planning a presentation individually. Working individually each student should plan the first version of his or her presentation. Each student should try to meet the criteria for the assignment set by the teacher. Any version, however, is better than no version. Students should plan something.

Step 7. Presenting the initial version. Combine one pair of students with another pair into a group of four. Have each person give his or her presentation. The other three members carefully analyze the presentation (using the assessment rubric) and make suggestions as to how it may be improved. The teacher rotates throughout the class and samples as many presentations as he or she can. When all four members have finished, the group discusses how each may revise his or her presentation to make it better.

Step 8. Replanning the presentation (the second version!). Things get better the second time around. Working individually, students should carefully consider the suggestions made by their groupmates to improve their presentation, deciding which ones they want to use. Students then revise their presentation to make it better and to better meet the criteria set up by the teacher.

Step 9. Giving the presentation. Combine one pair of students with a different pair to form a new group of four. Each member gives his or her presentation. The other three members critically analyze the presentation (using the assessment rubric) and consider how the presentation may be improved. The teacher rotates throughout the class and samples as many presentations as he or she can. Students should listen carefully to the feedback they receive from the other three members on how to improve their presentation. The teacher may wish to collect the assessment forms completed by the group members to help him or her assess the quality of each student's presentations.

Step 10. Discussing the quality of the partnership (How well did the students work together?). With their partner, students should discuss the effectiveness of their partnership. They can list specific actions each did that helped the other to make a high-quality presentation. They can think about how they could work together even better next time. Students thank each other for the help and assistance received, and celebrate the success of their partnership.

You can review how well you organize and prepare your classroom and your students by maintaining a checklist of the various components of cooperative learning that contribute to success in your class. Such a checklist is provided in Activity 5.2.

PREPARATION PAPERS AND PRESENTATIONS

To prepare for each lesson, students write a short paper and present it to their cooperative base group. Even if the papers and presentations are not graded, the assignment compels students to do their homework, organize their thoughts, and take some responsibility for the lesson's success.

1. Students' tasks are to write a short paper (one to two pages) on an aspect of the assigned readings and to prepare a 2- to 3-minute presentation on the paper. Before each lesson (class session), students:
   a. Choose a major theory, concept, idea, or person discussed in the assigned reading
   b. Write a one- to two-page analysis of this theory, summarizing the relevant assigned readings and adding relevant material from another source (book, journal, magazine, newspaper) to enrich the analysis
   c. Prepare a 2- to 3-minute presentation on the paper.
2. Students meet in their cooperative base groups of four members. The base groups stay the same for the entire semester or year. Teachers create the cooperative structure by giving the base groups the responsibility of ensuring that each member's writing and presenting continuously improves throughout the semester. Bonus points may be given if all members' compositions and presentations meet the basic requirements for excellence. Students are given (or ideally help develop) a set of criteria with appropriate rubrics to assess the quality of each other's compositions and presentations.

   Students should bring a copy of their paper for each member of their base group and a copy for the teacher. The base group meets at the beginning of the class session. Each member hands out the copies of his or her paper and presents a 2- to 3-minute summary of the paper to the base group. The other group members assess the quality of the presentation and give suggestions for how it could be improved. Before the next class session, members of the cooperative group read, edit, and constructively criticize the paper. Members then sign each member's paper. The signature means that they have read the paper and have provided feedback to improve their groupmates' writing skills.
3. The cooperative groups summarize what they have learned from members' papers and how it applies to the topic of the lesson.

ACTIVITY 5.2 ■ TEACHER APPRAISAL SYSTEM

1. Provides opportunities for students to participate actively and successfully:

    _____ Varies activities appropriately

    _____ Structures cooperative groups appropriately

    _____ Monitors and interacts with cooperative groups appropriately

    _____ Intersperses pair discussions during lectures

    _____ Extends students' responses and participation

    _____ Provides time for thoughtful responses

2. Assesses and provides feedback on student progress during instruction:

    _____ Defines instructional task clearly

    _____ Defines criteria for success clearly

    _____ Systematically observes students at work in cooperative groups

    _____ Solicits responses, explanations, and demonstrations for assessment

    _____ Structures peer assessment and corrective feedback

    _____ Structures peer support for high-quality work

    _____ Reinforces correct responses and performances

    _____ Provides corrective feedback and clarifies

    _____ Reteaches when needed

3. Organizes students and materials:

    _____ Secures student attention

    _____ Gives clear directions

    _____ Maintains appropriate grouping and seating arrangements

    _____ Moves students into groups and from group to group smoothly

    _____ Has materials, aides, facilities ready

    _____ Provides clear cooperative structure for learning groups

SUMMARY

Two of the most important performances to be assessed are writing and presenting. Through compositions and presentations students demonstrate what they can do in actual performances. If students are to learn to write and present, they must write and present frequently, receive immediate and detailed feedback on the quality of their performances, and observe, analyze, and assess the performances of others. More time is needed to assess each student's work and provide the necessary feedback than any one teacher has. Teachers, therefore, may wish to involve students in observing, analyzing, and assessing each other's work.

For writing assignments, students are assigned to cooperative pairs and are given a writing assignment. Students help each other plan their compositions, ensuring that each has adequate material and a good start on his or her composition. Students write the composition individually and have their partner edit it. The student then rewrites the composition and has it reedited by his or her partner to ensure that the final draft is ready for the teacher to read.

For presentations, students are assigned to cooperative group of four and are given an assignment to prepare a presentation. Students help each other outline the presentations, ensuring that each has the information needed and a good start on his or her presentation. Each student prepares a presentation individually and gives the initial presentation to the group. The group gives feedback on how the presentation could be improved. Each student revises his or her presentation and then gives the presentation to another group of students.

Writing and presenting can be combined through preparation papers. Each day students write a short paper on some aspect of their homework and give a 3-minute presentation on their paper to their cooperative group. The group members assess the quality of the presentation and the paper and give feedback on how each could be improved.

PARTNERSHIP PROCESSING FORM

Student's Name: _____   Grade: _____   Date: _____

1. My actions that helped my partner learn:

a. _____

_____

_____

b. _____

_____

_____

c. _____

_____

_____

2. Actions I could add or improve on to be an even better partner next time:

a. _____

_____

_____

b. _____

_____

_____

c. _____

_____

_____

WRITING A PERSUASIVE ARGUMENT

Student's Name: _____   Grade: _____   Date: _____

THESIS STATEMENT   (A statement that you want others to agree with and accept, but expect others to challenge)

RATIONALE   (The facts, information, and theories gathered that validate the thesis statement, arranged in a logical order that leads to a conclusion)

CONCLUSION   (A statement that is logically derived from rationale and is the same as the thesis statement)

Author: _____   Editor: _____

PERSUASIVE ARGUMENT COMPOSITION RUBRIC

Name: _____   Grade: _____   Date: _____

Title of Composition: _____

SCORING SCALE: LOW   1   2   3   4   5   HIGH

For each criterion, rate the composition between 1 (very poor) and 5 (very good).

Criteria	Score	Weight	Total
Organization Thesis statement and introduction Rationale presented to support thesis Conclusion logically drawn from rationale Effective transitions		6	(30)
Content Topic addressed Reasoning clear with valid logic Evidence presented to support key points Creativity evident		8	(40)
Usage Topic sentence beginning every paragraph Correct subject-verb agreement Correct verb tense Complete sentences (no run-ons, fragments) Mix of simple and complex sentences		4	(20)
Mechanics Correct use of punctuation Correct use of capitalization Few or no misspellings		2	(10)
Scale 93–100 = A 85–92 = B 77–84 = C		20	(100)

COMMENTS:

PARTNERSHIP PROCESSING FORM

Student's Name: _____   Grade: _____   Date: _____

1. My actions that helped my partner learn:

    a. _____

        _____

        _____

    b. _____

        _____

        _____

    c. _____

        _____

        _____

2. Actions I could add or improve on to be an even better partner next time:

    a. _____

        _____

        _____

    b. _____

        _____

        _____

    c. _____

        _____

        _____

ORAL PRESENTATIONS RUBRIC

Name: _____   Grade: _____   Date: _____

Title of Presentation: _____

SCORING SCALE: LOW   1   2   3   4   5   HIGH

For each criterion, rate the presentation between 1 (very poor) and 5 (very good).

Criterion	Rating	Comments
Adresses subject, scholarly, informative		
Organized (introduction, body, conclusion)		
Creative reasoning and persuasiveness		
Intriguing (audience wants to find out more)		
Interesting, transitions, easy to follow, concise		
Volume, enunciation, eye contact, gestures		
Engaging (audience active, not passive)		
Visual aids, props, music		
Other:		
Total		

PREPARATION PAPER ASSESSMENT FORM

Name: _____   Date: _____

Course: _____   Preparation Paper Number: _____

Rated By: ☐ Self   ☐ Peer   ☐ Instructor   ☐ Other _____

Points Possible	Criteria	Points Earned
10	Has a clear, accurate, descriptive title	
10	Begins with a focus statement	
10	Major terms are defined	
10	Explains why the topic is of interest	
10	Includes analysis and critical thinking	
10	Ends with conclusions	
10	Includes information from two or more sources	
10	Each paragraph begins with a topic sentence	
10	Capitalization, appearance, punctuation, spelling	
10	Other:	
100	**Total**	

Comments or specific suggestions on how to improve paper:

REFLECTION ON MY STRENGTHS AND GROWTH GOALS

Student's Name: _____ Grade: _____ Date: _____

1. The best aspects of my skills in writing are…

2. An interesting part of my rationale is…

3. Things I learned from editing my partner's writing are…

4. My next step(s) in improving my writing are…

5. Aspects of writing on which I could be more skilled are…

CHAPTER SIX

PROJECTS

NATURE OF PROJECTS

A **project** is an assignment aimed at having students produce something themselves on a topic related to the curriculum rather than just "reproduce" knowledge on tests. Projects are a traditional part of the curriculum. Projects are assigned at all grade levels in subjects such as music, media, art, science, language arts, and social studies. Projects may involve models, maps, pictures, tables, graphs, collages, photographs, plays, films, or videotapes. The assignments are aimed at enhancing communication, reasoning, technical, interpersonal, organizational, decision-making, and problem-solving skills. Projects may be completed by individual students, cooperative learning groups, whole classes, schools, and communities. Projects may involve both in-class and out-of-class research and development. Projects allow students to be creative, use multiple modes of learning, and explore their own multiple intelligences. The disadvantages of projects are that they are difficult to assess and to store.

WHY USE PROJECTS?

Despite the assessment challenges posed by projects, they are useful assignments that achieve objectives that may not be achieved in any other way. Projects

1. Allow students to be creative and inventive in integrating diverse knowledge and skills
2. Allow students to demonstrate and clarify their multiple intelligences through the use of diverse medias (see Box 6.1)
3. Require students to use, integrate, apply, and transfer a wide variety of diverse information and skills into a final product
4. Require students to engage in procedures (such as scientific investigation and inquiry) that promote higher-level outcomes
5. Give students the opportunity to formulate their own questions and then try to answer them
6. Accommodate different achievement levels by allowing students to complete projects at varying levels of difficulty
7. Give students with reading and writing problems an alternative method of demonstrating learning and competencies, which may result in increased academic self-esteem
8. Provide opportunities for positive interaction and cooperation among classmates
9. Provide a forum for students to share their learning and accomplishments with other students, classes, parents, and the community

HOW TO ASSIGN PROJECTS

The wide variety of meaningful outcomes achieved by projects make them a valuable and flexible teacher tool. Their richness and complexity make them ideally suited for

■ ■ ■ ■ ■

BOX 6.1
MULTIPLE INTELLIGENCES

INTELLIGENCE	DEFINITION
Linguistic	Ease in producing language (writers, poets, storytellers); related to written and spoken words and language
Logical-mathematical	Ability to reason and to recognize abstract patterns (as in science, mathematics); often called "scientific thinking" because it deals with logical reasoning, numbers, and the recognition of abstract patterns
Musical/rhythmic	Sensitivity to pitch and rhythm (inherent in composers, instrumentalists); recognition of tonal patterns, including various environmental sounds
Visual/spatial	Ability to create visual/spatial representations of the world and to transfer these representations either mentally or concretely (architects, sculptors, engineers); relies on the sense of sight and being able to visualize an object and create internal mental images
Bodily/kinesthetic	Using the body to accomplish physical activity, to solve problems, to create products, and to convey ideas and emotions (athletes, surgeons, dancers); related to physical movement and knowing how the body, including the brain's motor cortex, controls body motion
Interpersonal	Ability to understand other people and to work effectively with them (salespeople, teachers, politicians); operates primarily through person-to-person relationships and communication; relies on all other intelligences
Intrapersonal	Personal knowledge about one's own emotions or self; relates to inner states of being, self-reflection, metacognition, and awareness of spiritual realities

Source: Adapted from White, Blythe, and Gardner, 1992.

cooperative learning groups. The steps for assigning a project for general use and specifically for cooperative learning groups follow.

Steps for General Projects

1. Assign a variety of projects throughout the year. Structure the projects so that students
   a. Have some choice in the focus or topic of their projects
   b. Can use a variety of intelligences in completing them
   c. Have to use higher-level reasoning skills such as induction and problem solving
   d. Can be creative and divergent in their approach to the assignment
2. For each project list the dates for when the project starts, when each part of the project should be completed, when the initial draft is submitted for peer editing and initial teacher reaction, and when the final product is due.
3. Show students samples or models of completed projects. A variety of projects ranging from excellent to poor will help students develop a frame of reference on what is and is not an acceptable finished product.
4. Have students develop specific criteria to assess the quality of the completed projects. Criteria may include timeliness, appearance, originality, quality, evi-

dence, reflection, richness of ideas, and presentation. Students develop indicators of excellent, fair, and inadequate products. If students want to make a video, for example, they can view several videos and then develop a rating scale that differentiates high-quality from medium- and low-quality videos. The best video they view can be the benchmark to which they aspire. Students need to understand the components of a good project and then use indicators to guide them in their work.

5. Teach students how to use a rubric supplied by you (the teacher) that is standardized for the school, district, or state. Learning how to use a standardized rubric for assessing the quality of projects gives students a more sophisticated frame of reference for reflecting on their own work.

6. Have students complete the project with help and assistance from faculty.

7. Have students present their completed projects to some or all of their classmates. In viewing classmates' projects, students use the rating scale developed and the standardized rubric to assess project quality. A peer-editing cycle is very useful at this point (see Chapter 5).

8. Students turn in their projects to be assessed by the faculty.

Steps for Group Projects

The usual rule for cooperative learning groups is that students learn in a group and are subsequently assessed as individuals (Johnson, Johnson, & Holubec, 1998). Whereas in school individual assessment is more common than group assessment, in real life it may be just the opposite. In most organizations, the success of each individual employee is less frequently focused on than is the success of the organization as a whole, or divisions in the organization, or teams in the division. Authentic assessment, therefore, most often means group assessment. Thus, a classroom assignment may be given that requires a group report, exhibit, performance, video, or presentation. An example of such a group project could be assigning groups to create a brochure for a vocational program. Each group would select and research a vocational program and prepare an instructional brochure to present to the class. (See Box 6.2 for more examples.)

Students and assessment procedures need to be clearly briefed when the purpose of assessment is to measure group productivity. Students are given the *task* of completing the assigned project. The *cooperative goal* is for group members to complete one project in which everyone has contributed a share of the work, everyone can explain its content and how it was conducted, and everyone can present it to the class. In addition to the general steps previously discussed, the *procedure* for groups projects includes

1. Students are assigned an initial project and are placed in cooperative learning groups to complete it. The required materials are provided.

2. The group completes the project, ensuring that all members contributed, agreed on, and can explain the results. The teacher systematically observes each group and provides feedback and coaching.

3. The group hands in their report to the teacher; each member presents the results to a section of the class; and a test may be given on the content of the project.

4. The assignment can be extended by the teacher presenting the relevant algorithm, procedure, concept, or theory required to complete the project. Students are then asked to apply what they have just learned to a more complex project.

Using the examples of group projects in Box 6.2 and the lists of steps for assigning general and group projects, you can practice doing so by completing Activity 6.1.

BOX 6.2
EXAMPLES OF PROJECTS

- Mythological rap song: write and present a rap song about the gods and goddesses in Greek mythology.
- Select a famous writer, artist, politician, or philosopher from the Renaissance period and become that person on a panel of experts.
- Teach cycles through gardening (different students are in charge of seeds, fertilizing, and so forth).
- Videotape a community project.
- Write plays, skits, role plays.
- Run a school post office.
- Have an international festival with multicultural activities.
- Groups write alternative endings with dramatizations.
- Turn a short story or event in history into a movie.
- Present a newscast.
- Pamphlet: select and research a disease and prepare an instructional pamphlet to present to the class.

- Research an international conflict in the world today (a student can research a different aspect of each country involved in the conflict—history, resolutions, maps, and so forth).
- Paint a mural of the history of the earth and humankind (each group takes an era—Greek, Roman, Middle Ages art)
- Create a timeline (personal, historical, literary, artistic, geological).
- Produce a school or class newspaper.
- Conduct a mock court.
- Create a mural based on reading.
- Create a new invention using the computer.
- Design an ideal school and have class enact it.
- Engage students in science fair projects.

ACTIVITY **6.1** ■ CREATE A PROJECT

1. List the projects you will assign students during the course.

   a. _____

   b. _____

   c. _____

   d. _____

2. Select one of the projects you listed. Write out the steps you will follow in assigning the project.

INDIVIDUAL ACCOUNTABILITY

What children can do together today, they can do alone tomorrow.   —*Vygotsky*

Assessing projects includes both group and individual accountability (Johnson, Johnson, & Holubec, 1998a). Teachers structure *group accountability* by assessing the overall performance of the group and giving the results back to group members to compare to a standard of performance. Criteria for excellence need to be established before the project is assigned and the quality of the group performance is assessed. A group grade or score is given, and every group member gets the same score.

A common concern with the use of projects is individual accountability. Teachers worry that some members will let others do all the work. Teachers structure *individual accountability* by assessing the performance of each group member and giving the results back to each member to compare to a preset standard of performance. There are a number of ways of doing this.

1. **Keeping the size of the group small.** The smaller the size of the group, the greater the individual accountability.

2. **Observing each group and group member.** Record the frequency with which each member contributes to the group's work. Knowing that the teacher is watching and collecting systematic data increases individual accountability.

3. **Assigning one student in each group the role of checker.** The *checker* asks other group members to explain the reasoning and rationale behind group decisions and answers.

4. **Giving random individual oral examinations.** Individual students are randomly selected to explain answers or present his or her group's work in the presence of the group or to the entire class.

5. **Having students teach what they learned to someone else.** Each group member can present the group's project to another group and teach that group what his or her group learned.

6. **Having students use what they have learned to solve a problem.** Each student can be given a problem that can only be solved by applying the knowledge and skills that were necessary to complete the project.

7. **Giving an individual test to each student.** After the group project is completed, an individual test on the knowledge and skills students were supposed to learn and use can be given. Bonus points can be given if all members of the group pass the test at a certain level (such as 90 percent correct).

SUMMARY

A project is an assignment aimed at having students produce a product on a topic related to the curriculum. Projects allow students to be creative and inventive by integrating diverse knowledge and skills, using diverse medias, using procedures such as the scientific method, formulating their own questions and answers, sharing their learning and accomplishments with others, and transfering and applying a wide variety of diverse information and skills. Projects are usually conducted by groups. When students are placed into groups to complete a project, both the group and the individual level assessments need to be conducted.

GROUP PROJECT RUBRIC

Students' Names: _____ Date: _____

Class: _____ Project: _____

DIRECTIONS:

For each criterion write the indicators for each of the three levels.

	Indicators		
Criteria	**Low**	**Middle**	**High**
Criterion 1	1. 2. 3.		
Criterion 2	1. 2. 3.		
Criterion 3	1. 2. 3.		
Criterion 4	1. 2. 3.		

Comments: _____

_____

_____

GROUP PROJECT SCORING RUBRIC

Students' Names: _____   Date: _____

Class: _____   Project: _____

Criteria	Score			
1. Quality of research	1————————2————————3————————4————————5 One source　　　　　Three sources　　　　　Five sources			
2. Question and answer section	1————————2————————3————————4————————5 Many factual errors　　　Some factual errors　　　No factual errors			
3. Graphics	1————————2————————3————————4————————5 No graphics　　　　　Good graphics　　　　Dazzling graphics			
4. Organization	1————————2————————3————————4————————5 Random　　　　　　Clear　　　　　　Overwhelming			
5. Oral presentation	1————————2————————3————————4————————5 Incomprehensible　　　　Clear　　　　　　Inspiring			

Comments:

GROUP GRADE

Score: _____

POINTS	GRADE
22–25	A
18–21	B
13–17	C
8–12	D

COLLEGE ADMISSIONS RATING FORM

Student's Names: _____   Date: _____

Please describe what you think is important about the applicant that will help us differentiate this student from other applicants. Describe the applicant's academic and personal qualities, especially his or her intellectual purpose, motivation, relative maturity, integrity, ability to work with others, interpersonal skills, leadership potential, independence, originality, capacity for growth, special talents, and enthusiasm.

Academic Skills and Potential	No Basis	Below Average	Average	Above Average	Top 5%
Creative, original thought					
Motivation					
Independence, initiative					
Intellectual ability					
Academic achievement					
Written expression of ideas					
Oral expression of ideas					
Disciplined work habits					
Potential for growth					
Ability to work with others					
Summary Evaluation					

CHAPTER SEVEN

STUDENT PORTFOLIOS

WHAT IS A PORTFOLIO?

Architects, artists, writers, and performers have used portfolios for some time to represent the quality of their work. Portfolios can also be used in collecting, assessing, and evaluating student work. A **portfolio** is an organized collection of evidence accumulated over time on a student's or group's academic progress, achievements, skills, and attitudes. It consists of work samples and a written rationale connecting the separate items into a more complete and holistic view of the student's (or group's) achievements or progress toward learning goals.

Portfolios can cover one semester, one year, or several years. They may represent student work in one, several, or all subject areas. They can include the work of one student or a group of students. They may be presented in file folders, notebooks, boxes, or video disks. They may be the property of the student, or they may be passed from teacher to teacher. There are no hard and fast rules as to the contents of a portfolio. Portfolios may contain any relevant item, such as

Completed homework, in-class assignments	Self-reflection and -analysis checklists
Tests (teacher made, curriculum supplied)	Group products
Compositions (essays, reports, stories)	Evidence of social skills
Presentations (recordings, observations)	Evidence of work habits and attitudes
Investigations, inventions, projects	Anecdotal records, narrative reports
Logs or journals	Standardized test results
Observation checklists (teacher, classmates)	Photo, autobiographic sketch
Visual arts (drawings, paintings, sculptures, pottery)	Performances (dances, thespian activities)

In elementary classes, portfolios can include all subject areas. In middle schools, students may keep a portfolio that reflects an integrated curriculum. In high schools, students may build employment portfolios to be used when students graduate. Some portfolios are graded whereas others help students reflect on their progress and set future learning goals. You can compare two different types of portfolios by studying Box 7.1, "The Best Works Portfolio" and Box 7.2, "The Process Portfolio." These types of portfolios reflect students' overall achievement in many subject areas. In contrast, Box 7.3 illustrates a portfolio that reflects student achievement in one subject area.

■ ■ ■ ■ ■

BOX 7.1
THE BEST WORKS PORTFOLIO

SUBJECT AREA	INDIVIDUAL STUDENT	COOPERATIVE GROUP
Science	The best solution to a scientific problem posed by the instructor, review of a scientific article, laboratory work conducted, original hypothesis formulated, position paper on a scientific issue, log or journal entry from a long-term experiment	The best scientific experiment conducted, project completed
Mathematics	The best solution to a problem posed by the instructor, description of how to solve a mathematical problem, review of a mathematics article, biography of mathematician, original mathematics theory developed, photo/diagram/ concept map of a mathematical idea investigated	The best project completed, small business planned and initiated
Language Arts	The best compositions in a variety of styles—expository, humor/satire, creative (poetry, drama, short story), journalistic (reporting, editorial columnist, reviewer), and advertising copy	The best dramatic production, video project, TV broadcast, newspaper, advertising display
Social Studies	The best historical research paper, opinion essay on historical issue, commentary on current event, original historical theory, review of a historical biography, account of academic controversy participated in	The best community survey, paper resulting from academic controversy, oral history compilation, multidimensional analysis of historical event, press corps interview with historical figure
Fine Arts	The best creative products such as drawings, paintings, sculptures, pottery, poems, thespian performance	The best creative products such as murals, plays written and performed, inventions thought of and built

CONTENTS OF PORTFOLIOS

The contents of a portfolio may be determined by

1. **The student.** Students can decide what to include in their portfolio.
2. **The cooperative learning group.** The student's cooperative learning group can recommend what the student includes in his or her portfolio.
3. **The teacher, school, and district.** Faculty can specify work samples or components to be included in the portfolio. Manhattan Community College faculty, for example, added an essay requirement to what was originally just a collection of

■ ■ ■ ■ ■

BOX 7.2
THE PROCESS PORTFOLIO

SUBJECT AREA	INDIVIDUAL STUDENT	COOPERATIVE GROUP
Science	Documentation (running records or logs) of using the scientific method to solve a series of laboratory problems	Documentation (observation checklists) of using the scientific method to solve a series of laboratory problems
Mathematics	Documentation of mathematical reasoning through double-column mathematical problem solving (computations on the left side and running commentary explaining thought processes on the right side)	Documentation of complex problem solving and use of higher-level strategies
Language Arts	Evolution of compositions from early notes through outlines, research notes, response to others' editing, and final draft	Rubrics and procedures developed to ensure high-quality peer editing
Social Studies	Evolution of speech from early notes through outlines, research notes, final draft, and response to critiques	Step-by-step documentation of historical research project
Fine Arts	"History" of any piece of student's creative work, from its original conception through first, second, third attempts and final product	Biography of school of artists who worked together to create a new form of artistic expression

■ ■ ■ ■ ■

BOX 7.3
MATH PORTFOLIO: POINTS OF FOCUS

Computations	Knowing basic computation procedures
Problem Solving	Developing and executing strategies
Mathematical Communication	Reading and writing in mathematics
Mathematical Disposition	Having healthy attitudes toward mathematics
Technology	Using computers and graphing calculators
Connections	Relating mathematics to other subjects
Teamwork	Working cooperatively with others to learn math
Growth over Time	Learning from mistakes

a student's work. A mathematics teacher might require a demonstration of the student's ability to make connections between two or more branches of mathematics (for example, an algebraic proof of a geometry theorem or a graphic solution of an algebra problem). In some school districts teachers are provided with a work sample menu, work sample descriptions, and supporting documentation. Teachers then decide which work samples they want their students to include in their portfolios and distribute the description assessment rubrics to students (see Box 7.4).

The contents of portfolios should include the following items:

1. *Cover sheet* that creatively reflects the nature of the student's (or group's) work
2. *Table of contents* that includes the title of each work sample and its page number
3. The *rationale* explaining what work samples are included, why each one is significant, and how they all fit together in a holistic view of the student's (or group's) work
4. The *work samples*
5. A *self-assessment* written by the student or the group members
6. *Future goals* based on the student's (or group's) current achievements, interests, and progress
7. *Other's comments and assessments* from the teacher, cooperative learning groups, and other interested parties such as the parents

WHY USE PORTFOLIOS?

1. **Portfolios give students the opportunity to direct their own learning.** Students can
   a. Document their efforts, achievements, development, and growth in knowledge, skills, expressions, and attitudes
   b. Use a variety of learning styles, modalities, and intelligences
   c. Assess their own learning and decide which items best represent their achievements and growth
   d. Set their future learning goals.
2. **Portfolios can be used to determine students' level of achievement.** Portfolios allow students to present a holistic view of their highest academic achievements, skills, and competencies.
3. **Portfolios can be used to determine students' growth over time.** Portfolios allow students to present their work over a period of time to show how they are progressing in achieving their learning goals (initial ideas, early drafts, first critiques, interim and final drafts, feedback from peers and teachers, and some suggestions of how one will build on the current project in future endeavors).
4. **Portfolios can be used to understand how students think, reason, organize, investigate, and communicate.** Portfolios can provide insight into students' reasoning and intellectual competencies by documenting students' progression of thought and work in achieving their learning goals.

■ ■ ■ ■ ■ ■
BOX 7.4
WORK SAMPLE

1. The skills and knowledge that are the focus of the description.
2. A summary statement of the materials expected from the student.
3. Several sample classroom assignments to help make the descriptions more concrete.
4. The scoring criteria for assessing the quality of the work sample.

5. **Portfolios provide an effective way of collecting and demonstrating achievement on a broad range of outcomes that cannot be assessed as effectively with paper-and-pencil methods.** Examples of these outcomes include persistence, growth, pride and ownership of work, problem solving, higher-level thinking, the ability to work with others, and self-evaluation.

6. **Portfolios can be used to communicate student efforts, progress toward accomplishing learning goals, and accomplishments.** Portfolios allow students to present their work as a whole in relation to standards and criteria to peers, teachers, parents, college admission officers, and so forth. In addition, portfolios allow teachers and other interested audiences to consider multiple sources of data when they examine what students know and can do.

7. **Portfolios can be used to evaluate and improve curriculum and instruction.** Portfolios provide a broad view on the effectiveness of the curriculum and instruction thereby allowing teachers to improve and enhance their instructional methods and curriculum materials. Portfolios have been found to change instruction as a result of changing the criteria against which student work is evaluated. The use of portfolios has also been found to change the way students' evaluate their own work. Students are taught the criteria against which their work will be judged. This improves their ability to think more deeply and creatively and analyze the strengths and weaknesses of their work.

This list identifies seven advantages for using portfolios. You may have reservations about using portfolios. Activity 7.1 provides the opportunity to reflect on your potential use of portfolios.

ACTIVITY **7.1** ■ REFLECTING ON PORTFOLIOS

Reflect on your potential use of portfolios. Write down the pluses and minuses of doing so along with any interesting ideas that come to mind.

Plus	Minus	Interesting
1.	1.	1.
2.	2.	2.
3.	3.	3.
4.	4.	4.
5.	5.	5.
6.	6.	6.

HOW TO USE STUDENT PORTFOLIOS

The student's portfolio represents the quality of student learning throughout the grading period. Although the teacher may give quizzes, tests, homework assignments, and projects during the course, the portfolio represents an overall, more holistic view of what the student has learned and accomplished. Important aspects of the teacher's role in using portfolios occur (a) before the instructional unit or grading period begins, (b) during the instructional unit or grading period, and (c) following the instructional unit or grading period.

The first step is to prepare for the use of portfolios. Before the term, semester, year, or course begins faculty must develop a portfolio program. Guidelines for doing so follow.

1. **Decide what type of portfolio to use.** Portfolios may be constructed by having
   a. Individual students keep personal portfolios with the input and help of teachers.
   b. Individual students keep personal portfolios with the input and help of their cooperative learning groups (the teacher monitors the process and provides help and assistance to the groups when it is needed).
   c. Cooperative base groups keep group portfolios with the input and help of teachers. Group portfolios include documentation of the work of the group as a whole and the work of each individual member.
2. **Identify the purposes and objectives of the portfolio.** Because there are so many varieties of portfolios, faculty should think through what they want portfolios to accomplish before requiring them. Will students hand in the portfolio to the faculty? Will it serve as the focus of a discussion with faculty? Will it be used in student–parent conferences? Or will students keep their portfolios?
3. **Select which categories of work samples should go into the portfolio.** What are the skills, competencies, and knowledge students should demonstrate and what assignments will show evidence of these skills, competencies, and knowledge? How much of a student's work should go into his or her portfolio? Will the portfolio include an assignment (such as an essay or a competency matrix) that helps students reflect on their learning?
4. **Have students select the pieces to include in their portfolio.** Whereas the teacher specifies the categories of work samples and the criteria by which they will be assessed and evaluated, students may select the individual pieces that best represent their work and meet the criteria for each category.
5. **Decide how the portfolio will be assessed and evaluated.** Who will develop the rubrics? Who will do the assessing and evaluating? Will students be involved?

In planning how to use portfolios as part of your assessment process, do not try to do too much with a portfolio program. Start out slowly. Do not try to use portfolios to assess everything. Activity 7.2 provides a list of questions to start you thinking about how to prepare and use portfolios.

The second step is to manage the portfolios during the semester or course. Portfolios are managed in the following way.

1. **The portfolio process.** Faculty explain to students the categories of work samples to be included in the portfolio.
2. **Rubrics.** Faculty develop rubrics to assess and evaluate the student's work samples. Students may participate in developing some or all of the rubrics (see Activity 7.3).
3. **Assignments.** Students complete assignments knowing that some or all of them will be included in the final portfolio. All assignments may be kept in a "working portfolio" during the grading period.

ACTIVITY **7.2** ■ PREPARING TO USE PORTFOLIOS

1. Who will construct the portfolios?

_____ Individual students with teacher input and help

_____ Individual students with the input and help of cooperative learning groups

_____ Cooperative base groups (whole group work and individual members' work) with teach input and help

2. What type of portfolio do you want to use?

_____ Best Works Portfolio _____ Process/Growth Portfolio

3. What are the purposes and objectives of the portfolio?

a. _____

b. _____

c. _____

4. What categories of work samples should go into the portfolio?

a. _____

b. _____

c. _____

d. _____

5. What criteria will students or groups use to select their entries?

a. _____

b. _____

c. _____

6. Who will develop the rubrics to assess and evaluate the portfolios?

_____ Faculty _____ Students

---

4. Self-assessment. Students reflect on and self-assess the quality and quantity of their work and progress toward their learning goals.

The third step is to manage the portfolio process at the end of the grading period. Once all the work samples have been completed, the selections for the portfolio must be made and organized into a coherent representation of the student's or group's work.

ACTIVITY **7.3** ■ INVOLVING STUDENTS IN DEVELOPING RUBRICS

1. Develop a list of potential criteria to use in evaluating portfolios. The potential criteria may be derived from having students interview each other about potential criteria and from the teacher supplying what he or she thinks are important criteria.

2. Have cooperative groups of students rank order the criteria from most important to least important. Then have the groups share their rankings and discuss until there is consensus on the criteria by the entire class.

3. Construct a rubric for each criterion starting with the one ranked most important by listing indicators of low, middle, and high proficiency.

4. Have students apply the rubrics to sample performances.

5. Have students apply the rubrics to their own and each other's work samples and portfolios.

Source: Based on procedure developed by Laurie Stevahn.

---

1. **Faculty specify a certain number and type of products to be included in the final portfolio.** One product, for example, might be included from each instructional unit conducted during the grading period.

2. **Students decide which items to include in their final portfolio.** The advice of the teacher and the student's cooperative learning group may be taken into account in selecting the final items. The student has the opportunity to revise his or her work and make the products better. The students understand what the criteria are for each assignment so they know the standards by which the teacher will grade them.

3. **Students describe the progress made in achieving their learning goals during the grading period.**

4. **The cooperative learning group describes the progress the student has made in achieving his or her learning goals during the grading period.**

5. **Faculty conduct a summative evaluation.** Faculty give a grade or score indicating their judgment as to the quality and quantity of the student's work. The scoring of student portfolios, however, often suffers from problems in reliability. Different teachers give different scores to the same portfolio and the same teacher may give the same portfolio different scores at different times. There are a number of options for grading:
   a. The portfolio is not graded because each entry has been previously graded during the grading period.
   b. Each individual entry is given a grade and the portfolio is not graded.
   c. One grade is given to the entire portfolio on the overall quality and quantity of the work products included.

6. **Postconferences are held.** The options for postconferences include
   a. The student and the teacher
   b. The student and the cooperative learning group
   c. The student (and the cooperative learning group) and his or her parents (with the teacher)
   d. The student and visitors at a portfolio exhibition

7. **A decision is made on whether, how, or what parts of the portfolio are to be passed on to the next teacher.** The portfolios of seniors may be used in the interview process for a job or college.

Individual Portfolios with Help from Cooperative Learning Group

The cooperative procedure for using portfolios is similar to that used for peer editing compositions. The *task* is for each student to create a portfolio. The *criteria for success* is a well-constructed portfolio by each student. The *cooperative goal* is for all group members to verify that each member's portfolio is perfect according to the criteria set by the teacher. Students receive an individual score or grade on the quality of their portfolio. The teacher can also give bonus points based on the quality of all members' portfolios. Each student is *individually accountable* for creating his or her own portfolio. The procedure follows (Johnson, Johnson, & Holubec, 1998a):

1. The teacher assigns students to cooperative base groups with at least one good reader and writer to each group.
2. The teacher explains individual portfolios. The teacher describes the categories of work samples that students will have to place in their portfolios and the criteria that will be used to assess and evaluate each sample.
3. Group members complete a series of individual assignments related to their learning goals with each other's help and assistance. Compositions, for example, go through a peer editing process to ensure that they meet the teacher-set criteria.
5. Faculty and group members monitor the groups as they work and collect data on interaction among members.
6. Students select work samples from each specified category to include in their portfolio. Each member explains his or her proposed portfolio to the group. Group members give the student feedback concerning the quality of his or her presentation and help him or her choose the specific pieces that best represent the quality of his or her work (taking into account the assessment criteria) and, therefore, should be included in the student's portfolio. If possible, a chart or graph is drawn showing the student's progress.
7. Faculty conduct a summative evaluation of the student's portfolio.
8. Postconferences are held between (a) the student and the faculty and (b) the student and his or her parents (possibly with the help of cooperative learning group but always with the assistance of the teacher).

Cooperative Group Portfolio

A **group portfolio** is an organized collection of group work samples and individual work samples of each member accumulated over time. The *task* is for each cooperative base group to create a group portfolio. A **cooperative base group** is a long-term, heterogeneous cooperative learning group with stable membership. It may last for one course, one year, or for several years. Its purposes are to give the support, help, encouragement, and assistance each member needs to make good academic progress and develop cognitively and socially in healthy ways.

The *criteria for success* is that the portfolio meets the criteria specified by the faculty and/or students. The *cooperative goal* is for all group members to verify that the group's portfolio meets the criteria. Each student is *individually accountable* for contributing his or her part of the portfolio and for helping to complete the overall group portions of the portfolio. The procedure follows.

1. The teacher assigns students to cooperative base groups with at least one good reader and writer to each group. The teacher structures identity interdependence by having groups choose names, create a group symbol, and so forth.
2. The teacher explains group portfolios. The teacher describes the categories of work samples that each group will have to place in their portfolio and the criteria that will be used to assess and evaluate each sample.

3. The group completes a series of group projects (that any one member could not complete alone) related to the learning goals of its members. Examples include creating a new invention using the computer, turning a short story or historical event into a movie/video, or researching a vocational program and creating an informational brochure about it.

4. Group members complete a series of individual assignments related to their learning goals with each other's help and assistance. Presentations, for example, go through a peer editing process to ensure that they meet the criteria set by the teacher.

5. Faculty and group members monitor the groups as they work and collect data on interaction among members.

6. Faculty specify the categories of group and individual work samples that go into the group portfolio.

7. Group members select the group projects to include in the group's portfolio that best represent the quality of learning or progress toward learning groups of the group as a whole (taking into account the assessment criteria).

8. The group includes in its portfolio evidence of teamwork such as charts and grafts documenting constructive patterns of interaction among members. The data result from members' and faculty's observations of the patterns of members' interactions and members' processing and self-assessments of how well the group is functioning. Descriptions of group celebrations are also included.

9. Members select individual work samples from each specified category to include in the group portfolio. Each member explains his or her proposed work samples to groupmates. Group members give each member feedback concerning the quality of his or her presentation and help the member choose the specific pieces that best represent the quality of his or her work (taking into account the assessment criteria) and, therefore, should be included in the group's portfolio. If possible, a chart or graph is drawn showing the student's progress.

10. Faculty conduct a summative evaluation of the group's portfolio.

11. Postconferences are held between (a) the group and the faculty and (b) the cooperative group and members' parents.

Similar to individual portfolios, the contents of group portfolios should include the following items:

1. Cover sheet that creatively reflects group's personality
2. Table of contents
3. Description of the group and its members
4. Introduction to portfolio and rationale for the work samples included
5. Group work samples (products by the group that any one member could not have produced alone)
6. Observation data of group members interacting as they worked on group projects
7. Self-assessment of the group by its members
8. Individual members' work samples that were revised on the basis of group feedback (compositions, presentations, and so forth)
9. Self-assessment of members, including their strengths and weaknesses in facilitating group effectiveness and other members' learning
10. List of future learning and social skills goals for the group and each of its members
11. Comments and feedback from faculty and other groups

SUMMARY

A portfolio is an organized collection of evidence (work samples and a written rationale) accumulated over time (a semester, year, or several years) of a student's or group's academic progress, achievements, skills, and attitudes. It provides a holistic view of the student's (or group's) achievements or progress toward learning goals. There are two major types of portfolios, one presenting the best works of a student or group and the other presenting a systematic view of the learning process by sampling a student's or group's work conducted over a semester or year to show the growth of the student or group over time. The work samples included may be selected by the student, the cooperative learning group, the teacher, or the school district. A portfolio may include a cover sheet, table of contents, rationale explaining what is included and why, work samples, a self-assessment, future goals, and comments from relevant others. There are three steps involved in using portfolios: Prepare for the use of portfolios, manage the portfolios during the semester or year, and manage the use of the portfolios at the end of the specified period.

FINAL PORTFOLIO

Student/Group: _____   Time Frame and Dates: _____

Grade Level: _____   Subject(s): _____

Purpose: _____   Best Work _____   Process/Growth

Selection	Points	Comments
1.		
2.		
3.		
4.		
5.		
6.		
7.		
Total Grade		

Comments:

Suggested Future Goals:

Final Portfolio Grade: _____   Faculty: _____

GROUP PORTFOLIO

Group: _____   Time Frame and Dates: _____

Grade Level: _____   Subject(s): _____

Purpose: _____   Best Work _____   Process/Growth

Group Projects	Assessment Criteria
Chosen to Be Included	**Rationale**
Student Teamwork Data	**Teacher Teamwork Data**

PORTFOLIO ORGANIZER

Name: _____   Class: _____   Date: _____

Reading	Writing
Science	**Math**
Social Studies	**Physical Education**

I believe I do the following well:

1. _____

2. _____

3. _____

Your comments and suggestions:

_____

_____

_____

CHAPTER EIGHT

OBSERVING STUDENTS

ASSESSMENT THROUGH OBSERVING STUDENTS LEARN

> The only thing that endures over time is the law of the farm: I must prepare the ground, put in the seed, cultivate it, water it, then gradually nurture growth and development to full maturity. There is no quick fix.
> —*Stephen Covey*

Teachers observe and notice what is going on around them. They watch students to see who is on task, who is out of his or her seat, who looks puzzled, and who is finished and waiting for his or her next assignment. Observation is a primary, yet often underutilized, tool of assessing learning and instruction. By and large, little attention has been devoted to training teachers how to engage in unbiased observation of student performances and students' efforts to learn. **Observation** is aimed at recording and describing behavior as it occurs (Johnson, Johnson, & Holubec, 1998a). Its purpose is to provide objective data in the following areas:

1. **The quality of student performances.** Many student performances may only be assessed through direct observation procedures. Many performances, such as giving a speech, playing tennis, helping a classmate, reciting a poem, or drawing a picture can only be assessed through observational methods.
2. **The processes and procedures students use in completing assignments.** To improve continually the process of learning, students must receive feedback concerning their actions in completing an assignment. The process of learning is primarily assessed through observation.
3. **The processes and procedures teachers use in conducting lessons.** If teachers are to improve continually, they need feedback on their actions in conducting class sessions and teaching a course. The process of instruction is primarily assessed through observation.

A major problem with observation is the potential for lack of objectivity by the observers. An example of biased observing may be seen in a study conducted by Hastorf and Cantril (1954). They asked Dartmouth and Princeton college students to watch a film of a football game between the two schools. The game was an unusually rough one in which many penalties had been called. The Princeton quarterback, an all-American, left the game in the second quarter with a broken nose and a mild concussion. The Dartmouth quarterback left the game in the third quarter with a broken leg.

The Dartmouth and Princeton college students were asked to watch the film and record the number and severity of the infractions committed by the two teams. Dartmouth won the game and its students saw the two teams committing an equal number of violations. The Princeton students saw the Dartmouth players as committing more than twice as many penalties as the Princeton team. A solution to the problem of bias is using a **structured coding system,** which requires observers to categorize each group behavior into an objectively definable category.

In using observation as an assessment tool, you need to (Johnson, Johnson, & Holubec, 1998a)

1. Understand the basics of observing.
2. Prepare for observing by
   a. Deciding which student behaviors, actions, and skills are to be observed
   b. Deciding who will be the observers
   c. Making a sampling plan
   d. Constructing an observation sheet to record the frequencies of targeted actions that are appropriate for the age of the students
   e. Training observers
3. Be an observer. Record how often each student performs the specified behaviors. (Observation procedures may be formal or informal.)
4. Summarize observations in a clear and useful manner to
   a. Give feedback to each student and group.
   b. Help students analyze the observation data.
   c. Help students reflect on how effectively they are learning and helping each other learn, and whether they may behave more effectively next time.

THE BASICS OF OBSERVING

To use observation for assessment purposes, it is necessary to understand the basic nature of observation (Johnson, Johnson, & Holubec, 1998a). (Box 8.1 provides a brief account of the observation process.) Working with a partner, complete the following activities that will define and explain the nature of observing.

1. Observe the Characteristics of Your Setting

Being aware of the setting in which observation takes place is important. Settings can be natural or simulations (see Box 8.2). The characteristics of the setting can influence observation in many ways. Complete Activity 8.1 to discover how your observations compare with others.

2. Differentiate between Objective and Subjective Observations

Ensure all triad members understand the difference between objective and subjective observations. *Objective* observations are factors or details all members can readily agree

---

■ ■ ■ ■ ■

BOX 8.1
FIVE-MINUTE WALK

1. Select actions to observe.
2. Construct observation sheet.
3. Plan route through the classroom.
4. Gather data on every group.
5. Feed the data back to the groups and/or to the class as a whole.
6. Chart or graph the results.

■ ■ ■ ■ ■ ■

BOX 8.2
SIMULATIONS, ROLE PLAYING, AND OBSERVATION

There are times when you wish to observe students engaging in a skill or pattern of behavior, but it will take far too much time to wait and observe the behavior occurring naturally. To save time, you create a simulation and observe what students do. Simulations and games are increasingly being used as training and assessment procedures. Simulations can vary widely in complexity of issues and number of participants, ranging from relatively simple simulations for an individual or small group to moderately complex computerized simulations requiring a number of groups to participate. For assessment purposes, students are placed within a simulation and their actions are monitored and observed so that behavioral measures of outcomes can be obtained.

Frequently in simulations, students role play the characters. Initial instructions are given, and the role players determine what happens. Role playing is a tool for

1. Bringing a specific skill and its consequences into focus so it may be practiced
2. Experiencing concretely the type of interaction under examination
3. Setting up an imaginary life situation so students can act and react in terms of the assumptions they are asked to adopt, the beliefs they are asked to hold, and the character they are asked to play
4. Giving students experience in discussing and identifying effective and ineffective behavior

Your tasks, as the coordinator of the simulated role play, are as follow:

1. Get students in "role." You help involve the role players in the situation by introducing it in such a way that the players are emotionally stimulated. Using name tags and asking the players questions to help them get a feeling for the part are helpful. Introduce the scene to the role players and the observers.
2. Conduct the simulation. While the students are engaged in the role play, you carefully observe and record the frequency of their effective and ineffective actions.
3. Get students out of "role." Always "de-role" after the role playing has ended.
4. Conduct a processing session in which students reflect on what happened and how to behave more effectively.

upon. *Subjective* observations are unique perceptions, biases, or individual points of view that all members may not agree upon. To test your knowledge of these differences, label each observation recorded in Activity 8.1 as either objective (O) or subjective (S).

3. Differentiate between Descriptions and Inferences

Ensure all triad members understand the difference between descriptions and inferences. Descriptions should be based on facts, details, or factors that can be observed. Inferences are conclusions about behavior that involve opinion and interpretation. Activity 8.2 is an exercise in distinguishing between descriptive and interpretive statements.

4. Phrase Questions Well

To observe in an objective and descriptive way, you must understand the specific purpose of the intended observations and focus on the behaviors that will provide

ACTIVITY 8.1 ■

You have 5 minutes to write down as many characteristics of your setting as possible.

1.	6.
2.	7.
3.	8.
4.	9.
5.	10.

Form a triad and compare your observations:

1. What did each of you observe? _____

_____

_____

2. In what sequence were your observations made? _____

_____

_____

3. How did you decide what to write down and what not to? _____

_____

_____

4. Did the format of the task influence what you observed? _____

_____

_____

the answer or solve the problem. This is best done by limiting observation to directly observable behaviors. Questions should be well phrased so that they allow the observer to focus on directly observable behavior. You should carefully evaluate how well you phrase questions (see Activity 8.3).

5. Differentiate between Category and Sign Systems

Category system requires the observer to list a set of categories so that every observed behavior can be recorded into one, and only one, of a series of mutually

ACTIVITY **8.2** ■

Identify the descriptive (D) and the interpretative (I) statements given below:

_____ **1.** Sam held his hand up 90 seconds before the teacher called on him.

_____ **2.** Helen made sarcastic remarks about the teacher.

_____ **3.** Roger laughed four times during the meeting.

_____ **4.** David was embarrassed when they sang "Happy Birthday."

_____ **5.** Roger is holding the golf club in his left hand.

_____ **6.** Keith does not like the lesson.

_____ **7.** Dale is confused by the teacher's explanation.

_____ **8.** Edythe is not talking enough.

_____ **9.** John has his back to his group.

ACTIVITY **8.3** ■ PHRASING QUESTIONS

DIRECTIONS:

Determine which of the following questions are well phrased and explain why you think so.

Questions	Well Phrased	Poorly Phrased	Reason(s)
1. Are males more restless than females during the lesson?			
2. How many questions did students ask during the lesson?			
3. Is the teacher encouraging students to disagree and challenge each other?			
4. How many students are studying during free time?			

exclusive categories. The categories must be exhaustive for a particular dimension so that every observed behavior can be categorized. (See Activity 8.4 for an example of how to implement the category system.)

A **sign system** involves listing beforehand a limited number of specific kinds of behavior of interest to the observer. An observer using a sign system approach records only those behaviors that fall into one of the preconceived categories listed. Many behaviors would not be recorded if they did not fit into the specified categories. (See Activity 8.5 for an example of how to implement the sign system.)

6. Understand Types of Categories

Mutually exclusive categories are precisely distinguishable and independent from other categories. Non–mutually exclusive categories are overlapping (a behavior can

---

ACTIVITY 8.4   ■   **CATEGORY SYSTEM OF OBSERVING**

Category	Member 1	Member 2	Member 3
Gives information			
Asks for other's information			
Gives direction to group's work			
Summarizes members' ideas			

ACTIVITY 8.5   ■   **SIGN SYSTEM OF OBSERVING**

Group Member	Explains Concept	Draws Representation	Withdraws
1.			
2.			
3.			
4.			

be coded in more than one category). **Exhaustive categories** exist when every instance of observed behavior can be classified in one of the available categories. Activity 8.6 provides examples of categories for which you can determine the type.

7. Understand Types of Sampling

Time sampling occurs when the observer records the occurrence or nonoccurrence of selected behavior(s) within specified, uniform time limits. **Event sampling** occurs when the observer records a given event or category of events each time it naturally occurs. You can use the observation forms for these types of sampling provided on pages 137 and 138 or you can construct your own.

The basics of observing include being aware of the characteristics of the setting, differentiating between objective and subjective observations, differentiating between descriptions and inferences, understanding the phrasing of questions, differentiating between category and sign systems, differentiating between mutually exclusive and overlapping and between exhaustive and nonexhaustive categories, and understanding the difference between time sampling and event sampling. Given your understanding of these basics, you are now ready to prepare for observing.

ACTIVITY 8.6 ■

Examine the categories. Decide whether they are (a) mutually exclusive or overlapping and whether they are (b) exhaustive or nonexhaustive. Write *yes* or *no* in each box.

Categories	Mutually Exclusive	Exhaustive
Asking a question Stating an opinion Explaining a concept Telling a joke		
Being silent Talking		
Looking out the window Looking at the book Looking at the teacher		
Standing Sitting Lying prone		

PREPARING FOR OBSERVING

In preparing for observing, you state your instructional objectives in the appropriate behavioral form. The objectives should describe student behavior that is observable and countable. Then you decide which actions to observe, who will observe, what the sampling plan will be, and how the observers will be trained. You then construct your observation form.

Deciding Which Actions to Observe

On or Off Task.   You can observe students' work to determine whether they are on task, completing their work, or are off task, engaging in some other activity than the prescribed academic learning.

Academic Efforts, Procedures, and Strategies.   You can assess many learning outcomes (such as depth of understanding, level of reasoning, mastery of problem-solving procedures, metacognitive thinking) only by opening a "window" into students' minds and observing students "thinking aloud." Cooperative learning groups provide such a window.

Social Skills.   One of the many advantages of cooperative learning is that it allows teachers, students, and other interested parties to assess students' mastery of the interpersonal and small group skills needed to work with others.

Deciding Who Observers Will Be

Teachers.   You, the teacher, are always an observer. In every lesson, you systematically roam from group to group. You gather specific information on the interaction of members in each group. When necessary, you intervene to improve students' efforts to learn and to help classmates learn.

Students.   When students become experienced in working in cooperative learning groups, you should train them to be observers. Students may be roving observers who circulate throughout the classroom and monitor all learning groups. Similar to the teacher, student roving observers need a sampling plan to ensure that they observe all groups an approximately equal amount of time.

Students may also observe their own groups (one observer per group). In this case, student observers remove themselves slightly from the group so they are close enough to see and hear the interaction among group members but are not tempted to participate in the academic task. Observers do not comment or intervene while the group is working. You set aside a time near the end of the class period for the learning groups to review the content of the lesson with the observer. The role of observer rotates so that each group member is an observer an equal amount of time.

Visitors.   Visitors should not be allowed to sit and watch a lesson passively. When someone visits your classroom, hand them an observation form, explain the role of the observer, and put them to work. Visitors may be roving observers or they may observe one single group, depending on the purpose of their visit.

Making a Sampling Plan for Roving Observers

Before the lesson begins you plan how much time you will spend observing each learning group. This is a **sampling plan.** You may observe one learning group for the entire class period, collecting information on every member. Or if the class period lasts for 50 minutes and there are ten groups in the class, you may decide to observe each group for 5 minutes. Or you may observe each group for 2 minutes and rotate through all the groups twice during one class period. If you decide you should intervene in a group or with a student, you temporarily suspend the sampling plan and then resume it after the intervention is over.

Constructing an Observation Form

Observation forms or check sheets are used to answer the question, How often are certain actions or events happening? An **observation form** is used to tally the number of times a behavior, action, or event is observed in a specified time period. An example is provided in Figure 8.1. The form has to be designed so that all potential observers can use it (that is, age appropriate). A structured observation form is created by

1. Defining exactly what behaviors, actions, skills, or events are being observed (all observers have to be looking for the same thing)
2. Determining the time period during which the data will be collected (minutes to weeks)
3. Entering the actions to be observed in the first column (each action or skill is placed in a separate row, the final row is reserved for the total of the columns)
4. Making an additional column for each member of the group, and making a final column to record the total for each row on the form
5. Making sure all columns are clearly labeled and wide enough to enter data

FIGURE 8.1 **Sample Observation Form**

OBSERVATION FORM

Observer: _____   Grade: _____   Date: _____

Actions	Edythe	Keith	Dale	Total
Contributes Ideas				
Encourages Participation				
Checks for Understanding				
Gives Group Direction				
Other:				
Total				

Training Observers

If students or visitors are to be used as observers, they must be trained to follow observation procedures, use the observation forms, and follow the sampling plan. Minimal training can make students quite proficient observers. After observers are appointed and the observation form is constructed, the form is explained to the observers and the class as a whole. Teachers should make sure that all students understand what the observation form is and how it will be used. The following steps should be used as a guideline for learning the observation procedures.

Take a few minutes after an observation period to chat with students about what they learned in doing the observing. Occasionally, sit side by side with a student observer and check your counts against his or hers. Discuss any discrepancies. Videotaping a group working and then having everyone in the class observe it and compare their observations with classmates is an excellent way of training students. An advantage of a videotape is that it may be replayed and analyzed several times.

1. Use one observation form for each group. Place a tally mark in the appropriate row and column when a student engages in one of the targeted actions. Look for patterns of behavior in the group. Do not worry about recording everything, but observe as accurately and rapidly as possible.
2. Make notes on the back of the observation form if something takes place that should be shared with the group but does not fit into the actions being observed.
3. Write down specific positive and important contributions by each group member (to ensure that every member will receive positive feedback).
4. After the learning session is over, total the columns and rows. Transfer the totals to long-term record sheets and the appropriate charts or graphs. The observation forms should be dated and kept to assess the growth of the students and groups. When a group is observed more than once during a class session, different colored ink may be used. This allows group members to assess their skill development at a glance.
5. Give the information gathered to the group and assist group members in deriving conclusions. Show the observation form to the group, holding it so all members can see it. Ask the group, "What do you conclude about (a) your participation in the group and (b) the group functioning in general?" Ensure all group members receive positive feedback about their efforts to learn and help their groupmates learn. After small group processing, there is whole class processing.
6. Help group members set goals for improving their competence in engaging in social skills during the next group meeting by asking, "What could you add to be even a better group tomorrow than you were today?" Have members discuss the goals and publicly commit to achieving them. Emphasize the continuous improvement of students' competencies and group effectiveness.

BEING AN OBSERVER

Observing Students' On-Task Behavior

The simplest use of observation procedures is to observe each student and determine whether the student is engaged in academic learning or is off task. These observations can be made while students work individually or in cooperative learning groups. The observation form consists of a list of students in the class, two columns to indicate either on-task or off-task behavior, and a column for comments (see Figure 8.2).

FIGURE 8.2 Sample Observing On-Task Behavior Form

OBSERVING ON-TASK BEHAVIOR FORM

Class: _____   Grade: _____   Date: _____

Students	On Task	Off Task	Comments
Frank			
Helen			
Roger			
David			
Edythe			
Keith			
Dale			
Tai			
Roberta			
Phillip			
Juan			

Observing Academic Efforts: Window into Students' Minds

Many students may be unaware of their reasoning processes while they are engaged in academic work. When asked, "How do you solve this problem?" many students may respond, "I don't know; I just do it." Such an answer is usually not acceptable. If students cannot accurately describe the reasoning procedures and sequences they use before, during, and after problem solving, they have not really learned the material.

The assessment issue is, How do you make covert cognitive reasoning overt and therefore open to correction and improvement? Although paper-and-pencil tests and homework assignments indicate whether students can determine the "correct" answer, they usually do not reveal students' cognitive reasoning and depth of understanding. The only way to determine whether students really understand a procedure or concept is to listen to them explain it to someone else. Such oral explanations can be obtained either by (a) listening to students' explanations as they work in cooperative learning groups or (b) interviewing a student and requesting a detailed explanation of reasoning processes.

Systematic observation of cooperative learning groups allows teachers to attain a "window" into students' minds and thereby

1. **Determine the extent to which students do or do not understand what they are studying.** This helps teachers to pinpoint areas of learning that need to be focused on or retaught.
2. **Make internal covert reasoning processes and procedures overt so they can be examined, corrected, and improved.** Many students, though able to derive the "correct answer," may misunderstand the basic principles and concepts involved. They may, for example, list correctly the phases of the moon without any understanding of what causes the moon to pass through different phases. Learning outcomes such as level of reasoning, mastery of problem-solving procedures, and metacognitive thinking cannot be measured by pencil-and-paper homework assignments and tests. They can only be assessed by observing students "think out loud" as they explain to each other how to solve a problem or complete the assignment.
3. **Assess aspects of learning and intelligent behavior.** Such aspects include persistence, using a variety of strategies, flexibility in thinking, metacognition, commitment to high-quality work, and commitment to continuous improvement.
4. **Assess performances.** Any performance (e.g., singing, dancing, playing an instrument, enacting dramas, giving a speech, or demonstrating athletic skills) may be better assessed with observation than with any other assessment procedure.
5. **Assess transfer and application of what is being learned.**

The procedure for obtaining a window into students' minds follows

1. Assign students to small cooperative groups and give them an academic assignment that requires them to use problem-solving and reasoning procedures.
2. Assign one member of each group the role of checker for understanding. The checker for understanding is responsible for asking other group members to explain the procedures and processes they are using to solve a problem or complete a task.
3. Construct an observation checklist. An **observation checklist** is a record-keeping device for teachers to use to keep track of the degree to which each student has demonstrated a targeted behavior, action, skill, or procedure. Checklists include students' names, space for four to five targeted behaviors, a code or rating scale to signify the level of mastery (+ = frequently; @ = sometimes; – = not yet), a space for comments or anecdotal notes, and a space to record the date so that developmental growth can be examined. Checklists may be used to observe students during lessons, on the playground, on field trips, in hallways. They can be used to observe students individually, in groups, with younger students, with older students, or with adults. An example is a checklist for observing student persistence (see page 139).
4. Move from group to group gathering observation data about the quality of the explanations and intellectual interchange occurring among group members.
5. Summarize and analyze the data to assess the effectiveness of students' efforts to learn and that of the instructional program, give students appropriate feedback, and help them reflect on how to improve their learning efforts.

Cooperative learning groups offer a unique opportunity for immediate (a) diagnosis of level of understanding, (b) feedback from peers, and (c) remediation to correct misunderstandings and fill in gaps in students' understanding. Training students to observe each other's cognitive reasoning and strategies for solving problems and completing assignments facilitates the cycle of diagnosis–feedback–remediation.

Observing Social Skills

The third use of observation procedures is to assess students' social skills. In addition to evaluating efforts to achieve academically, teachers need to assess and evaluate students' efforts to work together cooperatively. This is covered in Chapter 9.

Unstructured Observations

The use of structured observation schedules is not the only way to observe pupil behavior. As long as you are listening to or watching the class, you are observing. Informal, off-the-cuff observation is always taking place; the challenge is to become aware of it and make it as accurate and helpful as possible. Becoming more precise in your natural observing of pupils is called informal or unstructured observation. **Unstructured observation** is the recording of significant, specific events involving pupils. The emphasis is on the significant; it is not necessary to record an observation for each pupil each day. Teachers "eavesdrop" by making observations that

1. Are specific (they don't degenerate into generalities)
2. Are brief enough to write down quickly
3. Capture an important aspect of the behavior of one or more pupils
4. Provide help in answering questions about (a) students' efforts to maximize their own and each other's learning and (b) the successful implementation of instructional strategies and procedures.

Eavesdropping differs from the use of structured observation schedules in that it is concerned primarily with qualitative incidents, which may occur somewhat infrequently. You will want to develop a procedure for unstructured observation that allows you to make a permanent record of incidents as they are taking place. A stenographer's notebook, a few 3- × 5-inch index cards in a pocket, or scratch paper can facilitate the immediate recording of observations (see Figure 8.3). Such notes need to be placed in a log to organize them in a permanent way. You may want to write down positive incidents on cards and file them under the student's name (after they have

FIGURE 8.3   Sample Anecdotal Observations Record

Observer: _____   Date: _____

Note 1:   Group: _____   Student(s):_____

Note 2:   Group: _____   Student(s):_____

Note 3:   Group: _____   Student(s):_____

Note 4:   Group: _____   Student(s):_____

been used to give the student feedback). You can then access the cards during parent conferences for examples of a student's competencies and positive qualities.

Guidelines for Observing

Guideline 1. Use a formal observation sheet to count the number of times students engage in targeted behaviors. The more concrete the data is, the more useful it is to you and your students. A variety of observation instruments and procedures that you can use for these purposes appear in Johnson, Johnson, and Holubec (1998a, 1995).

Guideline 2. Try not to count too many different behaviors at one time. You may want to choose two to four behaviors from your observation sheet to record the first few times you observe. Once you have used the observation sheet several dozen times, you will be able to keep track of all the behaviors included.

Guideline 3. Sometimes you may use a simple checklist in addition to a systematic observation form. You can practice using a simple observation checklist in Activity 8.7.

Guideline 4. Focus on positive behaviors that are cause for celebration when present and cause for discussion when absent.

Guideline 5. Supplement and extend the frequency data with notes on specific student actions. Especially useful are skillful interchanges that you observe and, using objective praise, can later share with students. You can also share them with parents during conferences or telephone conversations.

Guideline 6. Train students to be observers. Student observers can obtain more complete data on each group's functioning. For very young students you must keep the system simple, perhaps having them record only who talks. Many teachers have

ACTIVITY **8.7** ■ OBSERVATION CHECKLIST

Behavior	Yes	No	Comments
1. Do students understand the task?			
2. Are students thinking out loud by explaining step by step how to complete the assignment?			
3. Are students challenging each other's reasoning and searching for new information and understandings?			
4. Are students engaging in the social and cognitive skills they are expected to practice in this lesson?			

had success with student observers, even in kindergarten. One of the more important things for you to do is to give the class adequate instructions (and perhaps practice) on gathering observation data and sharing it with the group. The observer is in the best position to learn about group working skills.

Consider one first-grade teacher who had a student who talked all the time (even to himself while working alone). He tended to dominate any group he was in. When she introduced the practice of having student observers in the class, she made him an observer. One important rule for observers was not to interfere in the task but to gather data without talking. He was gathering data on who talked and he did a good job, noticing that one student had done quite a bit of talking in the group whereas another had talked very little. The next day when he was a group member, and there was a different student observer, he was seen starting to talk, clamping his hand over his mouth, and glancing at the observer. He knew, from his own experience as an observer, what was being observed, and he didn't want to be the only student with marks. The observer often benefits by learning how to behave more competently.

Guideline 7. When you use student observers, allocate several minutes at the end of each group session for the group to teach the observer what members of the group have just learned. Often important changes are made during this review.

Guideline 8. You may want to use cooperative learning enough so that students understand how it works and how they should behave in helping each other learn before introducing student observers. Whether or not you use student observers, however, you should always monitor cooperative learning groups while they work.

Guideline 9. Be open to discovering unexpected and unplanned outcomes. Unexpected outcomes can be the most interesting, and you may want to include them in the list of expected outcomes for the next time you teach the same lesson.

SUMMARIZING OBSERVATIONS, GIVING FEEDBACK, FACILITATING ANALYSIS

Aesop tells of the consequences of not processing the effectiveness with which group members work together. A lion had been watching three bulls feeding in an open field. He had tried to attack them several times, but they had kept together and helped each other to drive him away. The lion had little hope of eating them, for he was no match for three strong bulls with their sharp horns and hoofs. He could not keep away from that field, however, for he could not resist watching a good meal, even when there was little chance of his getting it.

One day, however, the bulls had a quarrel. When the hungry lion came to look at them and lick his chops (as he was accustomed to doing), he found them in separate corners of the field. They were as far away from one another as they could get. It was then easy for the lion to attack them one at a time. He did so with the greatest satisfaction and relish. In failing to resolve their problems by working together and hence increase continually the effectiveness of their cooperation, the bulls forgot that their success came from their unity.

At the end of a lesson, (a) observations are summarized and organized to present to students and other stakeholders (such as parents), (b) each student receives (and gives) feedback on the effectiveness of his or her efforts to learn and help classmates learn, (c) students are helped to analyze and reflect on which actions were helpful and unhelpful in contributing to the achievement of their goals, (d) students make decisions about which actions to continue or change and to set goals for improving the quality of their work, and (e) students celebrate their success.

Summarizing Observation Data

Imagine you have finished observing a cooperative learning group composed of four members. You can either provide direct feedback to each student or you can show them the data and ask them to reach their own conclusions about their participation (see Figure 8.4). If you decide to give direct feedback, you might say:

> Helen contributed ten times, Roger seven times, Edythe five times, and Frank twice. Frank encouraged others to participate ten times, Edythe five times, and Roger and Helen twice. Roger summarized five times, Frank twice, and Helen and Edythe once.

If you decide to let students reach their own conclusions, you might say:

> Look at the totals in the rows and columns. What conclusions can you make concerning

> 1. Your participation in the lesson
> 2. The effectiveness of the group in completing the assignment

In summarizing, you might say:

> Each of you will want to set a personal goal for how you can be even more effective tomorrow than you were today. What actions did you engage in most and least? What actions were more and least appropriate and helpful under the circumstances? (Summarizing right after someone else summarizes may be inappropriate and not very helpful.) What other actions would have helped the group work more effectively? Decide on a personal goal to increase your effectiveness and share it with the other group members.

FIGURE 8.4   Sample Observation Form

OBSERVATION FORM

Students	Contributes Ideas	Encourages Others to Contribute	Integrates, Summarizes	Totals
Frank	11	卅卅	11	14
Helen	卅卅	11	1	13
Roger	卅 11	11	卅	14
Edythe	卅	卅	1	11
Totals	24	19	9	52

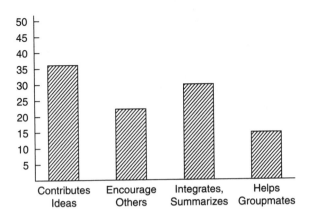

FIGURE 8.5 **Weekly Bar Chart**

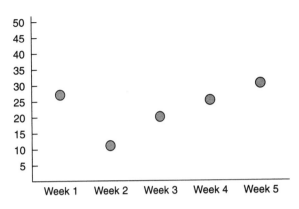

FIGURE 8.6 **Run Chart**

Charts and Graphs

Two charts are helpful to display the results of observations so that students, parents, and other interested parties may interpret them: the bar chart and the run chart (see Figures 8.5 and 8.6).

Constructing a Bar Chart.

Step 1. List the actions, conditions, or causes you wish to monitor.

Step 2. Collect the data on the number of times the actions, conditions, or causes occurred in a predetermined period of time.

Step 3. On the *y*-axis, list the measurement scale by recording the total number of actions, conditions, or causes.

Step 4. Under the *x*-axis, write the actions, conditions, or causes observed. They may be placed in descending order (the most frequently occurring action to the left and the least occurring to the right):

  a. Identify the action, condition, or cause with the largest total. Working from left to right,
     (1) Label the first bar on the *x*-axis of the chart with the action, condition, or cause.
     (2) Record the total in the blank space.
     (3) Draw a vertical bar stretching from 0 to the total frequency of occurrence using the measurement scale on the *y*-axis as a guide.
  b. Identify the action, condition, or cause with the second largest total.
     (1) Label the second bar on the *x*-axis of the chart with the action, condition, or cause.
     (2) Record the total in the blank space.
     (3) Draw a vertical bar stretching from 0 to the total frequency of occurrence using the measurement scale on the *y*-axis as a guide.
  c. Continue this procedure until every action, condition, or cause has been recorded on the chart in sequence from most to least frequently occurring.

Step 5. Students and/or other audiences make an action plan by noting which actions are engaged in at an appropriate level and which should be increased or decreased.

Constructing a Run Chart.
A **run chart** is used to monitor the process over time to see whether the long-range average is changing. In a run chart data points are plotted

on the *x*- and *y*-axes in chronological order. There are two guidelines for identifying meaningful trends or shifts in the average. First, when monitoring any process, an equal number of points should fall above and below the average. When nine points "run" on one side of the average, it indicates both a statistically unusual event and the average has changed. Second, when six or more points steadily increase or decrease with no reversals, it indicates a statistically unusual event. Both cases point toward an important change the team needs to investigate. You create a run chart by following five steps.

Step 1. Mark off the time period to be used along the *x*-axis.

Step 2. Enter the unit of measurement along the *y*-axis.

Step 3. Enter the data as it becomes available.

Step 4. Analyze the (historical) trend revealed by the position of the data points (each point can be compared to the overall average).

Step 5. Make a plan as to how either to increase or decrease the frequency of occurrence of the targeted action, condition, or cause.

Giving and Receiving Feedback

Students should receive feedback on the quality of their efforts to learn and help classmates learn so they can continually improve both. **Feedback** is information on actual performance that individuals compare with criteria for ideal performance. When feedback is given skillfully, it generates energy, directs the energy toward constructive action, and transforms the energy into action toward improving the performance of the teamwork skills. (Activity 8.8 provides a list of pointers for giving feedback in helpful, nonthreatening ways.) The results may include a decrease in the discrepancy between actual and real performance, increased self-efficacy, and empowerment to be even more effective next time.

Reflecting On and Analyzing Feedback

A common teaching error is to fail to provide a time and structure for students to reflect on and analyze the quality of their efforts to learn and to help classmates learn

ACTIVITY **8.8** ■ GIVING PERSONAL FEEDBACK IN A HELPFUL, NONTHREATENING WAY

_____ **1.** Focus feedback on behavior (not on personality traits).

_____ **2.** Be descriptive (not judgmental).

_____ **3.** Be specific and concrete (not general or abstract).

_____ **4.** Make feedback immediate (not delayed).

_____ **5.** Focus on positive actions (not negative ones).

_____ **6.** Present feedback visually (such as with a graph or chart) as well as auditorially (not just spoken words alone).

and make decisions about what actions to continue or change. A list of ways to facilitate and assess this process follow.

1. Each student summarizes (a) the feedback received, (b) what actions were helpful and unhelpful in increasing his or her own and others' academic learning, and (c) what actions he or she decides to continue or change. The student then places the reflections in a folder with his or her completed academic work and hands it in to the teacher.
2. The student creates a mind map representing the secrets to his or her success.
3. The student rates him- or herself on a series of dimensions on a bar chart.

Varying the procedures for reflection and analysis keeps the processing vital and interesting. The feedback checklist in Activity 8.9 may help in assessing the effectiveness of feedback. At the end of the processing, students should set goals for improving the effectiveness of their efforts to learn and for helping others do likewise.

Setting Improvement Goals

After reflecting on the feedback received, students set improvement goals specifying how they can act more skillfully in the next course session. Students should publicly announce the behavior they plan to increase. The goal should be written down and reviewed at the beginning of the next class session. Goal setting is the link between how students perform today and how well they perform tomorrow. Goal setting can have a powerful impact on students' behavior because it creates a sense of ownership of and it establishes commitment to actions that students decide to engage in (as opposed to assigned behaviors).

Celebrating

Lessons end with students celebrating their hard work and success. Celebrations are key to encouraging students to persist in their efforts to learn. Individual, small group,

ACTIVITY **8.9** ■ FEEDBACK CHECKLIST

Feedback	Yes	No, Start Over
Is feedback given?		Was not given or received
Is feedback generating energy in students?		Students are indifferent
Is energy directed toward identifying and solving problems so performance is improved?		Energy used to resist, deny, avoid feedback
Do students have opportunities to take action to improve performance?		Students are frustrated and feel like failures

and whole-class celebrations should occur. Feeling successful, appreciated, and respected builds commitment to and enthusiasm for learning as well as self-efficacy about mastering subject matter and cooperating with classmates.

SUMMARY

Observation is aimed at recording and describing behavior as it occurs. Its purpose is to provide objective data about the quality of student performances, the processes and procedures students use in completing assignments, and the processes and procedures teachers use in conducting lessons. Using observation as an assessment tool requires that teachers understand the basis of observing, know how to prepare for observing, know how to observe, and know how to summarize and organize the data for use by students, parents, and other stakeholders.

The basics of observing include being aware of the characteristics of the setting, differentiating between objective and subjective observations, differentiating between descriptions and inferences, the phrasing of questions, differentiating between category and sign systems, differentiating between mutually exclusive and overlapping categories and between exhaustive and nonexhaustive categories, and understanding the difference between time sampling and event sampling.

Preparing for observing involves deciding what actions to observe, who will observe, what the sampling plan will be, constructing an observation form, and training observers to use the form. Conducting observations may focus on students' on-task behavior, academic efforts, or social skills. Observations may be formal or informal and structured or unstructured. In summarizing observations, the data may be displayed in bar or run charts; feedback is then given to the students or other interested parties; and recipients reflect on the feedback and set improvement goals.

TIME SAMPLING OBSERVATION FORM

Observer: _____ Grade: _____ Date: _____

Group Member	10:00	10:15	10:30	11:00	Total

EVENT SAMPLING OBSERVATION FORM

Observer: _____   Grade: _____   Date: _____

Group Member	Sits Down	Reads	Writes	Draws	Total

CHECKLIST FOR PERSISTENCE

Student's Name: _____   Date: _____

Indicators	Observed Frequently	Observed Sometimes	Not Yet Observed
Accesses Information			
Does Not Give Up			
Tries Several Strategies			
Seeks Several Solutions			
Other:			
Other:			

Comments:

WEEKLY REPORT FORM

Name: _____   Class: _____   Date: _____

Date	On-Task Work	Contributes Ideas	Integrates, Summarizes	Helps Classmates	Completes Assignments
Totals:					

Comments:

OBSERVATION PLANNING FORM

1. I will be observing the following student actions:

_____

_____

2. I will assign the following observers:

_____

_____

3. I will use the following sampling plan:

_____

_____

4. I will use the following observation form:

_____

_____

5. I will train the observers in the following way:

_____

_____

6. I will focus on the following observations:

_____

_____

7. I will portray the results as follows:

_____

_____

8. I will present the results to the following interested parties:

_____

_____

9. I will facilitate reflection and goal setting in the following ways:

_____

_____

MY CHECKLIST FOR COOPERATIVE GROUPS

Name: _____   Class: _____   Date: _____

1. When I knew an answer or had an idea, I shared it with the group.

    Never   1——2——3——4——5   Always

2. When my answer did not agree with someone else's, I tried to find out why.

    Never   1——2——3——4——5   Always

3. When I did not understand something, I asked others to explain.

    Never   1——2——3——4——5   Always

4. When someone else did not understand something, I explained it until he or she did.

    Never   1——2——3——4——5   Always

5. I tried to make the people in the group feel appreciated and respected.

    Never   1——2——3——4——5   Always

6. Before I signed my name to our paper, I made sure that I understood everything, agreed with the answers, and was confident that all other members understood the answers.

    Never   1——2——3——4——5   Always

OBSERVATION FORM

Observer: _____   Grade: _____   Date: _____

Assignment: _____

DIRECTIONS:

1. Write the names of the group members above each column.

2. Put a tally mark in the appropriate box each time a group member contributes.

3. Make notes on the back of the form when interesting things happen that are not captured by the categories.

4. Write down one (or more) positive contribution made by each group member.

Action					Total
Contributes Ideas					
Describes Feelings					
Encourages Participation					
Summarizes, Integrates					
Checks for Understanding					
Relates New to Old Learning					
Gives Direction to Work					
Total					

OBSERVING INDICATORS OF CRITERIA

Name: _____ Grade: _____ Date: _____

Assignment: _____

DIRECTIONS:

List the criteria you wish to observe and specify indicators that describe the criteria. Then observe the student and record the frequency with which he or she engages in each indicator action.

Criteria				Total
1.				
a.				
b.				
c.				
2.				
a.				
b.				
c.				
3.				
a.				
b.				
c.				
4.				
a.				
b.				
c.				

Comments:

WEEKLY OBSERVATION FORM

Teacher: _____   Class: _____   Date: _____

Assignment: _____

DIRECTIONS:

1. List the students to be observed in column 1.

2. List the social skill in which each student is supposed to engage in column 2.

3. Note the frequency of the use of the skill for each day of the week.

4. Total the daily frequencies.

Student	Social Skill	Mon	Tues	Weds	Thurs	Fri	Total

Comments:

TEACHER OBSERVATION FORM

Teacher: _____   Class: _____   Date: _____

Assignment: _____

Groups	Explaining Concepts	Encouraging Participation	Checking for Understanding	Organizing the Work
1				
2				
3				
4				
5				

CHAPTER NINE

ASSESSING SOCIAL SKILLS

WHAT ARE SOCIAL SKILLS?

> From the standpoint of everyday life…there is one thing we do know; that man is here for the sake of other men—above all, for those upon whose smile and well-being our own happiness depends, and also for the countless unknown souls with whose fate we are connected by a bond of sympathy. Many times a day I realize how much my own outer and inner life is built upon the labors of my fellow men, both living and dead, and how earnestly I must exert myself in order to give in return as much as I have received.
>
> —*Albert Einstein (scientist and philosopher)*

Success in life depends on social skills. An example is Abraham Lincoln. During his four years as president, Lincoln spent most of his time interacting with the people he believed were going to get the job done—the troops. He met with his generals and cabinet members in their homes, offices, and in the field. He toured the Navy Yard and the fortifications in and around Washington and conversed with the troops. He inspected new weaponry and discussed its use with the soldiers in charge. He visited key individuals in government, such as members of Congress, and toured hospitals to visit and interview the sick and the wounded. He virtually lived in the War Department's telegraph office so he could communicate with individuals in every part of the war. Lincoln even went with the troops into several battles, coming under fire at least once (one of the few American presidents to do so while in office).

In establishing human contact with the individuals actually carrying on the war effort, Lincoln was able to provide extraordinary leadership. One hundred years later, Lincoln's philosophy became part of the revolution in modern leadership and was named MBWA (management by wandering around) by Thomas Peters and Robert Waterman in their 1982 book, *In Search of Excellence*. Without valuing relationships and his high level of interpersonal skills, Lincoln may not have been such a success.

Individuals learn social skills to gain social competence (Johnson, 2000). **Social competence** is the extent to which the consequences of a person's actions match his or her intentions. Individuals who are socially competent have acquired a broad range of interpersonal and small group skills that they can apply appropriately in interactions with others, thereby creating the joint outcomes they intend. The use of social skills in a fluent and flexible way help people establish positive relationships with others and successfully achieve joint outcomes. Social skills range from simple (i.e., making eye contact with the person to whom you are talking) to complex (i.e., criticizing ideas while confirming the competence of the person). Students' interpersonal and small group skills determine their ability to initiate, develop, and maintain caring and productive relationships and their ability to work effectively with others. Social skills can be classified in a number of ways.

The small group skills students need to master include setting goals, communicating effectively, providing leadership, making effective decisions, managing conflicts constructively, and using power appropriately (Johnson & F. Johnson, 2000). Johnson, Johnson, and Holubec (1998a) classify social skills students need to work together in cooperative groups as *forming, functioning, formulating,* and *fermenting* skills.

1. **Forming skills.** Skills needed to establish a cooperative learning group, such as members staying with their group and not wandering around the room, using quiet voices, taking turns, and using each other's names.
2. **Functioning skills.** Skills needed to manage the group's activities in completing the task and maintaining effective working relationships among members, such as sharing one's ideas and conclusions, providing direction to the group's work, and encouraging everyone to participate.
3. **Formulating skills.** Skills needed to build deeper-level understanding of the material being studied, to stimulate the use of higher-quality reasoning strategies, and to maximize mastery and retention of the assigned material. Examples are explaining step by step one's reasoning and relating what is being studied to previous learning.
4. **Fermenting skills.** Skills needed to stimulate reconceptualization of the material being studied, cognitive conflict, the search for more information, and the communication of the rationale behind one's conclusions. Examples are criticizing ideas (not people) and not changing your mind unless you are logically persuaded (majority rule does not promote learning).

Interpersonal skills individuals "dare" to learn follow (Johnson, 1991; 2000):

D   Disclosing ourselves to and trusting each other. Openness in letting others get to know you is based on self-awareness, self-acceptance, and the willingness to take the risk of trusting others.

A   Accurately communicating with each other. You must be able to send messages that are phrased so that the other person can easily understand them and listen in ways that ensure you fully understand the other person.

R   Resolving conflicts and relationship problems constructively. The more committed the relationship is, the more frequently conflicts tend to occur. When conflicts are managed by engaging in problem-solving negotiations or smoothing, the relationship tends to be strengthened.

E   Encouraging and appreciating diversity. There is strength in diversity. You encourage others to be themselves and you appreciate the wide variety of attitudes and perspectives brought to the relationship. It takes considerable skill in building and maintaining relationships with individuals from backgrounds and cultures different from yours.

WHY TEACH AND ASSESS SOCIAL SKILLS?

> I will pay more for the ability to deal with people than any other ability under the sun.
> —*John D. Rockefeller*

Social skills are the connections among people. They are key to all aspects of our lives. Any time students talk to, play with, interact with, or work with others, they are using social skills. Increasingly, however, large numbers of children, adolescents, and young adults do not possess the social skills necessary to establish and maintain positive relationships with their peers. Because of changes in the structure of family, neighborhood, and community life, many students have never been taught how to interact effectively with others. Without direct instruction many students may never become socially competent. The severity and persistence of social problems among children, adolescents, and young adults necessitate that schools become more involved in teaching social skills. Yet in many classrooms, social skills are neglected and almost never taught.

Social skills are not a luxury, to be learned when time allows. They are necessary to all aspects of living. The importance of social skills cannot be overstated, as they are related to the following issues (Johnson, 2000; Johnson & F. Johnson, 2000; Johnson & R. Johnson, 1999):

1. **Personal development and identity.** Our identity is created out of relationships with others. As we interact with others we note their responses to us, we seek feedback as to how they perceive us, and we learn how to view ourselves as others view us. Individuals who have few interpersonal skills have distorted relationships with others and tend to develop inaccurate and incomplete views of themselves.

2. **Employability, productivity and career success.** Social skills may be even more important than education and technical skills for employability, productivity, and career success. Recent national surveys found that (a) when hiring new employees, employers value interpersonal and communication skills, responsibility, initiative, and decision-making skills and (b) 90 percent of the people fired from their jobs were fired for poor job attitudes, poor interpersonal relationships, inappropriate behavior, and inappropriate dress. In the real world of work, the heart of most jobs, especially the higher-paying, more interesting jobs, is getting others to cooperate, leading others, coping with complex power and influence issues, and helping solve people's problems in working with others.

3. **Quality of life.** There is no simple recipe for creating a meaningful life, but the research indicates that for almost everyone a necessary ingredient for a high quality of life is some kind of satisfying, close, personal, intimate relationship.

4. **Physical health.** Positive, supportive relationships have been found to be related to living longer lives, recovering from illness and injury faster and more completely, and experiencing less severe illnesses. Physical health improves when individuals learn the interpersonal skills necessary to take more initiative in their relationships and become more constructive in the way they deal with conflict. Loneliness and isolation kill. High-quality relationships create and extend life.

5. **Psychological health.** When individuals do not have the interpersonal skills to build and maintain positive relationships with others, psychological illness results. The inability to establish acceptable relationships often leads to anxiety, depression, frustration, alienation, inadequacy, helplessness, fear, and loneliness. The ability to build and maintain positive, supportive relationships, on the other hand, is related to psychological health and adjustment; lack of neuroticism and psychopathology; reduction of psychological distress; coping effectively with stress; resilience; self-reliance and autonomy; a coherent and integrated self-identity; high self-esteem; general happiness; and social competence.

6. **Ability to cope with stress.** Positive and supportive relationships help individuals cope with stress by providing caring, information, resources, and feedback. Supportive relationships decrease the number and severity of stressful events, reduce anxiety, and help with the appraisal of the nature of the stress and one's ability to deal with it constructively. Discussions with supportive peers help individuals perceive

the meaning of the stressful event, regain mastery over their lives, and enhance their self-esteem.

Overall, social science research indicates that life without a modicum of social skills is not much of a life. The inability to relate to other people leads to loneliness and isolation. Loneliness and isolation can stunt growth, spark failure, make life seem meaningless, create anxiety and depression, result in an obsession with the past, increase fragility, increase inhumaneness, and even shorten life.

HOW TO ASSESS SOCIAL SKILLS

To assess students' social skills, you engage in the following tasks (Johnson, Johnson, & Holubec, 1998a, 1998b):

1. Review the assumptions that underlie teaching social skills.
2. Teach the targeted social skills to students.
3. Structure a cooperative learning situation in which the targeted social skills can be observed. Observe students working in cooperative learning groups (see Box 9.1).
4. Intervene to ensure appropriate use of social skills.
5. Assess knowledge of social skills.
6. Facilitate self-diagnosis of social skill mastery.
7. Set goals for continuous improvement.
8. Report on students' social skills to interested stakeholders, such as students, parents, and potential employers.

Basic Assumptions

The assumptions underlying the assessment of students' social skills follow (Johnson, Johnson, & Holubec, 1998a).

1. **Social skills must be learned.** Placing socially unskilled students in a group and telling them to cooperate does not guarantee that they will be able to do so. We are not born instinctively knowing how to interact effectively with others. Interpersonal and small group skills do not magically appear when they are needed. You must teach students the social skills required for interacting effectively with others and motivate students to use the skills if students are to become socially competent.
2. **Every cooperative lesson is a lesson in social skills as well as academics.** Students must learn both academic subject matter (taskwork) and the interpersonal and small group skills required to work with classmates (teamwork). Coopera-

■ ■ ■ ■ ■ ▬▬▬▬▬▬▬▬▬▬▬▬▬▬▬▬▬▬▬▬▬▬▬▬▬▬▬▬▬▬▬▬

BOX 9.1
GROUPS

When we work in groups, we

- **G**   Give encouragement.
- **R**   Respect others.
- **O**   Stay on task.
- **U**   Use quiet voices.
- **P**   Participate actively.
- **S**   Stay in our group.

tive learning is inherently more complex than competitive or individualistic learning because students have to engage simultaneously in taskwork and teamwork. If group members are inept at teamwork, their taskwork tends to be substandard. The greater are the members' teamwork skills, the higher is the quality and quantity of their learning. Ways of deciding which interpersonal and small group skills need to be emphasized include

   a. Observing students at work to determine which social skills they lack.

   b. Asking students which social skills would increase their productivity (see Box 9.2).

   c. Drawing a flow chart of how the group actually completes the assignment. On the basis of the process required, certain social (and cognitive) skills may be suggested or even required.

3. You must understand what teamwork skills to teach and how to teach them.

4. You must follow the three rules of teaching teamwork skills:

   a. Be specific. Operationally define each social skill with a T-chart.

   b. Start small. Do not overload your students with more social skills than they can learn at one time. Emphasizing one or two skills for a few lessons is enough. Students should not be subjected to information overload.

   c. Emphasize overlearning. Having students practice skills once or twice is not enough. Keep emphasizing a skill until the students have integrated it into their behavioral repertoires and do it automatically and habitually.

TEACHING SOCIAL SKILLS

When police evaluate potential suspects, they look for the joint presence of three characteristics: opportunity, motive, and means. Engaging in an interpersonal action requires the opportunity of contact with other people for the act to occur, a reason sufficient to motivate the act, and access to a method or procedure whereby the act can occur. For students to work as a team, they need (a) an opportunity to work together cooperatively (where teamwork skills can be manifested), (b) a motivation to engage in the teamwork skills (a reason to believe that such actions will be beneficial to them), and (c) some proficiency in using teamwork skills. After providing students with the opportunity to learn social skills in cooperative groups, you must provide students with the motive and means for doing so. There are five steps in teaching social skills (Johnson, 1991, 2000; Johnson & F. Johnson, 2000; Johnson & R. Johnson, 1999; Johnson, Johnson, & Holubec, 1998a, 1998b).

The first step is to ensure that students see the need for the teamwork skill. To establish the need for the teamwork skill, you can

1. Ask students to suggest the teamwork skills they need to work together more effectively. From the skills suggested, choose one or more to emphasize.

■ ■ ■ ■ ■

BOX 9.2
KISSES

- **K** Keep on task.
- **I** Include everyone.
- **S** Speak in 6-inch voices.
- **S** Stay with your group.
- **E** Encourage everyone.
- **S** Share ideas.

2. Present a case to students that they are better off knowing, than not knowing, the chosen skills. You can display posters, tell students how important the skills are, complement students who use the skills.
3. Setting up a role play that provides a counterexample in which the skill is obviously missing in a group is a fun way to illustrate the need for the skill.

The second step is to ensure that students understand what the skill is, how to engage in the skill, and when to use the skill.

1. Operationally define the skill as verbal and nonverbal behaviors so that students know specifically what to do. It is not enough to tell students what skills you wish to see them use during the lesson ("Please encourage each other's participation and check each other's understanding of what is being learned"). What is encouraging to one student may be discouraging to another. You must explain exactly what they are to do. One way to explain a social skill is through a **T-chart** (see Box 9.3). You list the skill (e.g., encouraging participation) and then ask the class, "What would this skill look like [nonverbal behaviors]?" After students generate several ideas, you ask the class, "What would this skill sound like [phrases]?" Students list several ideas. You then display the T-chart prominently for students to refer to (see Figure 9.1 for further examples of T-charts).
2. Demonstrate and model the skill in front of the class and explain it step by step until students have a clear idea of what the skill sounds and looks like.
3. Have students role play the skill by practicing the skill twice in their groups before the lesson begins.

The third step is to set up practice situations and encourage mastery of the skill. To master a skill, students need to practice it again and again. You can guide their practice by doing the following (see Box 9.4):

1. Assign the social skill as either a specific role for certain members to fulfill or a general responsibility for all group members to engage in. You may wish to introduce one or two new skills each week, review previously taught skills, and repeat this sequence until all the skills are taught.

■ ■ ■ ■ ■

BOX 9.3
T-CHART FOR ENCOURAGING PARTICIPATION

Encouraging Participation

Looks Like	Sounds Like
Smiles	"What is your idea?"
Eye contact	"Awesome!"
Thumbs up	"Good idea!"
Pat on back	"That's interesting"

FIGURE 9.1   **Examples of Other T-Charts**

Checking for Understanding

Looks Like	Sounds Like
Eye contact Leaning forward Interested expression Open gestures and posture	"Explain that to me please." "Can you show me?" "Tell us how to do it." "How do you get that answer?" "Give me an example please." "How would you explain it to the teacher?"

Contributing Ideas

Looks Like	Sounds Like
Leaning forward Open gestures and posture Taking turns Member talking while others listen	"My idea is…" "I suggest…" "We could…" "I suggest we…" "This is what I would do…" "What if we…"

Summarizing

Looks Like	Sounds Like
Leaning forward Pleasant expression Open gestures and postures	"Our key ideas seem to be…" "Let's review what we have said so far…" "At this point, we have…" "The points we have made so far are…" "Our thinking is…"

BOX 9.4
STERN

- **S**   Show need for skill.
- **T**   Teach T-chart skill.
- **E**   Engage students in practice.
- **R**   Reflect on success.
- **N**   Practice until using skill is natural.

2. Observe each group and record which members are engaging in the skill with what frequency and effectiveness. Utilize student observers as soon as possible. You may want to begin with a simple observation form that only has 2 to 4 skills on it. When you become used to the observation process, you may expand to an intermediate observation form that has 6 to 8 actions listed and then to an advanced observation form that has 10 to 12 actions on it (see Figure 9.2). Student observers are trained in the same sequence of simple to intermediate to advanced observation forms. The procedures for observing may be found in Chapter 8.

FIGURE 9.2   Examples of Observation Forms, from Simple to Advanced

	Jose	Tia	Helen	Total
Who Talks				

(a) Simple Observation Form

	Dale	Frank	Edythe	Total
Contributing Ideas				
Encouraging Participation				
Total				

(b) Intermediate Observation Form

	Frances	Juan	Gia	Total
Contributes Ideas				
Checks for Understanding				
Encourages Participation				
Supporter, Praiser				
Total				

(c) Advanced Observation Form

3. Cue the use of the skill periodically during the lesson by asking a group member to demonstrate the skill.
4. Intervene in the learning groups to clarify the nature of the social skill and how to engage in it.
5. Coach students to improve their use of the skill.

The fourth step is to ensure that each student (a) receives feedback on his or her use of the skill and (b) reflects on how to engage in the skill more effectively next time. Practicing teamwork skills is not enough. Students must receive feedback on how frequently and how well they are using the skill. Organize the observation data into bar graphs and run charts and report the data to the class, groups, and individuals. Help students analyze and reflect on the data. The observer reports the information gathered to the group and group members report their impressions as to how they behaved. The observer shows the observation form to the group, holding it so every group member can see it. He or she then asks the group, "What do you conclude about (a) your participation in the group and (b) the group functioning in general?" The observer ensures that all group members receive positive feedback about their efforts to learn and help their groupmates learn. (Activity 9.1 offers suggestions for ensuring positive feedback.) After small group processing, there is whole-class processing in which the teacher shares his or her feedback to the class as a whole.

Reflection is needed to discover what helped and hindered students in completing the academic assignment and whether specific actions had a positive or negative effect. The observer helps group members process how well the group functioned, how frequently and well each member engaged in the targeted skill, and

---

ACTIVITY 9.1 ■ ENSURING EVERY GROUP MEMBER RECEIVES POSITIVE FEEDBACK

1. Each group focuses on one member at a time. Members tell the target person one thing he or she did that helped them learn or work together effectively. The focus is rotated until all members have received positive feedback.

2. Members write a positive comment about each of the other member's participation on an index card. The students then give their written comments to each other so that every member will have, in writing, positive feedback from all the other group members.

3. Members comment on how well each other member used the social skills by writing an answer to one of the following statements. The students then give their written statements to each other.

   a. "I appreciated it when you…"
   b. "I liked it when you…"
   c. "I admire your ability to…"
   d. "I enjoy it when you…"
   e. "You really helped out the group when you…"

This procedure may also be done orally. In this case students look at the member they are complimenting, use his or her name, and give their comments. The person receiving the positive feedback makes eye contact and says "Thank you." Positive feedback should be directly and clearly expressed and should *not* be brushed off or denied.

how the interaction among group members should be modified to make it more effective. On the basis of the feedback received and their own assessment of skills used, the students reflect on how to use skills more effectively in the future and set improvement goals. Finally, the groups should celebrate their hard work in learning and using the targeted social skills. Play Mystery Person in Activity 9.2 to highlight how well students analyze and reflect on each other's social skills learning.

The fifth step is to ensure that students persevere in practicing the skill until the skill becomes a natural action. With most skills there is a period of slow learning, then a period of rapid improvement, then a period where performance remains about the same, then another period of rapid improvement, then another plateau, and so forth. Students have to practice teamwork skills long enough to make it through the first few plateaus and integrate the skills into their behavioral repertoires. Most skill development goes through stages:

1. Self-conscious, awkwardly engaging in the skill
2. Feelings of phoniness while engaging in the skill. After a while the awkwardness passes and enacting the skill becomes more smooth. Many students, however, feel inauthentic or phony while using the skill. Students need teacher and peer encouragement to move through this stage.
3. Proficient but mechanical use of the skill
4. Automatic, routine use where students have fully integrated the skill into their behavior repertoire and feel like the skill is a natural action to engage in.

Encourage students to improve continually their teamwork skills by refining, modifying, and adapting them. See Box 9.5 for a recap of the five steps in teaching social skills outlined in this section.

CREATING COOPERATIVE SITUATIONS IN WHICH SOCIAL SKILLS CAN BE USED

To assess students' social skills, a situation must be created in which students work together to achieve a common goal. Cooperative learning situations are structured so that students can learn social skills and demonstrate their level of mastery of the skills. While the students learn together, you observe to assess the quality and quantity of their use of the targeted social skills. You can adopt the verbal responses to appropriate and inappropriate group work detailed in Activity 9.3.

ACTIVITY **9.2** ■ MYSTERY PERSON

1. Inform the class that you will be focusing on one student whose name will be kept secret.

2. Select a student randomly or select a student who will be a positive role model or who could benefit from some recognition.

3. Observe during the lesson without revealing whom you are observing.

4. Describe to the whole class what the person did (frequency data) without naming the person.

5. Ask students to guess who the mystery person is.

BOX 9.5
FIVE STEPS OF TEACHING SOCIAL SKILLS

STEPS IN TEACHING A SKILL	TEACHER ACTIONS
Step 1. Establish the need for the skill.	**1.** Students choose needed skills. **2.** You choose and persuade. **3.** Role play the absence of skill.
Step 2. Define the skill.	**1.** Define with T-chart. **2.** Demonstrate, model, explain.
Step 3. Guide practice of the skill.	**1.** Assign the social skill as a role. **2.** Record frequency and quality of use. **3.** Periodically cue the skill.
Step 4. Guide feedback and reflection.	**1.** Structure feedback sessions. **2.** Structure reflection (processing).
Step 5. Repeat steps 3 and 4 repeatedly.	Emphasize continued improvement while proceeding through the stages of skill development.

INTERVENING TO IMPROVE USE OF SOCIAL SKILLS

While observing students engage in learning activities, you may see patterns of behavior interfering with learning or teamwork. You may then wish to intervene for the following reasons:

1. To correct misunderstandings or misconceptions about task instructions and the academic concepts and procedures being learned
2. To correct the absence, incorrect use, or inappropriate use of interpersonal, small group, and cognitive skills
3. To reinforce, encourage, and celebrate the appropriate or competent use of skills and procedures

Teachers decide when and at what level they want to intervene:

1. Should I intervene now or wait for group processing time? You may want to stop the group's work and intervene immediately, or you may want to wait until processing time and then intervene.
2. Should I intervene in this group or should I have the entire class focus on the issue? Sometimes the problem is specific to a group and sometimes it is a generic problem that all groups may be experiencing.

Teachers have to decide how to intervene effectively. Ineffective or weak interventions include (a) telling students how to be more effective, (b) solving the problem for the group, (c) rescuing floundering groups. Instead, you should highlight the problem for the group to solve and guide them to a solution that they themselves discover and implement (see Box 9.6). You teach students how to diagnose and solve their problems in group functioning by

1. Using the language or terms relevant to the learning. Instead of saying, "Yes, that is right," you should say something more specific to the assignment, such

ACTIVITY **9.3** ■ IDEAS FOR MONITORING AND INTERVENING

Check for...	If Present...	If Absent...
Members seated closely together	"Good seating."	"Draw your chairs closer together."
Group has correct materials and are on correct page	"Good, you are all ready."	"Get what you need—I will watch."
Students who are assigned roles are doing them	"Good! You're doing your jobs."	"Who is supposed to do what?"
Groups have started task	Good! You've started.	"Let me see you get started. Do you need any help?"
Cooperative skills being used (in general)	"Good group! Keep up the good work!"	"What skills would help here? What should you be doing?"
A specific cooperative skill being used	"Good encouraging! Good paraphrasing!"	"Who can encourage Lamar? Repeat in your own words what Lamar just said."
Academic work being done well	"You are following the procedure for this assignment. Good group!"	"You need more extensive answers. Let me explain how to do this again."
Members ensuring individual accountability	"You're making sure everyone understands. Good work!"	"Juan, show me how to do #1. Keisha, explain why the group chose this answer."
Reluctant students involved	"I'm glad to see everyone participating."	"I'm going to ask Helen to explain #4. Get her ready and I will be back."
Members explaining to each other what they are learning and their reasoning processes	"Great explanations! Keep it up."	"I want each of you to take a problem and explain to me step by step how to solve it."

Check for...	If Present...	If Absent...
Group cooperating with other groups	"I'm glad you're helping the other groups. Good citizenship!"	"Each of you go to another group and share your answer to #6."
One member dominating	"Everyone is participating equally. Great group!"	"Sarah, you are the first to answer every time. Could you be the accuracy checker?"
Groups that have finished	"Your work looks good. Now do the activity written on the board."	"You are being very thorough, but time is almost up. Let's speed up."
Group working effectively	"Your group is working so well. What behaviors are helping you?"	"Tell me what is wrong in the way this group is working. Let's make three plans to solve the problem."

■ ■ ■ ■ ■

BOX 9.6
INTERVENING IN COOPERATIVE LEARNING GROUPS

- **O**   Observe.
- **IDQ**   Intervene by sharing data and/or asking a question.
- **SP**   Have students process and plan how they will take care of an issue.
- **BTW** Tell students to go back to work.

as, "Yes, that is one way to find the main idea of a paragraph." Using the more specific statement reinforces the desired learning and promotes positive transfer by helping students associate a term with their learning.

2. Interviewing members of a cooperative learning group about their reasoning processes. Ask,
   a. "What are you doing?"
   b. "Why are you doing it?"
   c. "How will it help you?"
3. Showing group members the observation data and asking them to identify the problem. Often just the awareness of the recorded information (for example, showing data that indicates group members are not sharing or helping) will get group members back on the right track.
4. Guiding them towards several alternative courses of action when group members cannot identify a clear procedure to correct the problem. Highlighting a problem may only create helplessness, demoralization, and frustration if students believe

nothing can be done to solve it. In such a case, giving them several strategies will empower them.

5. Joining the group and
   a. Having group members set aside their task ("pencils down, close your books")
   b. Point out the problem ("Here is what I observed")
   c. Asking them to create three possible solutions
   d. Asking them to decide which solution they are going to try first
6. Having students role play the situation and practice new behaviors that can solve the problem

ASSESSING KNOWLEDGE OF SOCIAL SKILLS

To assess students' knowledge about the social skills being taught, objective tests may be given. Such a test on leadership skills is provided in Activity 9.4.

SELF-ASSESSMENT OF SOCIAL SKILLS MASTERY

A self-diagnosis questionnaire for leadership skills is provided in Activity 9.5. Students complete a checklist or questionnaire about their actions in the group to assess how often and how well they individually performed the targeted social skill and other small group skills. Students can diagnose the level of their social skills in at least two ways. You may have students complete a self-diagnosis questionnaire or engage in a learning activity as a participant–observer to diagnose their social skills.

Each group member can complete a checklist or questionnaire. The focus of the questions could be on what the member did (*I, me*), what other members did (*you, they*), or what all members did (*we*). Self-assessments ("I" statements) are gathered from group members about how often and how well they individually performed the targeted social skills and other expected behaviors. The "you" statements give students an opportunity to give other group members feedback about which actions were perceived as helpful or unhelpful. The "we" statements provide an opportunity for group members to reach consensus about which actions helped or hurt the group's work. The results are used to help analyze how well group members worked together. For each question the frequencies can be summed and divided by the number of members to derive an average.

Or each group member can publicly share his or her answers in a "whip." The group whips through members' answers, one question at a time, by giving each group member 30 seconds to share his or her answer to each question with no comment allowed from other group members.

A third procedure is having each group member name actions he or she performed that helped the group function more effectively, and then name one action the member to his or her right (or left) performed that also helped the group. Another procedure is to have students (a) complete the self-assessment, (b) engage in a cooperative learning activity in which they have the opportunity to use the skills (the activity is observed and feedback is given to each student), and (c) compare their self-perceptions of how they used the skills with the data gathered by the observer on how they actually behaved in the situation.

SETTING GOALS FOR CONTINUOUS IMPROVEMENT

Group members need to set goals for improving their competence in engaging in social skills during the next group meeting. Members discuss the goals and publicly

ACTIVITY 9.4 ■ **TEST FOR UNDERSTANDING FUNCTIONING (LEADERSHIP) SKILLS**

Task and maintenance leadership skills are listed in column 1; statements that reflect expressing the skills appear in column 2. For each task or maintenance action, indicate which statement (*a* through *l*) expresses it.

Task Actions	Task Statements
_____ 1. Information and opinion giver	a. "Julie, my understanding of you is that you are suggesting that we define the problem before we try to solve it."
_____ 2. Information and opinion seeker	b. "How about giving our report on yoga while standing on our heads?"
_____ 3. Direction and role definer	c. "Dale thinks we should play football, Jose thinks we should go to lunch, and Tai believes we should write a story."
_____ 4. Summarizer	d. "I think we should help resolve the conflict between David and Linda."
_____ 5. Energizer	e. "George Washington was the first president of the United States and, in my opinion, the best one."
_____ 6. Checker for understanding	f. "Francene has not said anything for the past 5 minutes. Is there a problem?"
Maintenance Actions	**Maintenance Statements**
_____ 7. Encourager of participation	g. "That is an important insight Roger. It indicates you have really worked hard on the homework."
_____ 8. Communication facilitator	h. "Fire up! We can find a good solution. Let's put a little more effort into it."
_____ 9. Tension reliever	i. "Frank, explain to us step by step how to solve question 12."
_____ 10. Process observer	j. "We should first define the problem and second suggest solutions. We can then decide which solution to adopt."

(continued)

ACTIVITY 9.4 *Continued*

Maintenance Actions	Maintenance Statements
_____ 11. Interpersonal problem solver	k. "Jim, do you know who the fourth president of the United States is and what he is famous for?"
_____ 12. Supporter and praiser	l. "Meisong, I would like to hear what you think about this; you have good ideas."

Answers: 1. e, 2. k, 3. j, 4. c, 5. h, 6. i, 7. l, 8. a, 9. b, 10. f, 11. d, 12. g.

commit to achieving them. The observer helps the group set a growth goal by asking, "What could you add to be even a better group tomorrow than you were today?" The continual improvement of students' competencies and group effectiveness is emphasized. The procedures for setting goals are detailed in Chapter 2. A goal-setting form is included at the end of this chapter.

REPORTING ON STUDENTS' SOCIAL SKILLS

Besides reporting the results on assessing students' social skills to students during and immediately following the lesson to help students improve their skills, periodic summaries of students' social skills may need to be reported to other interested stakeholders, such as parents and potential employers. Students, for example, will want to include data on their social and teamwork skills in their portfolios and discuss them in student-led conferences and employment interviews. Teachers may summarize social skill data on charts and graphs, write a narrative on each student's social skills, or complete a checklist for a parent conference or report card. An example of a social skills report card is given at the end of this chapter.

SUMMARY

One of the most important student performances to assess is students' social competence. **Social competence** is having the consequences of your actions match your intentions. Your social competence is determined by your ability to use social skills appropriately in interactions with others. One of the most useful ways of classifying social skills is to divide them into forming, functioning, formulating, and fermenting skills. Assessing social skills is important as they largely determine personal development and identity, employability and career success, quality of life, physical health, psychological health, and ability to cope with stress. The inability to relate to others stunts growth, sparks failure, makes life meaningless, kills, creates anxiety and depression, and makes one more fragile, lost in the past, and inhumane.

The assessment of social skills consists of several steps. First, you review the assumptions underlying the teaching of social skills. Social skills must be learned. Every cooperative lesson is a lesson in social skills as well as academics. You must

ACTIVITY **9.5** ■ UNDERSTANDING YOUR LEADERSHIP ACTIONS QUESTIONNAIRE

A group member provides leadership any time he or she engages in an action that (a) helps the group complete its task or (b) helps the group maintain effective working relationships among its members. When you are a member of a group, which leadership actions do you engage in? How do you influence other group members to complete the task and work together effectively?

RANKING THE QUALITY OF YOUR LEADERSHIP ACTIONS

Each of the following items describes the quality of a leadership action. For each leadership action listed below, rank from 1 to 5 the quality of that action using the following scale.

5 if you always behave that way   2 if you seldom behave that way
4 if you frequently behave that way   1 if you never behave that way
3 if you occasionally behave that way

_____ 1. I offer facts and give my opinions, ideas, feelings, and information to help the group discussion.

_____ 2. I warmly encourage all members of the group to participate. I am open to their ideas. I let them know I value their contributions to the group.

_____ 3. I ask for facts, information, opinions, ideas, and feelings from the other group members in order to help the group discussion.

_____ 4. I help communication among group members by using good communication skills. I make sure that each group member understands what the others say.

_____ 5. I give direction to the group by planning how to go on with the group work and by calling attention to tasks that need to be done. I assign responsibilities to different group members.

_____ 6. I tell jokes and suggest interesting ways of doing the work to reduce tension in the group and to increase the fun we have working together.

_____ 7. I pull together related ideas or suggestions made by group members and restate and summarize the major points discussed by the group.

_____ 8. I observe the way the group is working and use my observations to help discuss how the group can work together better.

_____ 9. I give the group energy. I encourage group members to work hard to achieve our goals.

_____ 10. I promote the open discussion of conflicts among group members to resolve disagreements and to increase group cohesiveness. I mediate conflicts among members when they seem unable to resolve them directly.

(continued)

ACTIVITY 9.5 *Continued*

_____ **11.** I ask others to summarize what the group has been discussing to ensure that they understand group decisions and comprehend the material being discussed by the group.

_____ **12.** I express support, acceptance, and liking for other members of the group and give appropriate praise when another member has taken a constructive action in the group.

SCORING THE QUALITY OF YOUR LEADERSHIP ACTIONS

Each numbered item below corresponds to the leadership actions in the list above. The actions are categorized as task actions or maintenance actions. To obtain a total score for task actions and maintenance actions, write the score for each item in the appropriate column and then add the columns.

TASK ACTIONS	MAINTENANCE ACTIONS
____ **1.** Information and opinion giver	____ **2.** Encourager of participation
____ **3.** Information and opinion seeker	____ **4.** Communication facilitator
____ **5.** Direction and role definer	____ **6.** Tension reliever
____ **7.** Summarizer	____ **8.** Process observer
____ **9.** Energizer	____ **10.** Interpersonal problem solver
____ **11.** Comprehension checker	____ **12.** Supporter and praiser
____ Total for task actions	____ Total for maintenance actions

understand which social skills to teach and how to teach them. When teaching social skills, be specific, start small, and emphasize overlearning.

Second, you teach students each social skill. You show the need for the skill, define it with a T-chart, set up practice situations in which students can use the skill, ensure that students receive feedback on their use of the skill and reflect on how to improve, and ensure that students persevere in practicing the skill until it becomes automatic.

Third, as part of teaching students social skills, you structure cooperative learning situations so students can use social skills and you can observe them doing so. Fourth, you intervene in the cooperative learning groups to ensure that members are using social skills appropriately and to reinforce them for doing so. Fifth, you facilitate students' self-diagnoses of their level of mastery of the targeted social skills. Students can complete checklists or questionnaires to do so.

Sixth, you assign students the task of setting improvement goals to increase their social competence. Seventh, you assess students' knowledge of social skills. Finally, you report on the level of students' social skills to interested stakeholders, such as students, parents, and potential employers.

CONTINUALLY IMPROVING MY SOCIAL SKILLS

Student's Name: _____ Grade: _____ Date: _____

Skills Targeted	Checklist	Questionnaire	Observed Behavior
1.			
2.			
3.			
4.			

Conclusions:

Plan for improving my social skills:

The timeline for achieving my goals:

SOCIAL SKILLS REPORT FORM

Student: _____   Grade: _____   Date: _____

DIRECTIONS:

For each of the social skills below, rank the student's performance using the following scale:

N = Needs improvement   *P* = Making progress   *S* = Satisfactory   *E* = Excellent

**Cooperative Attitude
(Forming) Skills**

_____   Moves into group quietly

_____   Stays with group; no wandering

_____   Uses quiet voice in group work

_____   Takes turns

_____   Uses others' names

_____   Respects rights of others

_____   Positive about working
          in group

_____   Is willing to help others

_____   Follows directions

_____   Shows courtesy toward others

**Leadership
(Functioning) Skills**

_____   Clarifies goals

_____   Gives direction to group's work

_____   Contributes ideas, opinions

_____   Requests others' ideas, opinions

_____   Summarizes, integrates

_____   Encourages others' participation

_____   Supports; gives recognition,
          praise

_____   Paraphrases

_____   Facilitates communication

_____   Relieves tension

**Facilitating Understanding
(Formulating) Skills**

_____   Summarizes, integrates

_____   Seeks accuracy (corrects)

_____   Relates new learning to old

_____   Helps group recall knowledge

_____   Checks for understanding

_____   Makes covert reasoning overt

**Intellectual Challenge
(Fermenting) Skills**

_____   Criticizes ideas, not people

_____   Differentiates members' ideas

_____   Integrates members' ideas

_____   Asks for rationale, justification

_____   Extends others' reasoning

_____   Probes, asks complex questions

WORK HABITS AND PERSONAL DEVELOPMENT REPORT FORM

Student: _____ Grade: _____ Date: _____

DIRECTIONS:

For each of the work habits below, rank the student's performance using the following scale:

N = Needs improvement   *P* = Making progress   *S* = Satisfactory   *E* = Excellent

Work Habits	October	February	May	Total
_____ Completes work on time				
_____ Uses time wisely				
_____ Checks work				
_____ Welcomes challenges				
_____ Listens carefully				
_____ Takes risks in learning				
_____ Makes effort needed				
_____ Meets responsibilities				
_____ Strives for high-quality work				
_____ Appropriately asks for help				
_____ Appropriately uses materials				
_____ Participates in discussions				
_____ Seeks extra credit, extensions				
_____ Follows rules				

CHAPTER TEN

ASSESSING STUDENT ATTITUDES

IMPORTANCE OF STUDENT ATTITUDES

W. Edwards Deming was fond of saying, "The primary responsibility of a teacher is to create a love of learning." If he visited your class, he would ask, "Do your students like or dislike your class? Do they like the subject you teach? If given a chance, would they give up some of their free time to study further the topics you discuss in class? Or do they perceive your class as being boring, uninteresting, and filled with busy work?" ∎

All learning has affective components. Whenever a student masters knowledge or skills, she or he develops an attitude toward subject area and the processes of learning. Because students' attitudes influence future behavior, the development of positive attitudes may be more important than mastery of specific knowledge and skills. It does little good to teach a student to read if she or he ends up disliking and avoiding reading whenever possible.

Because the overall purpose of schools is to develop each student to maximum capacity as a productive and happy member of society, an important measure of success is not the degree to which students master knowledge and skills, but whether the students voluntarily use such knowledge and skills in their daily life outside of school and in their lives after they have finished school. Besides positive attitudes toward subject areas and skills such as reading, writing, and math, schools are supposed to inculcate positive attitudes toward (a) self, (b) diverse others, (c) potential careers, and (d) positive attitudes toward being "role responsible" (having the capacity to live up to general expectations of appropriate role behavior such as promptness and cleanliness) and "role readiness" (having the ability to meet the demands of many organizational settings with the proper cooperation). Perhaps most important of all, schools are supposed to ensure students develop positive attitudes toward our pluralistic, democratic society, freedom of choice, equality of opportunity, self-reliance, and free and open inquiry into all issues.

To achieve instructional objectives such as creating lifelong learners or a commitment to scholarship, the development of positive attitudes may be more important than the actual mastery of facts and knowledge (see Boxes 10.1 and 10.2). An **attitude** is a positive or negative reaction to a person, object, or idea. It is a learned predisposition to respond in a favorable or unfavorable manner to a particular person, object, or idea. Attitudes are important determinants of behavior. When instruction creates interest and enthusiasm, learning will be easier, more rapid, and result in higher achievement than when instruction promotes disinterest and negativism (Bloom, 1976; Johnson, 1970).

■ ■ ■ ■ ■ ━━━━━━━━━━━━━━━━━━━━━━━━━━━━━━━
BOX 10.1
READING OBJECTIVES

1. Students should use reading as a tool for acquiring information.
2. Students should develop a lifelong habit of reading good books of fiction and nonfiction.
3. Students should find relaxation and enjoyment in reading good books.

━━

■ ■ ■ ■ ■ ━━━━━━━━━━━━━━━━━━━━━━━━━━━━━━━
BOX 10.2
MUSIC OBJECTIVES

1. Students should appreciate music as an important part of our cultural heritage.
2. Students should cultivate a taste for good music.
3. Students should develop a lasting joy for good music.

━━

Students should regard learning as an enduring quest for meaning and understanding, not as credit accumulation or a bureaucratic requirement. Students may only learn effectively when they are open to instruction, desire to learn the material being taught, and have sufficient confidence in themselves to put forth the necessary energy and resources to overcome difficulties and obstacles. A strong desire to learn science leads to science achievement; a strong liking for Shakespeare leads to frequent reading of his plays; and a strong dislike for school leads to absenteeism, refusal to do homework, and withdrawal. The attitudes students develop toward a class, subject area, learning, and school determine academic achievement, educational aspirations, and academic self-esteem. Lifelong learners who desire to investigate, explore new fields of thought, and gain new insights develop more through positive attitudes than through mastering material.

ASSESSING STUDENT ATTITUDES

Because of their importance on so many educational outcomes, student attitudes toward the subject area you teach, the instructional activities you use, school personnel (including you), other students, and their ability to complete assignments successfully should be assessed regularly. The information can then be used to modify and improve instructional programs so that they influence students to adopt positive attitudes toward learning. Attitudes, of course, should usually have no effect on students' grades. Components of instructional programs such as teaching strategies and curriculum materials, however, can be modified on the basis of students' attitudes.

A teacher, school, or school system can assess student attitudes through observational procedures, questionnaires (standardized or teacher made), and interviews. Because observing and interviewing are discussed in other chapters, this chapter focuses on using questionnaires to assess students' attitudes. In planning how to use questionnaires (or observations and interviews) to measure student attitudes, you may use the following procedure:

1. **Decide on which attitudes to measure.** Minimally, you may want to measure attitudes toward the subject area, the instructional methods used, and learning

in general. You may also want to determine attitudes toward classmates, academic self-esteem, and so forth.

2. **Construct a questionnaire by writing specific questions to measure the targeted attitudes.** In constructing your own questionnaires and writing your own questions,
   a. Decide on what types of questions to use.
   b. Decide which forms of response to elicit.
   c. Write well-worded questions.
   d. Arrange the questions into the optimal sequence.
   e. Ensure the physical layout is appealing and facilitates completing and scoring the questionnaire.

3. **Select the standardized attitude measures you want to use, if any.** Whether you use a standardized attitude measure depends on your instructional goals and expertise in using the results to improve instruction.

4. **Give your questionnaire near the beginning and then near the end of an instructional unit, semester, or year.** From such spacing, you can calculate whether attitudes have improved or deteriorated. If you use the same questions for a few years, you can build norms as to how most students respond. Such multiyear comparisons are helpful in interpreting how positive students' attitudes are.
   a. Use more than one question and use different types of questions in measuring student attitudes toward any one aspect of your class. A combination of observations and questionnaires is often helpful.
   b. Ensure and protect student anonymity. Do not ask students to put their names on the questionnaires. This increases the likelihood of getting honest responses. You can create a system of identification that allows you to compare pre- and postattitudes for each student by having students make up a number combination at the beginning of the course to put on the questionnaires. Because you do not know which student is using which number combination, student anonymity is protected. You may also have each cooperative learning group decide on a number combination. Each student then writes his or her group number and his or her personal number on each questionnaire. This allows you to analyze the pre- and postdata for each group as well as for each individual. If trust is high, names can be used.
   c. Emphasize that you are asking students to indicate their attitudes to improve instruction and not to evaluate students. Make it clear that students' attitudes will have no impact on their grades. Ask for student cooperation in giving honest reactions.

5. **Analyze and organize the data for feedback to interested stakeholders and to make instructional decisions.** Calculate the means and standard deviations for each question and scale and place the results in bar and run charts.

6. **Give the feedback in a timely and orderly way and facilitate stakeholders' use of the data.** Establish a rapid feedback system so that students (and other stakeholders) see the results (a) portrayed in an easily understandable way and (b) used in ways that clearly change the course. The data gathered are only as good as students' motivation to give accurate information. The care and honesty with which students complete attitude questionnaires is influenced heavily by the ways in which they see the data being used. Sharing the results indicates that their cooperation is appreciated. The major flaw with most large testing programs is the failure to provide feedback concerning results and uses of the information, which decreases respondents' motivation to provide accurate and valid information. Much care and attention must be given to the delivery of testing results to interested stakeholders.

7. **Use the data on student attitudes to modify and improve the course and your teaching.** Vary your instructional methods and curriculum materials to inculcate more positive attitudes toward the subject area and learning in general.

DECIDING WHICH ATTITUDES TO MEASURE

Which attitudes you want to measure depends on your instructional goals and the subject matter you teach. Minimally, however, you may want to measure attitudes toward the subject area, the instructional methods used, and learning in general. You may also want to determine attitudes toward social support, academic self-esteem, and class cohesion.

CONSTRUCTING YOUR OWN QUESTIONNAIRE

For most classes, you will want to construct your own questionnaire to measure specific aspects of the course and your success in getting students to love learning and love learning your subject area. In preparing your own questionnaire, three types of questions can be used: open-ended questions, closed-ended questions, and semantic-differential questions.

Open-ended questions call for the student to answer by writing a statement that may vary in length. They may require respondents to give a free response or supply a word or phrase to fill in the blank. Examples of open-ended questions follow:

My general opinion about English is _____.

My teachers are _____.

If someone suggested I take up American history as my life's work, I would reply,

_____.

History is my _____ subject.

Such open-ended questions provide the teacher with interesting samples of student attitudes. Open-ended questions are a good way to obtain new ideas about what to ask to measure student attitudes and values. Student responses are scored by counting the number of times a word or phrase occurs. A mean and standard deviation may then be calculated. Open-ended questions, however, tend to be hard to analyze and often are not fully answered.

Closed-ended questions require the student to indicate the alternative answer closest to his or her internal response. The response they require can be dichotomous, multiple choice, ranking, or scale. Here are some examples:

English is my favorite school subject.   ___ True   ___ False

Do you intend to take another course in English?   ___ Yes   ___ No   ___ Don't know

Circle each of the words that tell how you feel about English:

> interesting   very important   worthless   difficult
>
> dull   weird   exciting   boring   useful

Rank these subject areas from most interesting (1) to least interesting (6) to you:

_____	Social Studies	_____	English
_____	Science	_____	Mathematics
_____	Physical Education	_____	Foreign Language

How interested are you in learning more about English?

Very uninterested   1   2   3   4   5   6   7   Very interested

The questions are scored by counting the frequencies of each response and then calculating the mean response and the standard deviation.

Perhaps the most general method for the measurement of attitudes is the **semantic differential** (Osgood et al., 1957). This type of question allows the teacher to present any object (be it a person, issue, practice, subject area, or anything else) and obtain an indication of student attitudes toward it. A semantic-differential question consists of a series of rating scales of bipolar adjective pairs describing a concept the teacher wants to obtain student attitudes toward. An example is:

POETRY

Ugly	1	2	3	4	5	6	7	Beautiful
Bad	1	2	3	4	5	6	7	Good
Worthless	1	2	3	4	5	6	7	Valuable
Negative	1	2	3	4	5	6	7	Positive

The teacher then sums the response to obtain an overall indication of attitudes toward the concept. Almost any concept of interest can be used in this type of question. Each concept is listed separately accompanied by the same sets of adjectives. If a teacher does not use adjective pairs that are generally evaluative, such as those given above, he or she may wish to score the responses to each adjective pair separately instead of summing them.

HOW GOOD ARE YOUR QUESTIONS?

Writing good closed-ended and open-ended questions takes some expertise and practice. Write a series of questions to measure students' attitudes toward one of the classes you teach. Then evaluate each question by considering the following points:

1. Is the question worded simply with no abbreviations and difficult words?
2. Are all the words in the question familiar to the respondents?
3. Is the question worded without slang phases, colloquialisms, and bureaucratic words?
4. Are any words emotionally loaded, vaguely defined, or overly general?
5. Does the question have unstated assumptions or implications that lead respondents to give a certain response? (Is it desirable to rewrite the syllabus for this course?)
6. Does the question presuppose a certain state of affairs? (Has your instructor improved the format of assignments?)
7. Does the question ask for only one bit of information? (Rate the *quality* and *relevance* of this class.)
8. Is only one adjective or adverb used in the question? (Is the teacher *helpful* and *sensitive*?)
9. Does the wording of the question imply a desired answer?
10. Do any words have a double meaning that may cause misunderstandings? (e.g., *liberal, conservative, traditional*)
11. Are the response options mutually exclusive and sufficient to cover each conceivable answer?
12. Does the question contain words that tend not to have a common meaning, such as *significant, always, usually, most, never,* and *several*?

If you are satisfied that your questions pass this test, they are ready to be pretested. A well-conducted pretest will disclose any further problems that may exist with a question.

DECIDING ON TYPES OF RESPONSES TO QUESTIONS

There are two general types of responses: open-ended responses and closed-ended responses. The types of open-ended responses are fill in the blank and free responses. The types of closed-ended responses include dichotomous, multiple choice, ranking, or scale. The following list of questions will help you determine which type of response you want to elicit.

1. Is the question best asked as an open-ended or closed-ended question?
2. For open-ended questions, should respondents give a free response or fill in the blank?
3. For closed-ended questions, should the response be dichotomous, multiple choice, ranking, or scale?
4. If a multiple-choice or scale check response is used, does it (a) cover adequately all the significant alternatives without overlapping, (b) provide choices in a defensible order, and (c) provide response alternatives of uniform value (distance)?

One of the most common approaches for writing closed-ended questions with a scaled response is the Likert method of summated ratings. The procedure for developing a **Likert scale** is to ask several questions about the topic of interest. For each question a response scale is given with anywhere from three to nine points. Questions with five alternatives are quite common. Two ways of presenting the alternatives follow:

Strongly disagree (1)	Agree (4)
Disagree (2)	Strongly agree (5)
Undecided (3)	

Strongly disagree   1   2   3   4   5   Strongly agree

A student's responses for all the questions are summed together to get an overall scale indicating the student's attitudes toward the issue being measured. The results for an entire class or school may be factor analyzed to build an attitude scale consisting of more than three items.

DECIDING ON QUESTION CONTENT

Define your goals for the questionnaire. Your goals will point toward the information you want to obtain (that is, the domains of information you want to sample). Write questions relevant to the domains. Then assess the quality of your questions against the following criteria.

Criterion 1: Is the question necessary? The question may ask for information that is (a) already covered in another question or (b) more detailed than necessary.

Criterion 2: Does the question cover too much material?
   a. Should the question be subdivided?
   b. Does the question adequately cover the ground intended?
   c. Is additional, related material needed to interpret the answers?

    d. Is further information needed on respondents' intensity of feelings?

    e. Is further information needed on how important the respondent considers the issue?

Criterion 3: Do respondents have the information necessary to answer the question?

    a. Does the question call for answers that the respondent either cannot give at all or cannot give reliably?

    b. Is the focus of the question such that it should be answered by some respondents and not others?

    c. Are alternative questions required to fit the content of the question with different types of respondents.

Criterion 4: Does the question need to be more concrete, specific, and closely related to the respondent's personal experience? Does it ask about specific recent events rather than what the respondent "usually" does?

Criterion 5: Is the question content sufficiently general and free from spurious concreteness and specificity? Do the replies express general attitudes and only seem to be specific?

Criterion 6: Is the question content biased or loaded in one direction without accompanying questions to balance the emphasis? Would the content be accepted as fair by an informed person with opposite views?

Criterion 7: Will the respondents give the information sought?

    a. Is the material too private, of an embarrassing nature, or otherwise likely to lead to resistance, evasion, or deception?

    b. Is the question likely to encounter emotional reactions and desires that will lead to falsification of answers?

DECIDING ON QUESTION SEQUENCE

A questionnaire (or interview) consists of a series of question sequences. The order of the sequences must be arranged so that responses are unbiased. In ordering your questions, you may want to use the "funnel" sequence with various "filter" questions. The **funnel sequence** starts off with broad questions and then progressively narrows down the scope of the questions until very specific questions are asked at the end. Suppose, for example, you wanted to know whether some students avoided English class because of the demands to learn grammar. You would not want to begin your questionnaire with questions that directly asked what you wanted to know, such as

Q1: Do you believe that English classes are too hard because of having to learn grammar?

Q2: Do you avoid taking English classes because you do not want to learn grammar?

These are grossly leading questions that rule out the possibility of other reasons why a student does not wish to take an English class. It would be more valuable if students spontaneously stated they avoided English class because it involves grammar before the students realized what the questions are really about. Therefore, you may want to start off with broad questions, such as

Q3: What is your opinion of English as a course of study?

Q4: What do you think of students who take lots of English classes?

Each question provides the respondent with an opportunity to mention the issue of grammar spontaneously. Next, you may wish to ask more restricted questions, such as

Q5: What English classes are you taking this year?

Q6: How many English classes have you taken in previous years?

Q7: Do you recommend English classes to your friends?

Each question should be followed up by asking why if the reply is negative, thus providing further opportunities for the grammar issue to emerge spontaneously. After that, you may narrow the questions still further:

Q8: Do you believe that English classes are undesirable in any way?

Q9: What are some of the difficulties in taking English classes?

Q10: Why do some students avoid taking English classes?

Note that the grammar issue still is not mentioned directly. Finally, you bring up the issue as nondirectively as possible:

Q11: Some students believe that English classes are too hard because you have to learn grammar, but others believe that learning grammar does not take away from the overall interesting and useful things you learn in English classes. What do you believe?

Q12: Do you believe that English classes are too hard because you have to learn grammar or do you believe that learning grammar does not take away from the interesting and useful things you learn in English?

By proceeding in this way you not only increase your chances of obtaining what you are seeking through a spontaneous reply, but also place the whole issue of grammar and English classes in the context of some of the other factors that determine whether students take English. This context is very important; it may be that other reasons for not taking English are mentioned far more frequently than grammar.

A **filter question** is used to exclude a respondent from a particular sequence of questions if the questions are not relevant to him or her. Thus, in the above example, you might wish to ask for some factual information about enrollment in English classes. Obviously, if the student is taking English then there is no point in asking him or her about why English classes are avoided.

Q1: Are you currently enrolled in an English class?

Q2: Have you taken an English class in the last year?

If the answer is yes, then the student can skip the next few questions and proceed to the beginning of the next question sequence.

In a questionnaire (or interview), try to avoid (a) putting ideas into respondents' minds and (b) suggesting that they have attitudes when they do not. With any issue, you want to start with open questions and only introduce more structured or precoded questions in a later stage.

Frequently, questions are grouped either by content or by response form. All questions dealing with attitudes toward English class may be grouped together, or all multiple-choice items may be grouped together. If all questions are of equal importance and specificity, and no logical grouping is apparent, the standard procedure is to arrange the questions in random order. The following criteria may help in deciding where to place a question in a sequence:

1. Did you begin the questionnaire with a few nonthreatening questions?
2. Is the answer to the question likely to be influenced by the content of the preceding questions?
3. Is the question led up to in a natural way? Is it in correct psychological order?
4. Does the question come too early or too late from the point of view of arousing interest, receiving sufficient attention, and avoiding resistance?
5. Are items grouped logically either by content or response form?
6. If all questions are of equal importance and no sequence is necessary, did you arrange the questions in random order.
7. Are appropriate filter questions used when appropriate?
8. Are questions arranged like a funnel with the most general questions first and the most specific questions last?
9. Are all personal questions placed last?

DECIDING ON PHYSICAL LAYOUT OF QUESTIONNAIRE

The following questions can help you sort out how you want your questionaire to look, and facilitate responses and response analysis.

1. Did you identify the nature of the questionnaire with a title in bold type on the first page?
2. Did you include brief but clear instructions?
3. Are the pages numbered?
4. Does the appearance of the questionnaire encourage respondents to spend the time and effort needed to complete it?
5. Is the layout of the questionnaire such that it will be easy to tabulate and summarize responses?
6. If you are using a long checklist, did you group the items in threes to help respondents keep their place?

DECIDING ON OVERALL FORMAT OF QUESTIONNAIRE

After you have built the questions, they need to be placed in a questionnaire. The overall format of the questionnaire will affect whether students complete it truthfully (See Figure 10.1 for an example of a questionaire.) Some general guidelines for evaluating your questionnaire as a whole follow:

1. Have you begun the questionnaire with interesting and easy-to-answer questions?
2. Does the questionnaire look as professional as possible?
3. Will the questionnaire appeal to students and motivate them to complete it?
4. Does the questionnaire contain brief and precise instructions where they are needed?
5. Is the format conducive to your chosen method of summarization (tabulating, key punching)?
6. Are students able to complete the questionnaire?

STANDARDIZED ATTITUDE MEASURES: CLASSROOM LIFE

To evaluate the impact of educational strategies and programs on student attitudes and values at the school and school district level, an instrument with established va-

FIGURE 10.1   **Sample Questionnaire**

MY VIEW OF THIS CLASS IS

Answer each question below with your best opinion. Do not leave any questions blank.

1. My general opinion about history is _____.

2. History is my _____ subject.

3. If someone suggested I take up history as my life's work, I would reply, _____.

4. History is my favorite school subject.   __ True   __ False

5. Do you intend to take another course in history?   __ Yes   __ No   __ I'm not sure

6. How interested are you in learning more about history?

Very interested   1   2   3   4   5   6   7   Very uninterested

7. I think history is

Ugly	1	2	3	4	5	6	7	Beautiful
Bad	1	2	3	4	5	6	7	Good
Worthless	1	2	3	4	5	6	7	Valuable
Negative	1	2	3	4	5	6	7	Positive

lidity and reliability is needed. The *Classroom Life* measure (Johnson & Johnson, 1983) contains 85 Likert-type questions on which respondents indicate on a 5-point scale the truth of the statement. A rating of 1 indicates that the statement is untrue and a rating of 5 indicates that the statement is true. It contains 15 factors that have been identified both theoretically and through previous factor analysis (Johnson & Johnson, 1983; Johnson, Johnson, & Anderson, 1983). The factors, their descriptions, their number of items, and their reliability coefficients may be found in Table 10.1. This survey was used to gather descriptive information about student interaction and perception of their evening study environment.

MAKING DECISIONS ON THE BASIS OF ATTITUDES

> If the school does not teach values, it will have the effect of denying them.
> —*Gordon Allport (1961, p. 215)*

The attitudinal data collected by teacher-constructed questionnaires and standardized attitudinal measures is organized to facilitate decisions concerning how to improve student learning and instruction. Once students have filled out the questionnaire(s), you complete the following tasks:

1. Score the questionnaires.
2. Calculate a mean for the class as a whole and for each learning group.

TABLE 10.1 Scales Included in the Classroom Life Measure

SCALE	DESCRIPTION	ITEMS	RELIABILITY
Cooperative Learning	Liking for and positive attitudes toward working cooperatively with other students	7	0.83
Positive Goal Interdependence	Perceptions of joint outcomes and ensuring that all group members learn the assigned material	6	0.61
Resource Interdependence	Perceptions of sharing materials, having a division of labor, and jigsawing materials	5	0.74
Teacher Academic Support	Belief teacher cares about how much one learns wants to help students learn	4	0.78
Teacher Personal Support	Belief teacher cares about and likes one as a person	4	0.80
Student Academic Support	Belief classmates care about how much one learns and want to help one learn	4	0.67
Student Personal Support	Belief classmates care about and like one as a person	5	0.78
Class Cohesion	Belief students in class are friends and like each other	5	0.51
Academic Self-Esteem	Belief one is a good student and is doing a good job of learning	5	0.61
Fairness of Grading	Belief students get the grades they deserve and hard work leads to success	5	0.61
Achieving for Social Approval	Belief one achieves to please teachers, parents, and peers	5	0.72
Alienation	Belief one is estranged from school, peers, and classroom activities	11	0.68
Learning with Heterogeneous Peers	Belief working with diverse peers is interesting and beneficial	4	0.51
Competitive Learning	Liking for and positive attitudes toward competing with classmates	8	0.80
Individualistic Learning	Liking for and positive attitudes toward learning alone	7	0.80

3. Organize feedback for the class, each cooperative learning group, and each student.
4. Give individual feedback to students and help plan how to increase their positive attitudes toward the subject area, the instructional experience, and learning.
5. Give groups feedback and help them plan how to increase members' positive attitudes toward the subject area, the instructional experience, and learning.
6. Give teachers feedback and help them plan how to improve the quality of (a) instruction and (b) specific interventions to increase students' positive attitudes toward the subject area, the instructional experience, and learning.

SUMMARY

Attitudes are learned positive or negative reactions to a person, object, or idea. They are one of the most important outcomes of instruction because they largely determine whether students continue to study the subject area, become uninterested, or wish to avoid it in the future. In assessing student attitudes, you (a) decide which attitudes to measure, (b) construct a questionnaire, (c) select a standardized measure if it is appropriate, (d) give the measures near the beginning and end of each instructional unit, semester, or year, (e) analyze and organize the data for feedback to interested stakeholders, (f) give the feedback in a timely and orderly way, and (g) use the results to make decisions about improving the instructional program.

When deciding which attitudes to assess, include attitudes toward the subject area, the instructional methods used, and learning in general. Then construct a questionnaire that may contain open-ended, closed-ended, or semantic, differential questions. Each question needs to be well worded and require either open-ended (fill-in-the-blank or free response) or closed-ended (dichotomous, multiple-choice, ranking, or scale) responses. The questions are then arranged in an appropriate sequence and given an attractive format. A standardized questionnaire, such as the Classroom Life measure, may be used to measure a broader range of attitudes.

QUESTIONNAIRE EXERCISE FORM

Students' Names: _____   Grade: _____   Date: _____

DIRECTIONS:

Given below are a number of poorly written questions. Your task is to identify the fault in each question. Find a partner and *cooperatively* decide on answers. Both of you must agree and be able to explain why each question is poorly written. Use the following scale to rank questions 1 through 10:

No   1   2   3   4   5   6   7   Yes

_____   **1.** Is the science text informative and interesting?

_____   **2.** Good health habits are a good thing, aren't they?

_____   **3.** Do you still fail examinations?

_____   **4.** Does the teacher give you instructions parsimoniously?

_____   **5.** Is it desirable to teach history?

_____   **6.** Does learning good health habits usually prolong one's life?

_____   **7.** Are history classes too liberal?

_____   **8.** Is mathematics a communist plot?

_____   **9.** Don't you believe that all high school students should not take advanced math courses?

_____   **10.** Does your math class stress competition?

Fill in the blanks appropriately for questions 11 through 16.

11. Think of the worst English class you have ever attended (do not identify the class). Very briefly and frankly describe what made the class so bad.

_____

_____

12. Which area of the country has the best health education program?

_____ Midwest   _____ Northeast   _____ West

13. Which of the following do you like the best?

_____ Quebec   _____ Manitoba

_____ British Columbia   _____ Canada

14. Science classes are taught in a way that is

_____ poor   _____ good   _____ satisfactory   _____ excellent

15. Do you like math?

_____ No   _____ Yes

16. What is your age?

ANSWERS

1. The first question is, in measurement terms, "doublebarreled"; it asks for two bits of information at once. The problem arises when the respondent thinks the science text was informative but boring, or interesting but uninformative.

2. The wording of this question implies a desired answer.

3. This question presupposes a certain state of affairs, namely that the respondent has previously failed examinations.

4. Many respondents may not know the definition of *parsimoniously.* The question is ambiguous because the word *parsimonious* is obscure.

5. The word *desirable* is overly general.

6. The word *usually* is too vague and does not have a common meaning.

7. The word *liberal* has a double meaning. It could mean "politically liberal" or it could mean "too generous."

8. The words *communist plot* are too emotionally loaded to obtain a valid response. Emotionally loaded words bias answers and slant the respondent for a particular answer.

9. This question has a double negative that is confusing.

10. This is a leading question that suggests competition is a possible emphasis of math courses.

11. This question contains long and difficult sentences that are likely to be misunderstood. It also is loaded with unstated assumptions. This question presupposes previous states of affairs. It presupposes that the respondent has attended several English classes and presupposes that one or more were "bad." The respondents may not have the information needed to answer the question.

12. The responses for this question are incomplete. All areas of the country need to be listed. It does not allow for every possible response.

13. The responses are not equal. Canada includes all of the other choices.

14. The responses are not balanced.

15. The problem with this question is response restriction. What if you do not care one way or the other?

16. This question is too private; may embarrass the respondent; or may lead to resistance, evasion, or deception.

CLASSROOM LIFE

Student's Name: _____ Grade: _____ Date: _____

DIRECTIONS:

Next to each statement, write the number that describes how well each of these statements applies to you.

1	2	3	4	5
False all the time	False some of the time	Neither false nor true	True some of the time	True all the time

_____ **1.** Other students in this class want me to do my best school work.

_____ **2.** My best friends are in this class.

_____ **3.** I am not doing as well in school as I would like to.

_____ **4.** I find it hard to speak my thoughts clearly when I am in this class.

_____ **5.** In this class, the other students like to help me learn.

_____ **6.** Schoolwork is fairly easy for me.

_____ **7.** Other students in this class think it is important to be my friend.

_____ **8.** When we work together in small groups, we try to make sure that everyone in the group learns the assigned material.

_____ **9.** I learn more from students who are similar to me.

_____ **10.** I do schoolwork to make my teacher happy.

_____ **11.** In this class it is important that we learn things by ourselves.

_____ **12.** I like to work with other students in this class.

_____ **13.** I should get along with other students better than I do.

_____ **14.** I do schoolwork because my classmates expect it of me.

_____ **15.** My teacher really cares about me.

_____ **16.** When we work together in small groups, our job is not done until everyone in the group has completed the assignment.

_____ **17.** In this class, we work together.

_____ **18.** In this class, we spend a lot of time working at our own desks.

1	2	3	4	5
False all the time	False some of the time	Neither false nor true	True some of the time	True all the time

_____ **19.** I learn new things from arguing with other students.

_____ **20.** My teacher thinks it is important to be my friend.

_____ **21.** In this class, everyone has an equal chance to succeed if they do their best.

_____ **22.** In this class, other students care about how much I learn.

_____ **23.** Whenever I take a test, I am afraid I will fail.

_____ **24.** When we work together in small groups, we all receive bonus points if everyone scores above a certain criteria.

_____ **25.** In this class, other students like me the way I am.

_____ **26.** When we work together in small groups, we all receive the same grade.

_____ **27.** My teacher cares about how much I learn.

_____ **28.** I do schoolwork to make my parents happy.

_____ **29.** I would rather work alone than argue.

_____ **30.** In this class, everybody is my friend.

_____ **31.** Other students in this class want me to come to class every day.

_____ **32.** I do schoolwork to keep my teacher from getting mad at me.

_____ **33.** In this class, students check answers with other students.

_____ **34.** In this class, we do not talk to other students when we work.

_____ **35.** When we work together in small groups, our grade depends on how much all members learn.

_____ **36.** My teacher likes to see my work.

_____ **37.** Other students in this class care about my feelings.

_____ **38.** I often get discouraged in school.

_____ **39.** Other students in this class like me as much as they like others.

_____ **40.** In this class, we help each other with our schoolwork.

_____ **41.** I like being in a group where students often disagree with each other.

_____ **42.** If a student works hard, he or she can definitely succeed in this class.

1	2	3	4	5
False all the time	False some of the time	Neither false nor true	True some of the time	True all the time

_____ **43.** My teacher likes to help me learn.

_____ **44.** When we work together in small groups, I have to make sure that the other members learn if I want to do well on the assignment.

_____ **45.** In this class, we work by ourselves.

_____ **46.** In this class, other students really care about me.

_____ **47.** I have a lot of questions I never get a chance to ask in class.

_____ **48.** I do schoolwork to be liked by other students.

_____ **49.** In this class, we learn more when we work with others.

_____ **50.** My teacher wants me to do my best schoolwork.

_____ **51.** When we work together in small groups, we cannot complete an assignment unless everyone contributes.

_____ **52.** My teacher likes me as much as he or she likes other students.

_____ **53.** I am often lonely in this class.

_____ **54.** In this class, students get the scores they deserve, no more and no less.

_____ **55.** My teacher cares about my feelings.

_____ **56.** All the students in this class know each other well.

_____ **57.** I deserve the scores I get in this class.

_____ **58.** I am a good student.

_____ **59.** When we work together in small groups, the teacher divides up the material so that everyone has a part and everyone has to share.

_____ **60.** I like being in a learning group with students who are different from me.

_____ **61.** I often feel upset in school.

_____ **62.** Arguing with other students makes me feel unhappy.

_____ **63.** I have more fun when I work with students who are different from me.

_____ **64.** I learn more from students who are different from me.

_____ **65.** Sometimes I think the scoring system in this class is not fair.

1	**2**	**3**	**4**	**5**
False all the time	False some of the time	Neither false nor true	True some of the time	True all the time

_____ **66.** When we work together in small groups, we have to share materials to complete the assignment.

_____ **67.** I like to share my ideas and materials with other students.

_____ **68.** It bothers me when I have to do it all myself.

_____ **69.** I like my work better when I do it all myself.

_____ **70.** I like the challenge of seeing who's best.

_____ **71.** I don't like to be second best.

_____ **72.** When we work together in small groups, everyone's ideas are needed if we are going to be successful.

_____ **73.** I am happiest when I am competing with other students.

_____ **74.** Competing with other students is a good way to work.

_____ **75.** I do not like working with other students in school.

_____ **76.** I can learn important things from other students.

_____ **77.** I work to get better grades than other students get.

_____ **78.** I like to help other students learn.

_____ **79.** I like to compete with other students to see who can do the best work.

_____ **80.** Working in small groups is better than working alone.

_____ **81.** I try to share my ideas and materials with other students when I think it will help them.

_____ **82.** When we work together in small groups, I have to find out what everyone else knows if I am going to be able to do the assignment.

_____ **83.** It is a good idea for students to help each other learn.

_____ **84.** I like to do better work than other students.

_____ **85.** I like to cooperate with other students.

_____ **86.** I like to work with other students.

_____ **87.** I do better work when I work alone.

_____ **88.** Students learn a lot of important things from each other.

1	2	3	4	5
False all the time	False some of the time	Neither false nor true	True some of the time	True all the time

_____ **89.** I would rather work on schoolwork alone than with other students.

_____ **90.** I like to be the best student in the class.

_____ **91.** I am doing a good job of learning in class.

CLASSROOM LIFE: SCALES

The Classroom Life questionnaire items can be sorted into the following categories, or scales.

TEACHER ACADEMIC SUPPORT

27. My teacher cares about how much I learn.

36. My teacher likes to see my work.

43. My teacher likes to help me learn.

50. My teacher wants me to do my best schoolwork.

TEACHER PERSONAL SUPPORT

15. My teacher really cares about me.

20. My teacher thinks it is important to be my friend.

52. My teacher likes me as much as he or she likes other students.

55. My teacher cares about my feelings.

STUDENT ACADEMIC SUPPORT

1. Other students in this class want me to do my best schoolwork.

5. In this class, other students like to help me learn.

22. In this class, other students care about how much I learn.

31. Other students in this class want me to come to class every day.

STUDENT PERSONAL SUPPORT

7. Other students in this class think it is important to be my friend.

25. In this class, other students like me the way I am.

37. Other students in this class care about my feelings.

39. Other students in this class like me as much as they like others.

46. In this class, other students really care about me.

COOPERATION

67. In this class, I like to share my ideas and materials with other students.

76. In this class, I can learn important things from other students.

78. In this class, I like to help other students learn.

81. In this class, I try to share my ideas and materials with other students when I think it will help them.

83. In this class, it is a good idea for students to help each other learn.

85. In this class, I like to cooperate with other students.

88. In this class, students learn a lot of important things from each other.

COOPERATION, SCALE 2

17. In this class, we work together.

33. In this class, students check answers with other students.

40. In this class, we help each other with our schoolwork.

49. In this class, we learn more when we work with others.

POSITIVE GOAL INTERDEPENDENCE

8. When we work together in small groups, we try to make sure that everyone in our group learns the assigned material.

16. When we work together in small groups, our job is not done until everyone in our group has finished the assignment.

24. When we work together in small groups, we all receive bonus points if everyone scores above a certain criteria.

66. When we work together in small groups, we have to share materials in order to complete the assignment.

72. When we work together in small groups, everyone's ideas are needed if we are going to be successful.

82. When we work together in small groups, I have to find out what everyone else knows if I am going to be able to do the assignment.

RESOURCE INTERDEPENDENCE

51. When we work together in small groups, we cannot complete an assignment unless everyone contributes.

59. When we work together in small groups, the teacher divides the material so that everyone has a part and everyone has to share.

66. When we work together in small groups, we have to share materials in order to complete the assignment.

72. When we work together in small groups, everyone's ideas are needed if we are going to be successful.

82. When we work together in small groups, I have to find out what everyone else knows if I am going to be able to do the assignment.

ALIENATION

3. I am not doing as well in school as I would like to.

4. I find it hard to speak my thoughts clearly when I am in this class.

6. Schoolwork is fairly easy for me.

13. I should get along with other students better than I do.

23. Whenever I take a test I am afraid I will fail.

38. I often get discouraged in school.

47. I have a lot of questions I never get a chance to ask in class.

53. I am often lonely in this class.

58. I am a good student.

61. I often feel upset in school.

65. Sometimes I think the scoring system in this class is not fair.

EXTRINSIC MOTIVATION, SOCIAL SUPPORT

10. I do schoolwork to make my teacher happy.

14. I do schoolwork because my classmates expect it of me.

28. I do schoolwork to make my parents happy.

32. I do schoolwork to keep my teacher from getting mad at me.

48. I do schoolwork to be liked by other students.

COHESION

2. My best friends are in this class.

12. I like to work with other students in this class.

30. In this class everybody is my friend.

53. I am often lonely in this class.

56. All the students in this class know each other well.

ACADEMIC SELF-ESTEEM

3. I am not doing as well in school as I would like to.

6. Schoolwork is fairly easy for me.

23. Whenever I take a test I am afraid I will fail.

58. I am a good student.

91. I am doing a good job of learning in this class.

FAIRNESS OF GRADING

21. In this class, everyone has an equal chance to succeed if they do their best.

42. In this class, if a student works hard, he/she can definitely succeed.

54. In this class, students get the scores they deserve, no more and no less.

57. In this class, I deserve the scores I get.

65. In this class, sometimes I think the scoring system is not fair.

INDIVIDUALISTIC LEARNING

11. In this class it is important that we learn things by ourselves.

18. In this class, we spend a lot of time working at our own desks.

34. In this class, we do not talk to other students when we work.

45. In this class, we work by ourselves.

68. It bothers me when I have to do it all myself.

69. I like my work better when I do it all myself.

75. I don't like working with other students in school.

80. Working in small group is better than working alone.

86. I like to work with other students.

87. I do better work when I work alone.

89. I would rather work on school work alone than with other students.

COMPETITIVE LEARNING

70. I like the challenge of seeing who's best.

71. I don't like to be second.

73. I am happiest when I am competing with other students.

74. Competing with other students is a good way to work.

77. I work to get better grades than other students get.

79. I like to compete with other students to see who can do the best work.

84. I like to do better work than other students.

90. I like to be the best student in the class.

CONTROVERSY

19. I learn new things from arguing with other students.

29. I would rather work alone than argue.

41. I like being in a group where students often disagree with each other.

62. Arguing with other students makes me feel unhappy.

VALUING HETEROGENEITY

9. I learn more from students who are similar to me.

60. I like being in a learning group with students who are different from me.

63. I have more fun when I work with students who are different from me.

64. I learn more from students who are different from me.

CHAPTER ELEVEN

INTERVIEWING STUDENTS

WHAT IS AN INTERVIEW?

Closely related to giving questionnaires is conducting interviews. An **interview** is a personal interaction between the interviewer (the teacher) and one or more interviewees (students) in which verbal questions are asked and verbal or linguistic responses are given. An interview may involve one student or a small group of students. The personal interaction between interviewer and the interviewee(s) and the verbal or linguistic nature of the data are what constitute the major strengths and weaknesses of the interview procedure.

Interviews may take place before, during, or after a lesson or instructional unit. Interviews can focus on a book read, a project completed, a research paper written, a film or video made, a field trip taken, a guest speaker heard, a composition written, a work of art seen, a piece of music heard, a foreign language learned, a problem solved, a scientific experiment conducted, a portfolio completed, or even the procedure used to fix a car.

The key difference between a questionnaire and an interview is that in an interview the interviewer and the respondent are both present as the questions are asked and answered. Questions and answers can thus be clearly communicated, and misunderstandings can be identified and immediately clarified. The interviewer has the opportunity to observe both the student and the total situation to which the student is responding. The key problem with interviewing is the subjective nature of asking questions and recording student responses.

Interviews are often structured according to what type of questions they contain. There are two types of questions: fixed-alternative (closed-ended) and open-ended questions. Fixed-alternative or closed-ended questions are used when possible alternatives are known, limited, and clear cut (e.g., *English class is lots of fun.* _____ *Yes* _____ *No*). They are well suited to obtaining factual information and knowledge. The advantages of closed-ended questions are that they (a) are easy to understand, (b) are easy to administer, (c) require the respondent, not the interviewer, to make judgments, (d) are quick and inexpensive to analyze, and (e) eliminate the possibility of irrelevant answers. Their disadvantages include (a) forcing respondents to give answers that do not reflect their true knowledge or opinion, (b) ommitting important alternative responses and (c) allowing alternatives to be interpreted differently by various respondents.

Open-ended questions are used when issues are complex, when relevant dimensions are not known, or when the purpose of the interview is exploration of students' knowledge and reasoning processes. Perhaps the best way to determine whether a student understands a subject or problem is simply to ask the student to explain what he or she knows. The advantages of open-ended questions are that they (a) provide information on students' reasoning, (b) do not bias responses by suggesting alternatives, and (c) provide the opportunity to clarify and probe a response. Disadvantages include that they (a) are difficult to administer, (b) require extensive training of the interviewer as well as competence, and (c) elicit responses that are complex and difficult to analyze.

WHY INTERVIEW STUDENTS?

Interviewing is an important assessment and teaching procedure. For assessment, interviewing students provides information concerning students' learning, level of understanding, reasoning processes, metacognitive thought processes, and retention. Any student of any age or ability level can be interviewed. The learning of preschool and primary students who cannot read or write can be assessed in an interview. The learning of unmotivated students who do not express what they know on tests can be assessed in an interview. **Oral examinations,** in which students are interviewed about what they have learned, are especially useful for students who have certain learning disabilities (such as dyslexia) that impair their ability to read or write. Paper-and-pencil tests may seriously understate such students' actual understanding of the material being studied. Through oral interviews, the students' true level of achievement may be identified.

For teaching, interviewing helps students (a) clarify their thinking, (b) reflect on their learning, (c) achieve new levels of understanding, (d) believe their ideas are valued, (e) appreciate their progress, and (f) set future goals. **Socratic interviewing,** for example, is a historical procedure of using an interview to lead students to deeper and deeper insights about what they know.

Imagine yourself standing on a street corner in Athens about 390 BC. You're thinking about how you're going to get a date for tomorrow's feast when along comes Socrates. Socrates asks you a question. To get rid of him so you can go back to the more important matter of who your date for tomorrow's feast is going to be, you give a short answer. He listens, then asks you another question. You tell him to leave. He repeats his question. You answer, but he immediately counters with another question. You find yourself intrigued. It is an interesting question he is asking. He waits for your response. After debating two or three possible answers, you finally give your best answer. "Aha!" he says. "That is a very interesting answer, but if it is true, it implies that the world is round! How do you reconcile that with the fact that when you look across a field, the world looks flat?"

Now he really has you hooked. You think. He waits. You think some more. He waits some more. Finally, you reply, "The world is so large that when you look across a field you see too small a segment of the world to perceive a noticeable curve." "That is a brilliant hypothesis," Socrates tells you, "why don't you skip the feast tomorrow and develop it so it can be tested?" You find yourself agreeing to do just that. Figuring out this problem is far more interesting than going to a feast. As Socrates walks away, you yell, "Why didn't you just tell me the world was large and round?" "I don't believe in putting ready-made ideas into students' minds," says Socrates. "The only true way students can learn is to be led by questioning to their own discoveries!"

While this example fictionalizes what Socrates actually did, it does reflect that Socrates (470–399 BC) believed that questioning students face to face was the means of inducing thinking and thereby leading the student to discover his or her own wisdom. Through direct questioning he would induce cognitive conflict within the student, which in turn would motivate the student toward further inquiry. In essence, the Socratic method of teaching is an oral interview in which the inconsistencies and conflicts in a student's reasoning are highlighted to motivate the student to engage in a deeper level of thinking. Activity 11.1 provides an exercise in the Socratic method.

This combination of assessing what students know and understand while teaching students "their own wisdom" by leading them into deeper insights and better conceptualized frameworks makes interviewing one of the most important assessment

ACTIVITY **11.1** ■ BEING A SOCRATES

1. Choose a topic being studied.

2. Develop two or three general questions on what the student knows about the topic to begin an interview.

3. After asking the opening questions, probe what the student knows while looking for inconsistencies, contradictions, or conflicts in what the student is saying.

4. Ask follow-up questions that highlight the conflicts within the student's reasoning and make the contradictions focal points for the student's attention.

5. Continue the interview until the student has resolved the conflicts by moving toward deeper-level analysis of what he or she knows and by arriving at greater and greater insights into the material being studied.

6. Conclude the interview by pointing the student toward further resources to read and study.

tools. The direct interaction in an interview provides more opportunity to motivate students to do their best, motivate students to supply accurate and complete information immediately, probe for attitudes and beliefs, reveal the complexity of students' reasoning, clarify communication, and guide students in their interpretations of the questions. Interviewing may provide the most flexibility in assessing and teaching students while at the same time giving teachers the most control over the assessment situation.

Perhaps the greatest strength of the interview is the opportunity it provides to build positive relationships between you (the teacher) and your students. Through the direct, face-to-face interaction, you can create a more personal, positive, supportive, and trusting relationship with the student. Supportive relationships improve the learning climate of the class and school. You can establish norms about the relationship, build rapport and closeness, and generally get acquainted with the student.

HOW TO INTERVIEW STUDENTS

The simplest way to interview students is to develop a questionnaire with closed-ended questions and read the questionnaire to the student while marking down their responses. Whereas this guarantees that students answer each question, this procedure does not capitalize on the flexibility and strengths of interviewing. (Box 11.1 describes guidelines for interviewing.)

The **focused interview** arranges questions like a funnel so that the initial questions are broad and general and subsequent questions require the student to be more and more precise and specific in his or her answers. The interviewer has the freedom to explore and probe in directions that are unanticipated. Only the initial questions are planned, as the subsequent questions are built on the statements made by the student being interviewed. Each student receives a different interview as each follow-up question is idiosyncratic to the student's previous response. You (the teacher), for example, may ask for the student's analysis of Shakespeare's *King Lear* and, according to what the student says in response, ask a series of questions that require the student to reveal more and more of his or her impressions of and reasoning about the play.

■ ■ ■ ■ ■

BOX 11.1
GUIDELINES FOR INTERVIEWING

1. Word and organize the questions so that the relationship between you and the student becomes more positive and trusting. A positive, trusting relationship encourages both you and the student to feel at ease, be spontaneous, respond honestly, and communicate effectively.
2. Phrase questions so that (a) students do not become defensive, (b) students' thoughts are clarified, (c) students have the opportunity to expand or modify, (d) you do not put ideas into students' minds, and (e) you do not suggest that students should have attitudes when they have none.
3. Begin the interview with simple, nonthreatening questions and save the more complex and threatening questions for the end of the interview.
4. Move from general to specific questions.
5. Make nonverbal cues that are helpful to eliciting full and complete responses from the student. Avoid smiling too much and excessive, affirmative nodding of the head.
6. Be quiet. What the student needs is a skillful, empathetic listener.
7. Allow sufficient wait time for students to formulate their thoughts and answer. Do not rush students' responses.

The primary purpose of a **small group interview** is to assess whether all group members have mastered and understood the assigned material. Conducting a small group interview begins with assigning students to cooperative learning groups. The groups should be heterogeneous. Give a set of questions to the groups on Monday. Instruct the students to prepare all group members to respond to the questions. Give time during each class period for the groups to practice their responses to the questions. On Thursday and Friday conduct an oral examination with the students, using the following procedure.

You meet with a group and randomly select one member to explain the answer to a randomly selected question. When that member finishes responding to the question, other group members can add to the answer. Judge the answer to be adequate or inadequate. Then ask another member a different question. Repeat this procedure until all questions have been answered or until you (the teacher) judge the group to be inadequately prepared. In this case, you ask the group to return to the assignments until members are better prepared. Give some guidance by identifying particular weaknesses and strengths in the members' answers. All group members are given equal credit for successfully passing the test. Among the many advantages of small group interviews are that you can quickly sample students' level of learning while making personal contact with each student. The disadvantages of the group interview are that (a) a chaining effect may bias responses and (b) the group may inhibit some individuals.

TYPES OF INTERVIEW QUESTIONS TO ASK STUDENTS

Different kinds of questions will elicit different kinds of information. The following list describes what kinds of information you may obtain through interview questions. Interview questions can

1. Prompt students to give information previously learned or to present information collected

2. Prompt students to add to their answers
3. Aim at prompting students to put together a sequence of at least two ideas
4. Encourage students to describe the sequence of their procedures
5. Prompt discussion and encourage students to listen to one another
6. Aim at prompting students to use evidence as a basis for stating relationships among variables
7. Encourage students to interpret new experiences using concepts they already have or to apply concepts they have just learned in a new situation

ANALYZING STUDENTS' RESPONSES

Responses to interview questions are scored similarly to essay questions. A content analysis is often conducted on the responses from which scoring rubrics are derived and applied. An example of a standardized scoring procedure is given in Box 11.2

SUMMARY

An **interview** is a personal interaction between a teacher and either one student or a small group of students in which verbal questions are asked and verbal responses are

---

■ ■ ■ ■ ■

BOX 11.2
NAEP SCORING SCALES: MATHEMATICS

LEVEL 200: BEGINNING SKILLS AND UNDERSTANDING
Learners at this level have considerable understanding of two-digit numbers. They can add two-digit numbers but are still developing an ability to regroup in subtraction. They know some basic multiplication and division facts, recognize relations among coins, use simple measurement instructions…

LEVEL 250: BASIC OPERATIONS AND BEGINNING PROBLEM SOLVING
Learners have an initial understanding of the four basic operations. They are able to apply whole number addition and subtraction skills to one-step work problems and money situations; in multiplication they can find the product of a two-digit and a one-digit number. They can compare information from graphs and charts, and are developing an ability to analyze logical relations.

LEVEL 300: MODERATELY COMPLEX PROCEDURES AND REASONING
Learners are developing an understanding of number systems. They can compute with decimals, simple fractions, and commonly encountered percentages. They can identify geometric figures, measure lengths and angles, and calculate areas of rectangles. They are also able to interpret simple inequalities, evaluate formulas, and solve simple linear equations. They can find averages…and are developing the skills to operate with signed numbers, exponents, and square roots.

LEVEL 350: MULTISTEP PROBLEM SOLVING AND ALGEBRA
Learners can solve routine problems involving fractions and percentages, recognize properties of geometric figures, and work with exponents and square roots. They can solve a variety of two-step problems using variables, identify equivalent algebraic expressions, and solve linear equations and inequalities…

given. Students may be interviewed before, during, or after a lesson or instructional unit. Interviews can contain fixed-alternative or open-ended questions. It is a highly flexible procedure that can be used for both assessment and teaching purposes. Students can be interviewed to assess their learning, cognitive reasoning, metacognitive thought, and retention. Students can also be interviewed to clarify their thinking, achieve new levels of understanding, reflect on their learning, believe their ideas are valued, appreciate their progress, and set future goals. Socrates is an example of a teacher who used oral interviews as the major instructional strategy. Interviews can also be used to build a more positive, supportive, and trusting relationship with each student.

Individual interviews may range from highly structured reading of a questionnaire with closed-ended questions to a focused interview in which the teacher unfolds the students' knowledge by progressively asking students to be more precise and specific in their answers. Small groups can be interviewed to assess their success in ensuring that all members have mastered the assigned material. The guidelines for interviewing include creating a supportive, nonthreatening climate, moving from simple to complex questions, moving from general to specific questions, and allowing sufficient wait time for students to formulate their thoughts and answers. The questions asked should prompt students to give information previously learned or collected, add to their answers, put a sequence of ideas together, provide evidence for their conclusions, and apply known concepts to new situations.

INTERVIEWING STUDENTS TO ASSESS REASONING

Class: _____   Project: _____   Date: _____

Group 1	Group 2	Group 3	Group 4
What are you doing?			
Why are you doing it?			
How will it help you?			

INTERVIEW ON "PERSONAL BEST" IN HELPING A CLASSMATE LEARN

Student's Name: _____ Grade: _____ Date: _____

1. Describe a situation in which you demonstrated a "personal best" in helping a classmate learn something important and valuable. Include *who, when, where,* and *what* your classmate learned.

2. Opportunities and Challenges
   a. What made the learning difficult for your classmate?
   b. How were you being innovative in your helping?

3. Costs and Gains
   a. What did it cost you to help? (time, energy, resources)
   b. What did you gain by helping? (satisfaction, pride, skills)

4. Involvement
   a. How did you energize to the learning situation?
   b. What did you do to empower your classmate?
   c. How did you keep your classmate involved in the learning?

5. Celebration
   a. How did you celebrate your classmate's success?
   b. How did you recognize the hard work the two of you put into the learning?

6. What did you learn about helping another person learn?

7. How would you sum up your experience in your own words? How did it represent your personal best?

CONFLICT REPORT FORM: INTERVIEW

Date: _____   Name: _____ _____ Male _____ Female

Grade: _____   Teacher: _____   Subject Area: _____

Who was involved in the conflict? _____

Class: _____   Project: _____   Date: _____

Relationship with other: _____ Friend _____ Nonfriend _____ Stranger _____ Adult

_____ Brother/Sister   Other: _____

What was the conflict about? _____

_____

_____

Where did the conflict take place? _____

What strategies were used to try to solve the conflict? _____

_____

_____

Was the conflict resolved? _____ Yes   _____ No

What was the solution? _____

_____

_____

How did you feel about the way the conflict was resolved?

1	2	3	4	5
Very unhappy	Unhappy	OK	Happy	Very happy

Conclusions:

CHAPTER TWELVE

LEARNING LOGS AND JOURNALS

WHAT ARE LEARNING LOGS AND JOURNALS?

Learning logs and journals are key tools for having students document and reflect on their learning experiences (Johnson & Johnson, 1998a). **Learning logs** are a self-report procedure in which students record short entries concerning the subject matter being studied. Log entries may be questions about material covered in lectures and readings, observations of science experiments, mathematics problem-solving entries, lists of outside readings, homework assignments, or anything else that lends itself to keeping records.

Learning journals are a self-report procedure in which students record narrative entries concerning the subject matter being studied. Journal entries may be personal observations, feelings, and opinions in response to readings, events, and experiences. A journal is a personal collection of writing and thoughts that have value for the writer about what the writer is learning and its personal relevance. These entries often connect what is being studied in one class with other classes or with life outside the classroom. Journal entries are usually more descriptive, longer, and more free-flowing than logs. Activity 12.1 is an exercise in keeping a journal for this course.

WHY USE LOGS AND JOURNALS?

Logs and journals are useful assessment tools for the following tasks:

1. Keeping track of the number of problems solved, books read, or homework assignments completed
2. Recording from lectures, movies, presentations, field trips, experiments, or reading assignments (a) key ideas, (b) questions, and (c) reflections
3. Responding to questions posed by the teacher or other students
4. Following the progress of an experiment; the weather; in-school, national, or world events, or even a story and (a) monitoring change over time or (b) making predictions about what will happen next
5. Connecting ideas presented to other subject areas
6. Brainstorming ideas about potential projects, papers, or presentations
7. Identifying problems and recording problem-solving techniques
8. Applying what is learned in the course to one's own personal life
9. Using what is learned in the course to clarify, update, and refine one's action theories (i.e., what actions are needed to achieve a desired consequence in a given situation)

As you complete this course you will be asked to keep a journal in which you record what you are learning about the subject matter covered and yourself as a person. A journal is a personal collection of writing and thoughts that have value for the writer about what he or she has learned in the course and its personal relevance. It has to be kept up on a regular basis. The journal is an important part of this course. It is not an easy part. The entries should be important to you in your effort to make this course useful. Because this is a cooperative course, journal entries should be useful to your fellow student colleagues. You may be surprised by how writing sharpens and organizes your thoughts. The journal will be of great interest to you after you have finished this course.

PURPOSES

1. To keep track of the activities related to this course (what you are doing to make the material useful in your teaching)

2. To answer in writing some of the questions that are important for a clear understanding of the course content (these will often be suggested, but others can be selected by you)

3. To collect thoughts that are related to the course content (the best thinking often occurs when you are driving to or from school, about to go to sleep at night, and so forth)

4. To collect newspaper and magazine articles and references that are relevant to the topics covered in the course

5. To keep summaries of conversations and anecdotal material that are unique, interesting, or illustrate things related to the content of the course

6. To collect interesting thoughts, articles, and conversations not especially related to the course, but important to you

DIRECTIONS:

1. Write a journal that includes at least one entry per week.

2. Summarize what you are learning in the course for the current week.

3. Describe how you behaved during an important experience you had during the week, including

   a. The nature of the situation
   b. The people involved
   c. The relationships among participants
   d. The strategies you used to manage the situation
   e. The feelings experienced
   f. The outcomes that resulted from your actions

4. From the description, summarize the implicit action theories that directed your behavior.

5. Use what you have learned in the course to describe how you could have behaved in a more effective and constructive way, including how you would modify your action theories.

Note: If you publish your journal, as did John Holt, Hugh Prather, and others, all we ask is a modest 10 percent of the royalties.

HOW TO USE LOGS AND JOURNALS

Learning logs and journals are usually considered formative assessment methods. It is difficult to assign point values or letter grades, but it can be done.

1. Assign students the task of keeping a journal (or a log) related to the content of the course. Explain what a journal is. Highlight the cooperative goal of ensuring that all group members keep journals that meet the specified criteria.
2. Inform students of when their entries should start, how often they are to write an entry, how long an entry should be, how often they will share their entries with groupmates and you (the teacher), how the entries will be assessed, and when the final journal or log is due.
3. Show students samples or models of completed journals or logs, ranging from excellent to poor. Students need to develop a frame of reference as to what is and is not an acceptable journal or log.
4. Have students develop (a) specific criteria to assess the quality of the completed journals or logs and (b) indicators of excellent, medium, and poor quality for each criteria. Teach students a standardized rubric if you, the school, the district, or the state has one.
5. Have students construct their journal or log (see Figures 12.1, 12.2, and 12.3 for examples). To help students make entries into their log or journal you may wish to give them a prompt or lead-in. Structure the first entry in the first class session. In each subsequent class session, give a prompt, lead-in, or a procedure for an entry. Examples of daily prompts or lead-ins follow:

An interesting part is…	I want to know more about…
I predict…	I wonder…
Three important ideas are…	The ways I helped others learn are…
I need to work more on…	I am excited about…
A connecting idea is…	I believe…

6. Have students share their journal or log entries with the other members of their cooperative learning group on a regular basis (e.g., daily, twice a week, once a week).
7. Have students turn in their journals or logs to you (the teacher) on a periodic basis for feedback and/or a grade based on the number of entries and their quality.
8. Have students complete a self-assessment on their journal or log entries based on the predetermined criteria.
9. Have students, with the help of their cooperative learning group and you (the teacher), select a few of the journal entries to be rewritten and placed in their portfolios.

HOW TO ASSESS LOGS AND JOURNALS

The quality of logs and journals can be assessed in two ways. First, rate entries against criteria of excellence. This method involves four steps: (1) specifying a number of criterion for quality, (2) developing indicators of high, medium, and low performance for that criterion, (3) rating a student's log or journal on each of the criterion, and (4) adding the ratings for each criterion together to determine a total score. An example of a rating sheet is provided in Figure 12.4.

Second, assign point values to each criterion. This method for assessing journals or logs allows you to rate different criteria with different weights. An example is provided in Figure 12.5.

FIGURE 12.1   Example of a Problem-Solving Log

PROBLEM-SOLVING LOG

Name: _____

Class: _____   Date: _____

1. My problem is…

2. The best way to analyze the problem is…

3. Something that is similar to the problem is…

4. Three ways to solve the problem are…

5. A question I still have about the problem is…

6. I need help with…

ACTION THEORIES AND JOURNALS

Several reasons for using journals in a class follow:

1. To increase students' awareness of their action theories
2. To make judgments about the effectiveness of their action theories
3. To update or refine their action theories on the basis of what is learned in the course

To accomplish these tasks, students have to understand what an action theory is and how they are to use a journal to examine and modify their action theories.

Action Theory

All humans need to become competent in taking action and simultaneously reflecting on their actions to learn from them. Integrating thought with action requires that we plan our behavior, engage in it, and then reflect on how effective we were. When we learn a pattern of behavior that effectively deals with a recurrent situation, we

FIGURE 12.2   **Example of a Reading Log**

READING LOG

Name: _____   Date: _____

1. Key ideas: _____

_____

2. Connections: _____

_____

3. Questions: _____

_____

4. Liked best: _____

_____

FIGURE 12.3   **Example of a Double-Entry Journal**

DOUBLE-ENTRY JOURNAL

Initial Entry	Upon Reflection

tend to repeat it over and over until it functions automatically. Such habitual behavioral patterns are based on theories of action.

An **action theory** is a theory that hypothesizes what actions are needed to achieve a desired consequence in a given situation. All theories have if–then constructs. An action theory states that in a given situation, if we do X, then Y will follow. Our theories of action are normative; they state what we "ought" to do to achieve certain results. Examples of action theories can be found in almost everything we do. If we smile and say hello, others are expected to return our smile and greeting. If we apologize, the other person is expected to forgive us. If we steal, we can expect to be punished. If a person shoves us, he or she can expect us to shove back. All our behavior can be explained by theories that connect our actions with certain circumstances.

FIGURE 12.4   Sample Criteria Rating Sheet

CRITERIA RATING SHEET

Criteria	Score		
1. Number of Entries	1————2————3————4————5 No entries Few entries All required entries		
2. Length of Entry	1————2————3————4————5 Less than one page One page Several pages		
3. Depth and Personalization	1————2————3————4————5 Surface, impersonal Partial, personal Deep, very personal		
4. Thoughtfulness	1————2————3————4————5 Response only Response, examples Response, examples, reflections		
5. Originality	1————2————3————4————5 Straightforward Some metaphors, images Highly creative		

Comments: Score: _____

POINTS	GRADE
22–25	A
18–21	B
13–17	C
8–12	D

As children we are taught action theories by parents, teachers, and other socializing agents. As we grow older we learn how to modify our action theories and develop new ones. We learn to try to anticipate what actions will lead to what consequences, to try out and experiment with new behaviors, to experience the consequences, and then to reflect on our experiences to determine whether our action is valid or needs modification. Education is based on the systematic development and modification of action theories.

We all have many action theories, one for every type of situation in which we regularly find ourselves. This does not mean that we are aware of our action theories. An action is usually based on tacit knowledge—knowledge that we are not always able to put into words. Because most of our action theories function automatically, we are rarely conscious of our assumed connections between actions and their consequences. One of the purposes of this class is to help you become more conscious of the action

FIGURE 12.5   Assigning Point Values to Criteria

Points	Criteria
20	Completeness of entries
10	Entries recorded on time
15	Originality of entries
15	Higher-level reasoning demonstrated
15	Connections made with other subject areas
25	Personal reflection
100	Total

theories that guide how you behave in certain situations, to help you test your theories against reality, and to help you modify them to make them more effective.

LOGS AND INFORMAL COOPERATIVE LEARNING

One of the most useful ways to use learning logs in a class is with informal cooperative learning. Whenever a lecture, demonstration, presentation, guest speaker, film, or video is used, the combination of learning logs and informal cooperative learning will enhance the quality of instruction and ensure high-quality assessment of learning. The nature of informal cooperative learning is explained in the next section, and the procedure for using learning logs with informal cooperative learning is discussed.

Informal Cooperative Learning

Reflective logs can be used very productively with informal cooperative learning (Johnson & Johnson, 1999; Johnson, Johnson, & Holubec, 1998b; Johnson, Johnson, & Smith, 1998). Informal cooperative learning groups are temporary, ad hoc groups that last for only one discussion or one class period. Their purposes are to (a) focus student attention on the material to be learned, (b) set a mood conducive to learning, (c) help organize in advance the material to be covered in a class session, (d) ensure that students cognitively process the material being taught, and (e) provide closure to an instructional session. Informal cooperative learning groups also ensure that misconceptions, misunderstanding, and gaps in understanding are identified and corrected, and learning experiences are personalized. They may be used at any time, but are especially useful during a lecture or direct teaching.

For lectures to be successful students must be cognitively active, not passive. The major problem with lecturing is that information passes from the notes of the professor to the notes of the student without passing through the mind of either one. During lecturing and direct teaching the instructional challenge is to ensure that students, not the faculty, do the intellectual work of conceptualizing and organizing material, explaining it, summarizing it, and integrating it into existing conceptual frameworks. Students are more intellectually active when they engage in advance organizing, process cognitively what they are learning, and provide closure to the lesson.

The following procedure can help you plan a lecture that keeps students actively engaged intellectually. It entails having focused discussions before and after the lecture (i.e., bookends) and interspersing pair discussions throughout the lecture.

1. **Introductory focused discussion.** Assign students to pairs. The person seated next to them will do. You may want to require different seating arrangements each class period so that students meet and interact with a number of other students in the class. Give the pairs the cooperative assignment of completing the initial (advance organizer) task. Allow 4 or 5 minutes to do this task. The discussion task is aimed at promoting advance organizing of what students know about the topic to be presented and establishing expectations about what the lecture will cover.

2. **Lecture segment 1.** Deliver the first segment of the lecture. This segment should last from 10 to 15 minutes. This is about the length of time an adult can concentrate on a lecture.

3. **Pair discussion 1.** Assign students a discussion task focused on the material you have just presented. The discussion must be completed in 3 or 4 minutes. Its purpose is to ensure that students are actively thinking about the material being presented. The discussion task may be to (a) answer a question posed by the instructor, (b) respond to the theory, concepts, or information being presented, or (c) relate material to past learning so that it is integrated into existing conceptual frameworks. Discussion pairs should use the formulate–explain–listen–create procedure:
   a. Each student formulates his or her answer.
   b. Students explain their answer with their partner.
   c. Students listen carefully to their partner's answer.
   d. Pairs create a new answer that is superior to each member's initial formulation through the process of association, building on each other's thoughts, and synthesizing.

   Randomly choose two or three students to give a 30-second summary of their discussions. It is important that students are randomly called on to share their answers after each discussion task. Such individual accountability ensures that the pairs take their tasks seriously and check each other to ensure that both are prepared to answer.

4. **Lecture segment 2.** Deliver the second segment of the lecture.

5. **Pair discussion 2.** Assign a discussion task focused on the second part of the lecture. (Repeat this sequence of lecture segment and pair discussion until the lecture is completed.)

6. **Closure focused discussion.** Assign an ending discussion task to summarize what students have learned from the lecture. Students should have 4 or 5 minutes to summarize and discuss the material covered in the lecture. The discussion should result in students integrating what they have just learned into existing conceptual frameworks. The task may also point students toward what homework will cover or what will be presented in the next class session. This provides closure to the lecture.

Learning Log Procedure

Require students to keep a learning log for the course. They are to bring their log to every class session. The log entries are completed as follows.

1. **Introductory focused discussion.** To prepare students for the class session you have them complete a short, initial, focused discussion task. Plan your lecture around a series of questions that the lecture answers. Prepare the questions on an overhead transparency or write them on the board so that students can see them. In pairs students (a) come to agreement on their initial answers to the questions and record the answers in their learning logs and (b) record in their logs questions they want to have answered about the topic. Doing so helps students organize in advance what they know about the topic to be studied and establish expectations about what the class session will focus on.

2. **Pair discussions interspersed throughout the lecture.** Ask students to engage in a 3-minute discussion with their partner and write their conclusions in their learning log. Pairs use the formulate–explain–listen–create procedure. The conclusions students write in their logs enables teachers to track students' reasoning and identify which parts of the material covered were and were not comprehended.

3. **Closure focused discussion.** Ask students to engage in a 5-minute discussion with their partner and write in their learning logs (a) a summary of what they have learned in the class session, (b) how it relates to what was covered the previous class sessions and the assigned reading, (c) any questions about the material covered today, and (d) how it relates to the material that will be covered in the next class session.

4. Partners read each other's log sheets to ensure that they are complete, readable, and reflect what was discussed. They sign their names to verify that they have checked the log entry.

5. Students hand in their log sheets. You (the teacher) read them to assess what students learned, what students did not comprehend accurately or completely, and what questions students still have about the material covered.

6. You return the entry sheets the next day and students place them in their logs.

SELF- AND OTHERS' RATINGS

Thomas Mann (1875–1955), a German writer, once said, "No one remains quite what he was when he recognizes himself." Having students rate themselves and their groupmates is an important addition to most instructional units (Johnson, Johnson, & Holubec, 1998a). First, students rate the quality and quantity of their learning. Second, students rate the quality and quantity of the learning of each of their groupmates. Third, students discuss and reflect on their learning experiences (under the guidance of an observant teacher), comparing their self-ratings with the ratings they receive from groupmates. These self- and others' ratings allow students to see how the quality of their work has evolved.

Teachers need to assess a number of factors besides test scores. Students need to arrive at class on time and be prepared to learn (have the essential materials, resources, and attitudes). Students need to provide academic help and assistance to groupmates and ask groupmates for help when they need it. In using a rating form students need to understand clearly the purpose of the form and how it will be used, the number of points (if any) the form counts in evaluating students, and the questions on the form.

SUMMARY

Learning logs and **journals** are key tools for having students document and reflect on their learning experiences. In logs students record short entries about what they are studying. In journals students record longer narratives about what they are studying. These activities help students (1) keep track of what they have completed, (2) respond to questions posed by the teacher, (3) identify problems to be solved, and (4) apply what they are learning to their own personal life. Students should look at completed journals and logs that range from excellent to poor as an example of how to write useful entries. Students should also be given specific criteria to assess entries. In addition, students should periodically be given prompts to indicate what they should write about. Entries are assessed against criteria, which may be given different weights. Keeping a log or journal may increase students' awareness of the actions that are needed to achieve a desired consequence in a given situation. Logs and journals can also be used with informal cooperative learning, in which pairs of students write entries before, during, and after a lesson. Keeping a log or journal helps students rate the quality of their learning experiences.

INFORMAL COOPERATIVE LEARNING LOG

Name: _____ Class: _____ Date: _____

DIRECTIONS:

Your task is to work with your partner in completing this log entry during the class session. At the end of the session, your partner will check your log page to ensure it is completed and you will check his or hers. You then hand in your log for the teacher to read. The teacher will give it back to you tomorrow and you will add it to your learning log.

1. **Introductory discussion.** The teacher has presented one to three questions for you to answer. You have 5 minutes to do so. Work cooperatively with your partner using the formulate–explain–listen–create procedure. Use what you know from the assigned readings and from your general knowledge to answer the questions.

   a. _____

   _____

   b. _____

   _____

   c. _____

   _____

2. **Pair discussions.** Use the formulate–explain–listen–create procedure to answer each question posed by the teacher during the class session.

   a. _____

   _____

   My answer: _____

   _____

   Your answer: _____

   _____

   Our answer: _____

   _____

   b. _____

   _____

   My answer: _____

   _____

Your answer: _____

_____

Our answer: _____

_____

c. _____

_____

My answer: _____

_____

Your answer: _____

_____

Our answer: _____

_____

d. _____

_____

My answer: _____

_____

Your answer: _____

_____

Our answer: _____

_____

3. **Closure focused discussion.** Writing on a blank piece of paper, you and your partner have 5 minutes to
   a. Summarize what you have learned during the class session.
   b. Relate your new learning with previous class sessions and the assigned reading covered.
   c. List any questions you still have about the material covered today.
   d. Predict what will be covered next.

   Read and verified by: _____

STUDENT SELF- AND PEER EVALUATION FORM

Student's Name: _____   Class: _____   Date: _____

Group: _____   Project: _____

This form will be used to assess the members of your learning group. Fill out one form on yourself. Fill out one form on each member of your group. During the group discussion, give each member the form you have filled out. Compare the way you rated yourself with the ways your groupmates have rated you. Ask for clarification when your rating differs from the ratings given you by your groupmates. Each member should set a goal for increasing his or her contribution to academic learning of all group members.

RATING YOURSELF AND YOUR GROUPMATES

Person Being Rated: _____   Date: _____

Use the following rating scale to determine the number of points earned by the group member:

4 = Excellent, 3 = Good, 2 = Poor, 1 = Inadequate

_____   On time for class

_____   Arrives prepared for class

_____   Reliably completes all assigned work on time

_____   Work is of high quality

_____   Contributes to groupmates' learning daily

_____   Asks for academic help and assistance when it is needed

_____   Gives careful step-by-step explanations (doesn't just tell answers)

_____   Builds on others' reasoning

_____   Relates what is being learned to previous knowledge

_____   Helps draw a visual representation of what is being learned

_____   Voluntarily extends a project

CHAPTER THIRTEEN

TOTAL QUALITY LEARNING AND STUDENT MANAGEMENT TEAMS

CONTINUOUS IMPROVEMENT OF QUALITY OF LEARNING

> We don't seek to be one thousand percent better at any one thing. We seek to be one percent better at one thousand things.
>
> —*Jim Carlzon (president of Scandinavian Air Systems)*

In the Bible is a parable about a person of high rank going on a journey. Before he leaves, he gathers his sons together and gives each a talent. On his return, he asks his sons what they have done with their talents. Each son who has increased his talents pleases him. The son who buried his talent angers the father so much that he takes that single talent away and gives it to the son who increased his talents the most. The moral of this parable is, *Those who develop and continually improve what they have will receive even more; those who do nothing with what they have will lose even that.* ■

Focusing on continuous improvement makes assessment the centerpiece of schools (Johnson & Johnson, 1994). Continuous assessment is needed to make small, incremental, daily improvements in learning and instruction. A teacher dedicated to continuous improvement of instruction will find some way to improve every day the quality of the way he or she teaches. A student dedicated to continuous improvement of learning will find some way to improve the quality of the way he or she learns each day. Changes do not have to be dramatic. Small, incremental changes are fine. Ideally, everyone in the school will dedicate themselves to continuous improvement of the quality of the processes of learning, instructing, and administrating. In Japan, this mutual dedication is called **kaizen,** a societywide covenant of mutual help in the process of getting better and better, day by day. **Continuous improvement** is the ongoing search by everyone involved for changes that can increase the quality of the process. A **process** is all the tasks, organized in a sequence, that contribute to the accomplishment of one particular outcome, such as learning a math procedure, teaching a lesson, or conducting a faculty meeting.

Continuous improvement of the processes of learning, teaching, and administrating begins with changing the organizational structure of the class and school. There are two types of organizational structures: (a) mass-production and (b) team-based, high performance. In a **mass-production organizational structure,** the quality of students' learning is determined by inspecting the final outcome to see if it is adequate or needs improvement. Examples are final examinations or competency tests. This is known as inspecting quality in. In a team-based, **high-performance organizational structure,** the quality of students' learning is determined by examining the process of learning to determine if it can be improved. This is known as *continuous improvement* or *total quality learning.* See Box 13.1 for historical origins of this concept.

Continuous improvement in learning occurs when a cooperative learning group plans how to complete an assignment, does the assignment, assesses their effectiveness in doing so, reflects on how team members can improve the process of learning, and then modifies members' behavior in completing the next assignment. If students continuously improve their process of learning for 12 years, so that each assignment is completed more effectively than the one before, great learning would be occurring every hour! This chapter focuses on the continuous improvement of the processes of learning. The same principles can be used for continuous improvement of teaching and administrating.

CONTINUOUS IMPROVEMENT PROCEDURE

The following steps define the procedure for improving continuously the learning and instructing that takes place in a school (Johnson & Johnson, 1994):

Step 1. Form teams.

Step 2. Select a process for improvement.

Step 3. Define the process.

Step 4. Engage in the process.

Step 5. Gather information about the process; display it; and analyze it.

Step 6. Plan for improvement.

Step 7. Repeat the learning process in a modified way.

Step 8. Institutionalize changes that work.

■ ■ ■ ■ ■
BOX 13.1
HISTORICAL ORIGINS OF CONTINUOUS IMPROVEMENT

The name most closely associated with the continuous improvement of organizational processes is W. Edwards Deming. Deming was born in Sioux City, Iowa. During World War II he taught members of industry how to use statistical methods to improve the quality of military production. Following World War II, Deming taught the Japanese his theories of quality control and continuous improvement. Many experts credit him (along with Joseph Juran and others) with laying the groundwork for Japan's economic boom.

Deming's thesis was that in most organizations, management tends to view what goes wrong as the fault of individual people, not the organizational structure, whereas in fact the opposite tends to be true. Deming and Juran formulated the 85/15 rule: 85 percent of the problems can only be corrected by changing the organizational structure (largely determined by management) and less than 15 percent of the problems can be solved by changing individual workers. When problems arise, therefore, management should look for causes in the organizational structure and work to remove them, before casting blame on workers.

STEP 1: FORM TEAMS

The first step in continuous improvement is to form teams. In a high-performance organizational structure, teams do all the important work. Continuous improvement of the process of learning is not possible without teams. Students, therefore, are assigned to cooperative learning groups and given the responsibilities of continuously improving the quality of their own and their groupmates' learning. To fulfill these responsibilities, students need to be trained in how to organize their work, assess its quality daily, and place the results in a quality chart.

STEP 2: ANALYZE ASSIGNMENT AND SELECT A LEARNING PROCESS FOR IMPROVEMENT

The second step is to analyze the current assignment and select a process of learning for improvement. The team selects a specific, definable process to work on, such as members' ability to read with comprehension, write, present, or reason scientifically. W. Edwards Deming believed that if students concentrated on the continuous improvement of the processes of learning, the outcomes of learning (how much they learn and their scores on achievement and retention measures) would take care of themselves. One of the most profound changes educators can make is to shift the focus from examination of what students know to processes of learning.

STEP 3: DEFINE THE PROCESS

The third step is to define the process clearly. The definition of the process guides the assessment of student efforts. The team cannot improve a process until it defines the process, preferably by drawing a picture of it. Two common ways to picture a process are the flow chart and the cause-and-effect diagram.

Flow Charts

The **flow chart** is a pictorial or visual representation showing all the steps of a process or procedure and how they relate to each other. A flow chart describes the flow of people, material, and information within a designated workspace. The level of detail varies based on the needs of the team. Even without significant detail, flow charts can help identify gaps, duplication, and other potential problems. In flow charts easily recognizable symbols are used to represent the type of activity performed (see Figure 13.1). A flow chart is created by

1. Clearly defining the boundaries: where the process begins and ends and what are the inputs and the outputs
2. Identifying all the steps the process actually follows (what are the key steps, who does what, when). There is usually only one output arrow out of a process box. Otherwise, it may require a decision diamond.
3. Drawing the steps in sequence
4. Observing what team members actually do
5. Comparing actual performance with the flow chart and either revising the flow chart or planning how to increase the quality with which group members engage in each step

A variation on the above procedure is to (a) draw a flow chart of what steps the process actually follows, (b) draw a flow chart of what steps the process should

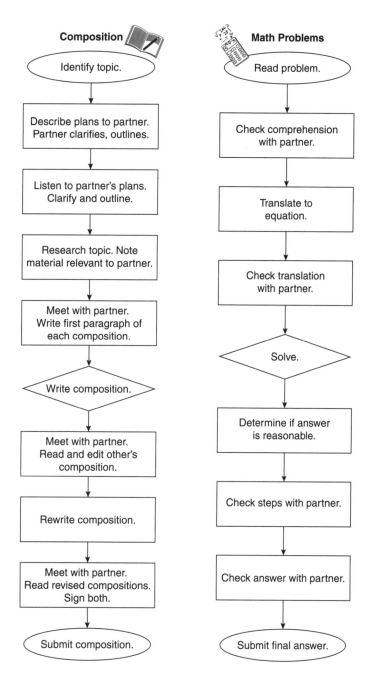

FIGURE 13.1   Flow charts

follow (if everything works right) and (c) compare the two charts to find where they are different because this determines where problems arise. This is sometimes called *imagineering*.

Cause-and-Effect Diagrams

A **cause-and-effect diagram** represents the relationship between some effect (the problem being studied) and all its possible causes (see Figure 13.2). The effect or problem is stated on the right side of the diagram and the major causes or influences are listed on the left. A cause-and-effect diagram is drawn to (a) illustrate clearly the

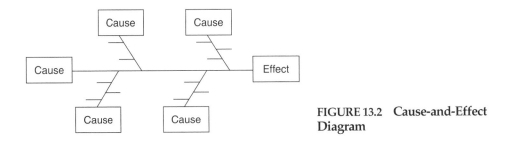

FIGURE 13.2   Cause-and-Effect Diagram

various causes affecting a process by sorting out and relating the causes and to (b) explore systematically cause-and-effect relationships so that the most likely causes of a problem or effect can be identified. Every effect is likely to have several major categories of causes. A team uses any category that emerges from the discussion or that helps team members think creatively. This charting technique is also referred to as a *fishbone diagram* due to its appearance when completed.

A team creates a cause-and-effect diagram by (a) defining the problem or effect clearly and placing it in a box on the right, (b) drawing a horizontal line or arrow, pointing to the effect, (c) determining the major categories of possible causes (use generic terms), (d) drawing a single line, for each major category, that branches off from the horizontal line, (e) thinking of possible causes in each category (ask questions, such as, Why? or, Why does this happen?) and adding each cause as a branch of the appropriate category, (f) identifying and circling the most basic (root) causes (start by looking for causes that recur), and (g) using a check sheet to gather data to verify the most likely root cause(s).

STEP 4: ENGAGE IN THE PROCESS

The fourth step is to engage in the process. Team members engage in the learning process so they can measure each step.

STEP 5: GATHER INFORMATION ABOUT THE PROCESS

The fifth step is to gather information about the process; display the data; and analyze it. This step involves three parts:

1. **The team identifies quantifiable factors.** If a factor cannot be counted, it cannot be improved (conversely, to be able to improve it, you must be able to count it).
2. **The team develops a design for gathering the relevant data.** This includes specifying what data will be collected, who will collect it, when it will be collected, and how it will be collected. A check sheet or observation form is a common way to gather objective data to answer the question, How often are certain events happening? A team uses the observation form to tally and count the number of times an event is observed in a specified time period (such as the number of times a social skill was used during a 50-minute period) or the amount of product (such as the progress in writing a composition).
3. **The team analyzes and portrays the data in ways that help members understand it easily.** Common ways to portray data are the Pareto chart, run chart, scatter diagram, and histogram.

Pareto Charts

The **Pareto chart** is a form of vertical bar chart that helps teams separate the vital few problems and causes from the trivial many. It takes its name from the Italian economist Vilfredo Frederico Damaso Pareto (1848–1923). While studying the unequal distribution of income, Pareto found that 80 percent of the wealth was controlled by only 20 percent of the population. In the late 1940s, Joseph Juran generalized Pareto's findings into the **Pareto principle (80/20 rule):** 80 percent of the trouble comes from 20 percent of the problems (the "vital few" should be separated from the "trivial many"). The Pareto chart is used to display the frequency and relative importance of problems, causes, or conditions to choose a starting point for improving process, monitoring progress, or identifying root causes of a problem. Pareto analysis allows the team to take data from basic tools (like check sheets and interviews) and present it in a simple bar graph format. The steps for developing a Pareto chart follow:

1. List actions, conditions, or causes you want to monitor.
2. Collect data on the number of times the actions, conditions, or causes occurred in a predetermined period of time.
3. Rank the various actions, conditions, or causes from highest to lowest as follows:
    a. Compute a total for each action, condition, or cause.
    b. Compute the total number of actions, conditions, or causes.
    c. Rank the action, condition, or cause from most frequently occurring to least frequently occurring.
4. On the y-axis, note the percentage scale (0 to 100 percent).
5. On the x-axis, list the measurement scale as follows:
    a. Record the total number of actions, conditions, or causes on the y-axis at the point that corresponds to 100 percent.
    b. Multiply the total number of actions, conditions, or causes by 0.75 to determine the number that corresponds to 75 percent.
    c. Multiply the total number of actions, conditions, or causes by 0.50 to determine the number that corresponds to 50 percent.
    d. Multiply the total number of actions, conditions, or causes by 0.25 to determine the number that corresponds to 25 percent.
6. Under the x-axis, write the actions, conditions, or causes in descending order (the most frequently occurring action to the left and the least occurring to the right):
    a. Identify the action, condition, or cause with the largest total. Working from left to right, (1) label the first bar on the x-axis of the chart with the action, condition, or cause; (2) record the total in the blank space; and (3) draw a vertical bar stretching from 0 to the total frequency of occurrence using the measurement scale on the y-axis as a guide.
    b. Identify the action, condition, or cause with the second largest total. Label the second bar on the x-axis of the chart with the action, condition, or cause. Record the total in the blank space. Draw a vertical bar stretching from 0 to the total frequency of occurrence using the measurement scale on the y-axis as a guide.
    c. Continue this procedure until every action, condition, or cause has been recorded on the chart in sequence from most to least frequently occurring.
7. Plot the cumulative frequencies of the data in a line graph:
    a. For the most frequent action, condition, or cause draw a point at its total frequency using the y-axis measurement scale as a guide (the point will be at the top of the bar graph).
    b. Add the frequency of the first and second most frequent actions, conditions, or causes, together for a cumulative total. Plot that point on the chart using the y-axis as a guide.

c. Add the frequency of the first, second, and third most frequent actions, conditions, or causes together for a cumulative total. Plot that point on the chart using the *y*-axis as a guide.

d. Continue this procedure until the cumulative total for all actions, conditions, or causes have been plotted on the chart. Draw a line connecting the cumulative points.

8. Make an action plan as follows:

a. Note how many of the actions, conditions, or causes account for 80 percent of the total.

b. Plan the actions required either to increase or decrease the frequency of the actions, conditions, or causes accounting for 80 percent of the total.

c. Plan the actions required either to increase or decrease the frequency of the actions, conditions, or causes accounting for 20 percent of the total.

A Pareto diagram is an extension of the cause-and-effect diagram in that the causes are not only identified but also listed in order of their occurrence (see Figure 13.3). Once team members gain some experience in making Pareto diagrams, members construct them quickly. The advantages of the Pareto diagram are that it can be used to analyze almost anything, it is easy to do, and easy to understand. The disadvantage is that only quantifiable data can be used in constructing it.

Run Chart

A run chart is used to monitor the process over time to see whether the long-range average is changing. It was discussed in Chapter 8.

Scatter Diagram

A **scatter diagram** displays the relationship between two actions, conditions, or causes (see Figure 13.4). A team uses a scatter diagram to display what happens to one variable when another variable changes, that is, to indicate the strength of a possible relationship between two variables. Usually, a team constructs a scatter diagram so that the *x*-axis represents the measurement values for the possible cause variable and the *y*-axis represents the measurement values for the possible effect variable.

A team creates a scatter diagram by (a) collecting paired samples that may be related (the more data points the better—50 to 100 are good), (b) constructing a data sheet that lists the values of variable 1 in one column and the values of variable 2 in

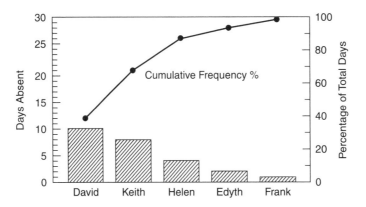

FIGURE 13.3   Pareto Diagram

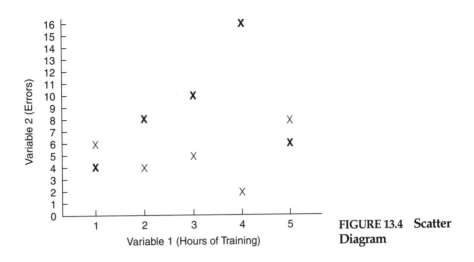

FIGURE 13.4   Scatter Diagram

another column, and (c) plotting the data on the chart by placing an X on the chart at each point where the paired data intersect (circle repeated data points). The ways the points are scattered about the chart indicate the relationship between the two variables. A randomly scattered pattern suggests they are unrelated. If the pattern moves from bottom left to top right, a positive correlation most likely exists. If the pattern moves from top left to bottom right, a negative correlation most likely exists. The more the cluster of data points resembles a straight line, the stronger the relationship.

Histogram

A **histogram** (history diagram) shows how continuous measurement data are clustered and dispersed (see Figure 13.5). It is used when the distribution and spread of data needs to be displayed. Histograms show the frequency of an occurrence and the dispersion between the highest and lowest values. By displaying measurement data across a range of values (spread), the team learns about the ability of the process to meet specifications, whether the distribution is centered in the right place, and whether the data points are evenly balanced or skewed. Histograms are useful when the team collects large quantities of data and simple tabulation does not provide easy analysis.

A histogram consists of a series of columns of equal width and varying height. The x-axis represents the range of data and the y-axis represents the number of data points in each interval. Each column represents an interval within the range of data. Because interval size is constant, so are the column widths. Because column height

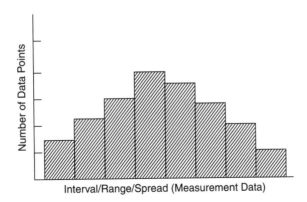

FIGURE 13.5   Histogram

represents the number of data points that occur within a given interval, column heights vary accordingly. The number of intervals (columns) determines how much of a pattern is visible. A team creates a histogram in the following way:

1. Collect the data to be analyzed.
2. Count the number of data points to determine the size of the data set (n).
3. Determine the range (R) by subtracting the smallest value from the largest.
4. Determine the number of classes (K) to use (such as less than 50 data points = 5–7 classes, 50–100 data points = 6–10 classes, 100–250 data points = 7–12 classes, and more than 250 data points = 10–20 data points).
5. Determine class width or interval size (H) by dividing the range (R) by the number of classes (K): $H = R/K$.
6. Determine class boundaries for each interval by (a) finding the lowest value data point (this is the start point for the first class boundary) and (b) finding the second class boundary by adding the class width (H) to the previous boundary's start point.
7. Make sure each data point can fit in one and only one class (the end point of each interval must always be slightly less than the start point of the next class).
8. Count and record the number of data points that fall within each class/interval.
9. Draw a rectangle/column above each class (x-axis) reflecting the appropriate frequency of occurrences.
10. Analyze the distribution and its implications.

Quality Chart Procedure

Using **quality charts** is the heart of the continuous improvement process (Johnson & Johnson, 1994). Each day (or week) the cooperative learning group rates the extent to which each member is meeting the learning criteria. The results are then charted each week to help the group (a) determine the frequency and fidelity with which each group member is implementing the targeted procedures and to help the group (b) set goals for implementation efforts for the coming week (see Tables 13.1 and 13.2). The procedure for creating a quality chart follows:

1. Each member shows his or her daily homework and work during class. The quality and quantity of work is assessed by the criteria contained in the appropriate rubrics.
2. Group members receive points according to the extent to which they reached each criterion. The individual student may keep a quality chart by entering the points received each day or the total points received during a week.
3. The points earned by group members are added together and divided by the number of members. The result is the group score. The score is plotted on the group's quality chart.
4. The group discusses the results and the long-term trend for each member and the group as a whole and plans either how to improve the quality and quantity of their learning efforts during the coming week or how to maintain their high level of learning.
5. Group members celebrate how hard they are working and how successful they are.

STEP 6: PLAN FOR IMPROVEMENT

The sixth step is to generate an improvement theory/plan based on the analysis of the data collected. The theory/plan specifies how the team plans to modify or replace the process to improve the quality of the team's work. The results of the current qual-

TABLE 13.1   Sample Data Summary Chart

DATA SUMMARY CHART

	David	Roger	Edythe	Dale	Total
Total					

(0 points = did not do, 1 point = half did, 2 points = did)

ity chart and the long-term trend of increasing or decreasing quality of work is examined. Plans are made to improve the processes of learning and thereby improve the quality and quantity of members' learning.

STEP 7: REPEAT LEARNING PROCESS IN A MODIFIED WAY

The seventh step is for the team to implement its plans. The focus is on making small, incremental improvements in a process day after day after day. The team carefully evaluates the implementation (members gather more data). If the modified process works, the team adopts it. If it does not work, the team redesigns it and tries it out again on a small basis.

STEP 8: INSTITUTIONALIZE CHANGES

The eighth step is to institutionalize the changes that work and the continuous improvement process. Ensure that no backsliding (reverting to the old practices) occurs by taking new data samples periodically, analyzing them, revising the theory/plan, revising the process, and so forth.

STUDENT MANAGEMENT TEAMS

Another procedure based on total quality management principles is student management teams (Johnson, Johnson, & Smith, 1998). A **student management team** consists

TABLE 13.2 Sample Quality Chart

QUALITY CHART

12										
11										
10										
9										
8										
7										
6										
5										
4										
3										
2										
1										
0	1	2	3	4	5	6	7	8	9	10

of three or four students plus the instructor who assume responsibility for the success of the class by focusing on how to improve either the instructor's teaching or the content of the course. The group members monitor the course through their own experience and the comments of classmates. They then make recommendations as to how to improve the course. The group meets weekly. The quality of the course is analyzed, suggestions for improving the course are developed, and plans are made for implementing the suggestions. The meetings usually last about 1 hour and occur on neutral territory, away from the classroom and the instructor's office. The group maintains a journal of suggestions on how to improve the course, the actions taken, and the success or failure of the implementation efforts. A student management team is implemented in four stages:

Stage 1. Forming. The instructor asks for students to volunteer to be on the committee and selects three or four members from the pool of volunteers.

Stage 2. Team building. The instructor meets with the team and presents the team goal of ensuring course success by continuously improving the instruction and course content. The initial task needs to be easy for the group to achieve and should highlight the interdependence between the instruction and the student members. In other words, the initial task should be such that the instructor cannot complete it without the help of the student members. Members should be accountable to contribute their share of the work, learn the teamwork skills required, and regularly process how effectively the team is functioning. At this point the instruction's receptivity to feedback, criticism, and encouragement for student members to improve the course either builds or destroys group trust.

Stage 3. Improving the course. To improve instruction, the instructor and the student members may want to

   a. Examine specific aspects of instruction the instructor wants feedback on
   b. Conduct a survey of previous classes to discover which aspects of instruction they should focus their attention on
   c. Conduct formative surveys of the effectiveness of instruction at various points throughout the semester, plot the data in quality charts, systematically implement team suggestions for change, and track the impact of the changes on the quality of instruction

To improve the content of the course, the team may

   a. Focus on improving the clarity and organization of the course material
   b. Evaluate the effectiveness of the texts
   c. Do a time-benefit analysis of course assignments

Stage 4. Reaping long-term gains. The team keeps a written log on the progress of the class with notes of insights and changes they have implemented. This written log provides guidelines for the instructor on how to revise the instruction and content of the course for the next semester.

SUMMARY

Faculty empower students by placing them in teams and assigning them the task of continuously improving the quality of the processes of learning. **Continuous improvement** is the ongoing search (made by everyone from students to school board members) for incremental changes that can increase the quality of the processes of learning, instructing, and administrating. Each time students write a composition, for example, they should find at least one way to improve their writing skills. The change does not have to be dramatic. Small, incremental changes are fine.

To improve continuously the process of learning, students need to engage in eight steps. First, they must form teams. Quality learning is not possible without cooperative learning groups. Second, team members analyze the assignment and select a learning process for improvement. Third, members define the process to improve, usually by drawing a flow chart or cause-and-effect diagram. Fourth, team members engage in the process. Fifth, students gather data about the process, display the data, and analyze it. Tools to help them do so include observation forms, Pareto charts, run charts, scatter diagrams, and histograms. Sixth, on the basis of the analysis, team members make a plan to improve the process. Seventh, students implement the plan by engaging in the learning process in a modified and improved way. Finally, the team institutionalizes the changes that do in fact improve the quality of the learning process.

Total quality learning may also be promoted through the use of student management teams. A **student management team** consists of three or four students plus the instructor who assume responsibility for the success of the class by focusing on how to improve either the instructor's teaching or the content of the course. The group members monitor the course through their own experience and the comments of classmates. There are four stages of using student management teams: forming the team by recruiting and choosing members, building a cooperative team by structuring the five basic elements, improving the instruction and content of the course, and reaping the long-term gains from the process by carrying on the improvements to the next course.

The process of continuous improvement needs to be placed in the context of improving the quality of learning. For students, this starts with cooperative learning groups. A constancy of purpose is created among students by structuring strong, positive goal interdependence. Students adopt the new philosophies of quality learning (each group member perfectly completes assignments every time) and continuous improvement (each day students improve their learning abilities). Students spend less time focused on test scores and more time on examining the process of learning and continuously improving it. Ongoing training in teamwork and academic skills is made an essential part of daily school life. Leadership is distributed among all group members. Fear is driven out of the classroom by eliminating all competition among students and increasing social support. Barriers among students are reduced by ensuring that the cooperative learning groups are heterogeneous and strong relationships are built among students.

CHAPTER FOURTEEN

TEACHING TEAMS AND ASSESSMENT

COLLEAGIAL TEACHING TEAMS

Assessment and reporting practices of schools have become so labor intensive and complex that one teacher cannot expect to do them alone. Realistically, colleagial teaching teams are needed to coordinate and continuously improve the instruction, assessment, and reporting process (Johnson & Johnson, 1994). **Colleagial teaching teams** consist of two to five faculty members who work together to implement instructional, assessment, and reporting procedures with fidelity and flexibility as well as solve any implementation problems that may arise.

The activities of a colleagial teaching team include (a) professional discussions in which faculty conceptually clarify the instructional, assessment, and reporting procedures, (b) coplanning, codesigning, and copreparing lessons, assessment procedures, and reporting procedures, (c) coimplementing the instructional, assessment, and reporting procedures, and (d) coassessing how successful the lessons and procedures are. The reasons for conducting assessments in teaching teams include the fact that, in general, team efforts are more productive than individual efforts (Johnson & Johnson, 1989), and the labor-intensive nature of many of the new assessment procedures is significantly reduced when teachers coordinate their assessment efforts.

Colleagial teaching teams focus on assessing the (a) quality and quantity of student learning and (b) quality of the overall instructional program. First, teacher teams are needed to assess the quality and quantity of student learning and communicate the results to interested audiences. Using a variety of alternative assessment methods allows you to know your students better and to provide them and other interested stakeholders such as their parents with more precise and descriptive information about the students' progress. The more intensive and varied the assessment procedures, however, the more time and effort it takes to implement them, and, therefore, the more help teachers need from colleagues.

Second, teacher teams are needed to assess the quality of instructional programs. Instructional programs consist of curriculum materials and instructional procedures. Pressures to assess and reform curricula and instructional methods come from many areas, not the least of which is the establishment of ambitious content knowledge standards at the district, state, and national levels. To ensure that students reach those content standards, new assessment procedures congruent with the standards are needed. Instructional programs extend beyond any one individual teacher, and, therefore, teacher teams (not individual teachers) should be responsible for collecting, organizing, and communicating data about the quality of instruction in a school and district.

In assessing the effectiveness of instructional programs, teacher teams have to be concerned with issues such as (a) the use of national standards to evaluate the quality of schooling, (b) comparisons being made among schools, school districts, and states, (c) accountability to a wider variety of audiences (such as business and industry, state legislators, and foreign companies who are considering locating a facility in the community), (d) accountability to achieve more diverse outcomes (such as ability to work effectively in teams and with diverse teammates), (e) broader definitions of achievement, and (f) the need to compete with schools in other countries.

Colleagial teaching teams focus on continuously improving the assessment of the (a) quality and quantity of student learning and the communication the results to interested audiences and (b) quality of instructional program. Regular meetings are necessary if team members are to create and operate assessment systems. Daily quick discussions between classes will supplement formal meetings. To better understand the dynamics of collegial teaching teams, complete the exercises in Activity 14.1. Team members may need further training, more practice, or visits to other schools to see various assessment systems in action. Plan what resources the team will need to ensure members continually grow in expertise in conducting high-quality assessments. Activity 14.2 offers a list of instructions for organizing a collegial support group meeting.

CONDUCTING THE ASSESSMENT AND REPORTING PROCESS

Once collegial teaching teams are organized and focused on the continuous improvement of student learning and the quality of instruction, the next step is to conduct the assessment and reporting process. The assessment and reporting process includes (a) developing rubrics, (b) applying the rubric in a reliable way, and (c) communicating the results to interested audiences.

To conduct a valid and reliable assessment, teachers need clearly defined rubrics that contain the criteria used in evaluating a student's work or the quality of the instructional program. In developing rubrics, two heads are better than one, especially if a number of teachers plan to use the same rubric in a reliable way. Whoever is going to use the rubric should have a part in developing it.

Developing rubrics is usually hard, time-consuming work. It is, however, one of the most important professional conversations that teachers can have. Developing rubrics requires teachers to think clearly and come to consensus about what is "quality" work. The best way to craft rubrics is for a team of teachers and others to meet regularly to decide on the relevant dimensions of a performance and draft possible criteria, try them out with their students, and revise them as needed. Activity 14.3 provides checklists and questions to help you start thinking about the process of creating rubrics.

Developing rubrics in teams increases teachers' coorientation and ability to apply the same rubric in the same way. Students may be confused, for example, if one teacher scores compositions with a heavy emphasis on writing mechanics whereas another teacher scores compositions with a heavy emphasis on ideas and creativity. Teachers need to become cooriented to the criteria used to evaluate and communicate students' work. In assessing students' learning and skills, a number of problems require teacher teams to solve.

1. **Generalizability of scores.** We know very little about the number of performances necessary to estimate a student's ability accurately. Shavelson, Gao, and Baxter (1991), for example, concluded that to estimate accurately a student's problem-solving ability in mathematics and science, 8 to 12 performances are needed. Such estimates, however, vary considerably by content areas, specific curriculum, and grade level. The circumstances under which the

ACTIVITY **14.1** ■ COLLEAGIAL TEACHING TEAMS

1. What is a colleagial teaching team?

2. What are the two purposes of the colleagial teaching team?

a. _____

_____

b. _____

_____

3. Fill in the chart below to select the members of your colleagial teaching team.

a. In column 1, list the names of the teachers in your school who are most competent.

b. In column 2, list the names of the teachers in your building who are most committed to assessment.

c. In column 3, list the teachers whose names appear in either column 1 or column 2 *and* who most like each other (i.e., are committed to each other as friends).

d. In column 4, write at least five names listed in column 3 to represent the teachers you will probably want to select for your team. (A minimum of five teacher choices is needed because one or more of the teachers may be unwilling or unable to volunteer the time needed for the team—at least one formal meeting per week and daily hallway meetings.)

Most Competent	Most Committed	Like Each Other	Teaching Team

4. When, where, and how often will the colleagial support group meet?

a. When: _____

b. Where: _____

c. How often (at least once a week is recommended): _____

(continued)

ACTIVITY 14.1 *Continued*

5. What are the resources the colleagial teaching team needs?

   a. _____

   b. _____

   c. _____

   d. _____

6. List the ways you will structure the five basic elements of cooperation into the teaching team.

   a. Positive interdependence: _____

   _____

   b. Individual accountability: _____

   _____

   c. Promotive (face-to-face) interaction: _____

   _____

   d. Social skills: _____

   _____

   e. Processing: _____

---

performances are made, furthermore, affect how reflective they are of what the students can do.

2. **Lack of interstudent comparisons.** Comparing the performances of one student with those of another can be very subjective.

3. **Student self-ratings.** It is unclear how student self-ratings contribute to assessments of academic or behavioral development.

4. **Score aggregation.** For each student performance, a series of criteria may be used in assessment. The resulting ratings are aggregated for any one performance and across all the student's performances to obtain a summary overall rating. What results is similar to a grade.

5. **Score reliability.** For scores to be reliable, (a) different teachers must give the student performance the same score or (b) the same teacher must give the student performance the same score on two different occasions. To achieve reliability, (a) criteria have to be anchored in observable and objective characteristics of a performance and (b) simple rubrics must be developed and used to guide assessment. The more complex criteria and rubrics are, the lower reliability tends to be. High interrater reliability may be achieved when a team of teachers score student performances together and discuss why each performance does or does not meet the criteria. Such discussions allow teachers to become cooriented as to what the criteria mean and how they may be applied to student performances.

6. **Time and other costs required for assessment activities.** There is very little data on the value of new assessment procedures weighed against the cost in teacher time and other resources required to implement them (see Activity 14.4).

ACTIVITY 14.2 ■ **COLLEAGIAL SUPPORT GROUP MEETING**

1. **Convener.** The role of convener is vital to effective meetings. Rotate this role among members. The convener is in charge of providing the meeting place, gourmet food, any materials required, a procedure for sharing new content, and keeping time so all agenda items are covered in the meeting.

2. **Membership grid.** Record in the grid what is shared by each group member. The topics should be personal rather than professional. Examples are favorite novel, poem, play, movie, or painting and why it is your favorite; most fun free-time activity; most vivid memory from elementary, junior high, or high school; most important, positive family memory in the past year.

3. **Share a success.** Think through what cooperative learning lessons and social skills you have taught during the past week. Share a success in using cooperative learning. Listen carefully to the successes related by your colleagues. In your classroom try to implement one good idea from what your colleagues shared. Then celebrate as a group.

4. **Goal setting.** To continuously improve your professional expertise and competencies (and to help your colleagues do likewise), set five goals to accomplish this week. One goal should deal with using cooperative learning. One goal should deal with teaching students social skills. One goal should deal with promoting the success of a colleague (another teacher). Two goals should reflect current issues in your classroom.

5. **Joint planning/contracting.** Each member shares his or her goals for the week. For each goal, another member volunteers to help. How the help is given and when and where it takes place are written down on the planning form. The help may range from providing relevant materials to coteaching a lesson. Be specific about the help you will give and when and where you will do so. Make sure that the work is divided so that everyone saves time and energy by being part of the team. Sign the joint-planning form with your colleagues to indicate that you understand what they are going to do and that you are willing to assist them.

6. **New content.** Share something new you have learned about cooperative learning in the past week. You could summarize an article you read, relate an insight gained from observing a colleague, provide a summary of a chapter of *Circles of Learning,* or suggest a new way to structure positive interdependence. Guests (such as an innovative teacher, a local businessperson committed to team-based organizations, or the superintendent) may be invited to speak during this part of the meeting. A barrier to creating a cooperative school may be identified and a series of strategies to resolving it may be generated.

7. **Current fires.** If there is a current crisis in the school or district, save the discussion of it until after all other agenda items have been covered.

8. **Celebrate.** Congratulate each member on a good week and send each other off happy, optimistic, and enthusiastic.

(continued)

ACTIVITY 14.2 *Continued*

MEMBERSHIP GRID

Group members names	Topic 1	Topic 2	Topic 3	Topic 4

JOINT-PLANNING FORM

Goal	Who	How	When/Where
Co-op learning			
Social skills			
Helped colleague			

7. **Teacher training required.** Teachers need training to conduct valid and reliable assessments. Even when clear scoring standards have been developed, teachers may not apply the standards consistently without direct, systematic, ongoing training. This training has to be ongoing—just because teachers achieve a high level of interrater reliability at one time does not mean it will continue forever. Even experienced teachers are often guilty of "scoring criteria drift" by developing idiosyncratic scoring rules or discontinuing to use recommended scoring criteria.

8. **Continual refining and upgrading.** Once established, a rubric is not written in stone. The criteria used in rubrics need to undergo a continuous improvement process whereby teachers regularly discuss them and refine, upgrade, and improve the criteria and the words and phrases used to describe them.

Communicating the results of assessments may involve helping others understand what is and is not quality work. The more thoroughly students understand criteria and rubrics, the more able they are to produce it. Well-defined criteria and rubrics,

ACTIVITY **14.3** ■ CREATING RUBRICS TO ASSESS STUDENT LEARNING

Step 1. Define the assessment procedure. Indicate on the checklist below the procedures the team will use to assess students' learning.

_____	Quizzes, tests, examinations	_____	Homework, extra credit
_____	Compositions	_____	Other:
_____	Presentations	_____	Other:
_____	Projects, experiments, surveys, historical research		

Step 2. Develop a set of criteria to use in evaluating student performance. A checklist of steps for doing so follow.

_____ **a.** Brainstorm a potential list of criteria.

_____ **b.** Rank order the criteria from most important to least important.

_____ **c.** Construct a rubric for each criterion. Begin with the criterion ranked most important by listing indicators of very poor, poor, fair, good, and very good levels of performance.

_____ **d.** Find some exemplary and very poor student performances and analyze them to help develop a set of indicators that accurately measures their strengths and weaknesses.

_____ **e.** Apply the rubrics to a set of sample performances.

Step 3. Construct rubrics. Rubrics are needed to assess the quality and quantity of each student's performance for each criterion. A checklist for constructing rubrics follows.

_____ **a.** Begin with the criterion ranked most important.

_____ **b.** List indicators of very poor, poor, fair, good, and very good levels of performance.

_____ **c.** Find some exemplary and very poor student performances and analyze them to help develop a set of indicators that accurately measures their strengths and weaknesses.

Step 4. Train teachers to use the criteria and rubrics. Make sure teachers are cooriented, consistent, and reliable in their use of the rubric. Teachers have to be able to apply the same rubric in the same way at different times. Different teachers have to be able to apply the same rubric in the same way. A checklist for one training procedure follows:

_____ **a.** Score a student performance together as a group, discussing how the performance should be assessed on each criterion.

_____ **b.** Score a set of student performances separately, with each team member scoring the performances on his or her own. Then compare the scoring to see whether team members are using the rubrics in the same way.

_____ **c.** Score all student performances with at least two team members scoring each performance. Any differences in the scoring are then discussed

(continued)

ACTIVITY 14.3 *Continued*

until two or more team members agree on the scoring of each student performance.

Step 5. Plan how to improve the instructional program. Use the assessment as the basis for your plan. List your suggestions below.

a. _____

_____

b. _____

_____

c. _____

_____

Step 6. Continually improve in using the rubrics to assess the quality and quantity of student learning. Improve the criteria, the indicators for each criterion, and the team members' skills in using rubrics.

_____   a. Beware scoring criteria drift.

_____   b. Periodically recalibrate team members' use of the scoring rubrics.

_____   c. Search for exemplary rubrics and scoring procedures in other teams and schools.

_____   d. Use these examples as benchmarks to improve your team's assessment practices.

---

furthermore, point students toward (a) what they need to do next to improve and (b) the support they need to do so. The more thoroughly parents understand criteria and rubrics, the more able they are to help students produce quality work. Potential employers are more able to recognize the quality work students do as their understanding of the criteria and rubrics increases. The use of charts and graphs to explain student performance over time is especially helpful in the communication process.

CONTINUOUS IMPROVEMENT OF INSTRUCTION, ASSESSMENT, AND REPORTING

The colleagial teaching team uses the continuous improvement procedure to improve learning, instruction, assessment, and reporting. The team (a) defines the process it is using to instruct, assess, and report the results by drawing a picture of it as a flow chart or cause-and-effect diagram, (b) engages in the process, (c) measures each of its steps, displays the data, and analyzes it, (d) creates and implements an improvement plan that focuses on making small, incremental improvements in the process day after day after day, and (e) repeats steps b, c, and d over and over again (Johnson & Johnson, 1994). This continuous improvement process needs to be institutionalized in the daily ebb and flow of school life.

A procedure for creating the criteria to assess the implementation of the targeted procedures is benchmarking (Johnson & Johnson, 1994). **Benchmarking** is establishing

ACTIVITY **14.4** ■ LOW-COST ARRANGEMENTS FOR WORKING TOGETHER

Given below are a number of low-cost arrangements for giving teachers time to coplan and coteach in their colleagial support groups. Give the pluses and minuses for using each arrangement.

1. Administrator takes one or more classes to free teachers to meet or coteach.

Pluses: _____

_____

Minuses: _____

_____

2. Teachers arrange a round-robin in which one teacher takes more than one class to free colleagues to meet or coteach.

Pluses: _____

_____

Minuses: _____

_____

3. Classes are sent to the library for study and research so teachers can meet or coteach.

Pluses: _____

_____

Minuses: _____

_____

4. Aides, parents, or student teachers take one or more classes so teachers can meet or coteach.

Pluses: _____

_____

Minuses: _____

_____

5. P.E. or music teachers take several classes at the same time so teachers can meet or coteach.

Pluses: _____

_____

Minuses: _____

_____

criteria based on best-known practices. First, you identify criteria by (a) surveying the research to see what has proven to be effective and (b) locating the schools where it is most successfully implemented. If you can, visit the schools. Second, you set a goal to achieve that level of performance as a minimum in your classroom and school. Third, you plan how to modify the processes of learning, instructing, and reporting to achieve the goals (see Activity 14.4). Fourth, you assess the effectiveness of what you are doing and adapt the procedures and strategies to your specific situation. Finally, you continue to move your benchmark higher as you reach your initial goals. For colleagial teaching teams continuously to improve instruction and student learning, members must collect data on a regular basis, portray the data in quality charts, and use benchmarking to determine the criteria for effectiveness.

ASSESSMENT TEAMS

Assessing students means moving from a solitary activity to a collaborative effort in which teachers work together to share and improve their assessment practices and student learning. A small group of three to six teachers and/or administrators meet for 45 to 90 minutes. Working together to assess students tends to sharpen, enhance, and refine teachers' assessment and instructional practices and improve student learning. The collaboration among teachers is enhanced when meetings are structured with the use of protocols.

A **protocol** is a set of guidelines; agreed on by the teachers involved that structure and guide teachers' conversations regarding assessment and students. Protocols help build the procedures, skills, and culture necessary for teachers to collaborate in assessing the outcomes of student instruction and development. The use of protocols results in more in-depth, insightful discussions about teaching and learning. The structure created by a protocol increases teachers' willingness to ask each other challenging questions and ensures equity and parity in attending to each teacher's issues and concerns.

There are two types of protocols. One focuses on the assessment and reporting procedures being used by teachers, and the other focuses on a specific student that all the teachers have in their classes.

Team Meeting on Assessment Procedures

The goals of the team meeting are (a) to improve and refine teachers' assessment procedures and instructional practices and (b) to improve student learning. Roles are initially assigned and then rotated each meeting so that each member enacts each role for the same amount of time. The roles are

- Presenter: A teacher presents an assessment of his or her class or of a subset of students.
- Facilitator: Chairs the meeting and ensures that the group has a productive discussion by keeping the group focused on the particular issue addressed by each step of the protocol and ensuring the protocol is completed.
- Prober: Asks probing questions to ensure that an in-depth discussion of the assessment procedures' strengths and weaknesses takes place.
- Encourager of participation: Ensures all members participate and feel good about their contributions to the discussion.

The steps of the protocol are as follows:

Step 1. One teacher distributes samples of students' work and describes the assignment and the criteria and rubrics being used to assess the quality and quantity of the work. Everyone reads or examines the work individually. The presenting teacher is silent.

Step 2. The facilitator asks, "How would you describe this work?" Group members describe (without evaluation) what they see in the students' work. The presenting teacher listens without responding. The consistency of descriptions by the teachers should be noted and disagreements should be explored to increase the understanding of the assignment and the assessment criteria and rubrics.

Step 3. The facilitator asks, "What questions do you have about this work?" Group members raise any questions they have about the work, the students, the assignment, the circumstances under which the work was done, and so forth. The presenting teacher answers these questions. The emphasis is on probing questions that require the presenting teacher to go beneath the surface.

Step 4. The facilitator asks, "What are the strengths and weaknesses of the criteria and rubrics that are being used?" The group members raise any questions they have about the criteria and rubrics and suggest ways they could be improved. It is often helpful if the teachers construct a new five-point rubric for each criteria to describe the ideal for the students' work to the minimal completion of the assignment. The new rubrics are then applied to several students' work (choose high-, middle-, and low-achieving students). This will give the team members insights into how the lesson may be improved.

Step 5. The facilitator asks, "How may the lesson, assignment, assessment procedures, reporting procedures, and instructional procedures be improved?" A general discussion is conducted in which the overall lesson is discussed. Each member should make one suggestion as to how he or she can help improve the assessment and instructional procedures. At least three conclusions should be formally adopted to help the teacher move to the next step in improving assessment and instruction.

Step 6. The group processes how well they have worked together, what they have learned, and how the protocol could be improved next time.

Team Meeting on Individual Student

A team of teachers who teach the same students meet regularly to discuss the academic and social development of each student. One student is selected to be the focus for each meeting. The goals of the conference are (a) to assess the quality and quantity of the student's current work and social development and (b) to make a plan to support and facilitate the student's learning and social development. Every teacher on the team brings in samples of the chosen student's work.

Step 1. Each teacher reports on the progress they are making with the student who was discussed in the previous meeting. Students who have been discussed in previous meetings may also be brought up for progress reports.

Step 2. One teacher (responsibility rotates each meeting) gives a brief introduction that identifies the target student and provides a short description of his or her background and previous achievement and behavior in the school.

Step 3. Each teacher provides a sample of the student's work and a description of his or her behavioral patterns in their class. No judgments are made at this time.

Step 4. There is a general discussion of the student's strengths and weaknesses. Teachers should ask each other probing questions that move the discussion below the surface in describing the student's work and behavior.

Step 5. A plan is formulated. First there is a general discussion of what the faculty can do to support the student's achievement and social development. Second, each teacher specifies what he or she can do to support the student's education and development.

Step 6. The student who will be discussed at the next meeting is identified so each teacher can prepare for the discussion.

Step 7. Processing of the effectiveness of the meeting and what can be done to improve the effectiveness of the assessment meetings.

SUMMARY

The days are gone when a teacher, working in isolation from colleagues, could instruct, assess, and report results by him- or herself. The practices have become so labor intensive and complex that one teacher cannot expect to do them alone. Realistically, **colleagial teaching teams** are needed to coordinate and continuously improve the instruction, assessment, and reporting process. Teachers need to begin their instruction, assessment, and reporting efforts by forming a colleagial teaching team. This allows them to capitalize on the many ways teams enhance productivity.

The team focuses its efforts on continuously improving both student learning and the quality of instruction. The team as a whole conducts the assessment and reporting process by developing rubrics, applying the rubrics effectively, and reporting results to interested audiences. The team then establishes a continuous improvement process focusing on maximizing the quality of instruction of each member. While engaging in the continuous improvement process, the team establishes a parallel, continuous retraining process whereby team members learn to use instruction, assessment, and reporting procedures more effectively and to adapt and refine them as conditions change in the school. The team enlists the aid of all other school faculty to ensure that the school ecology supports and enhances learning and instruction. Teachers also form assessment teams in which they follow protocols to share and improve their assessment procedures and to focus on each student to make an individual plan how the faculty could help the student achieve and develop in healthy ways. Finally, teachers have to remember that establishing and maintaining effective colleagial teaching teams is not easy. It takes continual effort.

ASSESSMENT RUBRIC

Student: _____   Class: _____   Date: _____

Project: _____

Write the indicators for each of the five levels of performance for each criterion.

Criteria	Indicators				
	Very Poor	**Poor**	**Fair**	**Good**	**Very Good**
Criterion 1					
1.					
2.					
3.					
Criterion 2					
1.					
2.					
3.					
Criterion 3					
1.					
2.					
3.					
Criterion 4					
1.					
2.					
3.					

Criterion 5					
1.					
2.					
3.					

Comments:

ASSESSMENT RUBRIC

Student: _____ Class: _____ Date: _____

Project: _____

Write the indicators for each of the three levels of performance for each criterion.

	Indicators		
Criteria	**Inadequate**	**Fair**	**Excellent**
Criterion 1			
1.			
2.			
3.			
Criterion 2			
1.			
2.			
3.			
Criterion 3			
1.			
2.			
3.			
Criterion 4			
1.			
2.			
3.			

Criterion 5			
1.			
2.			
3.			

Comments:

CHAPTER FIFTEEN

GIVING GRADES

WHAT IS GRADING?

The Committee on Grading was called upon to study grading
procedures. At first, the task of investigating the literature seemed to
be a rather hopeless one. What a mass and a mess it all was! Could
order be brought out of such chaos? Could points of agreement among
American educators concerning the perplexing grading problem
actually be discovered? It was with considerable misgiving and
trepidation that the work was finally begun.

—Warren Middleton (1933)

Although the quality of student learning and the instructional program can be assessed in many different ways, periodically teachers are asked to give an overall
summation of the learning achieved by each student. This grading is not necessary
for instructional or learning processes. Teachers can teach without grades and students can and do learn without grades. Giving grades does not improve teaching
and receiving grades does not increase learning. Most teachers, however, are required by their school districts to grade students at regular intervals. This requirement is not new. The issues of grading and reporting on student learning have been
with us a long time. Many great minds have tried to resolve the difficulties of grading. Yet the difficulties persist. What Middleton struggled with over 60 years ago, we
struggle with today (see Box 15.1 for a brief history of grading).

Grades are given because they are perceived as being the most effective way of
communicating summative evaluations. **Grades** are symbols (letters, numbers, words)
that represent a value judgment concerning the relative quality of a student's achievement during a specified period of instruction. In grading you summarize and combine
each student's performances on a variety of assignments. You may even add in bonus
points for other aspects of achievement, such as effort, attendance, and participation in
class. Participating in Activity 15.1 will help you decide for yourself the importance of
various reasons for giving grades.

WHY GRADES MUST BE FAIR

The real voyage of discovery consists not in seeking new landscapes, but in having new eyes.
—Marcel Proust (French novelist, 1871–1922)

Grades are important. A student's grades may determine whether he or she is admitted into gifted education and advanced placement classes. A student's grades

■ ■ ■ ■ ■ ▬▬▬▬▬▬▬▬▬▬▬▬▬

BOX 15.1
HISTORY OF GRADING

Pre-1850	Throughout human history, assessment of what students have learned has always occurred. The ancient Greeks, for example, had students orally explain what they knew so teachers could determine which topics the student had yet to master. Summative evaluation with the use of grades, on the other hand, is relatively new.
1850s	Summative grades were introduced in the United States. Before this time, grading was virtually unknown.
Late 1880s	Teachers were asked to issue progress evaluations on each student by writing down the skills the student had mastered. Students who completed the requirements for one level could move up to the next level.
Early 1900s	With the dramatic increase in secondary education, high school teachers introduced percentages as a way to certify students' accomplishments in specific subject areas. Elementary teachers continued to use written descriptions to document student learning.
1912	The use of percentage grades was challenged as being unreliable by studies that demonstrated that different teachers gave markedly different percentile grades to the same English, history, or geometry papers.
1918	Many teachers adopted grading scales with fewer and larger categories. A 3-point scale used the categories *excellent, average,* and *poor.* A 5-point scale used the categories *excellent, good, average, poor,* and *failing* corresponding to the letters *A, B, C, D,* and *F.*
Early 1930s	Norm-referenced grading became popular as a way to reduce the subjectivity of grading. Some advocates specified that 6 percent of students in a class should receive an A, 22 percent a B, 44 percent a C, 22 percent a D, and 6 percent an F. The rationale was that because scores on intelligence tests in the United States approximated a normal probability curve, the achievement scores of students within any class would also.
Late 1930s	The debate over grading became so intense that a number of schools abolished formal grades altogether and returned to using verbal descriptions of student achievement. Other districts adopted pass–fail grading systems whereas yet others adopted a mastery approach in which students had to master a skill or content area before they moved on to other areas of study.
1950s	Researchers who focused on how best to use grades concluded that a combination of grades with narrative feedback was more effective in increasing student learning than were grades by themselves.
1980s	Researchers concluded that the person assessing students' work and giving grades was learning more than were the students receiving the grades, and, therefore, students should be assessing and evaluating each other's work.
1990s	Alternative assessment procedures, such as portfolios, were recommended.

determine which educational and career opportunities are available to him or her. A student's grades determine whether he or she receives certain honors and recognition (such as being a National Merit Scholar). In the 1960s, grades were used to determine which male college students were drafted by the military. Because drafted males were

ACTIVITY **15.1** ■ WHY GIVE GRADES?

Rank the following reasons for giving grades from most important (1) to least important (8).

_____ **1.** To make students conform to the demands of the instructional program (value the goals, be involved, complete assignments, learn)

_____ **2.** To provide students access to certain educational programs and careers

_____ **3.** To give students information about their level of achievement so they can (a) gauge their strengths and weaknesses, (b) better understand what is expected of them, and (c) better understand how they may improve

_____ **4.** To communicate a student's level of achievement to parents and other interested parties (such as college admission officers and potential employers)

_____ **5.** To give students an extrinsic reward or incentive to learn

_____ **6.** To sort students into categories and identify students for particular educational paths or programs

_____ **7.** To evaluate the effectiveness of an instructional program

_____ **8.** To punish students who do not comply with requests or obey rules, or who display a lack of effort, responsibility, civility, and respect

often sent to Vietnam and often killed there, college grades literally determined in some cases who lived and who died. The power of grades to determine a student's educational and career opportunities as well as future earnings makes grading perhaps the most serious responsibility teachers have. This may be why giving grades is frequently cited as the most difficult and least desirable task teachers face.

The fairness of grading depends largely on the basis for which they are distributed. Three possible bases for distributing grades to students are (1) _equity_ (the person who contributes the most or scores the highest receives the greatest reward), (2) _equality_ (every person receives the same reward), and (3) _need_ (those who have the greatest need receive the greatest reward). All three systems of **distributive justice** operate within our society and all three systems have ethical rationales. Typically, the equality system assures people that their basic needs will be met and that diverse contributions will be equally valued. The need system assures people that in moments of crisis others will provide support and assistance. The equity system assures people that if they strive for excellence, their contributions will be valued and rewarded. Educators who give rewards in the classroom merely on the basis of equity may be viewing "fairness" from too limited a perspective.

Whether grades are perceived as fair may depend on several factors (Johnson & Johnson, 1989):

1. Students who "lose" in competitive learning situations commonly perceive the grading system as unjust and, consequently, dislike the class and the teacher.

2. Before a task is performed, group members generally perceive a competitive grading system as being the most fair, but after a task is completed, having all members receive the same grade or reward is viewed as the fairest.
3. The more frequently students experience long-term cooperative learning experiences, and the more cooperative learning was used in their classes, the more students believe that (a) everyone who tries has an equal chance to succeed in class, (b) students get the grades they deserve, and (c) the grading system is fair.

Not all purposes can be accomplished with any one grade. Different teachers will use grades to accomplish different purposes and, therefore, conflicts over grading can arise in a school or district. Many primary teachers report that they give grades because the school district requires it whereas many middle and high school teachers report that they give grades to inform students of their progress.

SUBJECTIVE NATURE OF GRADING

One of the criticisms of grading is that grades are too subjective (Guskey & Bailey, 2001). In 1912 Starch and Elliott shocked educators into considering subjectivity by publishing a study in which two papers written for a first-year English class in high school were sent to English teachers in 200 high schools for grading. Each teacher was asked to score the papers according to his or her school's standards. A percentage (0 to 100) scale was to be used, with 75 percent as a passing grade. Fifteen percent of the teachers gave one paper a failing mark whereas 12 percent gave it a score of 90 or more. The scores ranged from 64 to 98 percent, with a mean of 88.2. The other paper received a mean score of 80.2 with scores ranging from 50 to 97. Some teachers graded the papers on whether they communicated their message whereas other teachers took into account neatness, spelling, and punctuation. Defenders of percentage grading criticized this study on the basis that judging good writing is, by its very nature, subjective. In 1913 Starch and Elliott, therefore, repeated their study using history and geometry papers. For the geometry papers they found even greater variations, with scores on one paper ranging from 28 to 95. Some teachers took neatness, form, and spelling into account whereas others graded only for correct answers.

No matter what you do, grading and reporting will *always* involve some degree of *subjectivity.* Subjectivity opens the door to bias. Teachers' prejudices and expectations can influence their judgments of students' achievements and performances, and certain characteristics (such as handwriting) can significantly influence a teacher's judgment. Subjectivity of grading is increased when ambiguous student behaviors are included in the grade estimates. Subjectivity can be reduced by (a) making the criteria contained in the scoring rubric specific and detailed and (b) ensuring that all teachers in the school district use the same criteria. Having each student performance evaluated by more than one teacher can also reduce subjectivity.

TYPES OF GRADING SYSTEMS

Two types of grading systems are single grade and multigrade. Most commonly, teachers have used a single-mark system of grading in which students receive an A, B, C, D, or F. The single-mark system of grading is simple, concise, and convenient. The most common single-mark system is letter grades:

A	Excellent, outstanding work	Distinguished	4 Points
B	Good, noteworthy work	Proficient	3 Points

C	Average, competent work	Apprentice	2 Points
D	Poor, minimally acceptable work	Novice	1 Point
F	Failing, unacceptable work		0 Points

In elementary school, teachers sometimes use single-mark system of outstanding/satisfactory/unsatisfactory. Some secondary schools use a pass–fail or pass–no credit system.

The advantages of the single-mark system are that grades (a) provide a succinct description of achievement, (b) are generally understood, (c) predict future grades and how many years of conventional education students can attain, (d) motivate students to expend more effort to achieve (perhaps more to avoid the consequences of low grades than to attain high grades), and (e) are positive recognition of success.

The disadvantages of the single-mark system are that single grades (a) cannot give a full picture of the many facets of achievement, (b) are limited to one particular frame of reference, (c) are inherently ambiguous as to what they represent (as they are not keyed to any common standard), and (d) may discourage effort to learn by creating a ceiling for high achievers and demoralizing lower-achieving students.

Grading involves other problems as well. One is that a grade is essentially arbitrary. There is no way to make meaningful "break points" between the different grades. If a grade of B ranges from 80 to 89 percent, students at both ends of that range receive the same grade even though their scores differ by nine points, but the student with a score of 79 (a 1-point difference) receives a grade of C. A second problem is that grades are often overgeneralized so that they are taken as an indication of a student's total competence and worth as an individual, rather than as a summative evaluation of the student's mastery of certain limited knowledge and skills.

A third problem is the wide diversity among teachers as to the criteria they use when assigning grades. Although the criteria for awarding grades is sometimes specified by the school district, most often each teacher uses very broad guidelines in deciding what criteria to use in grading students. A teacher may be questioned if he or she gives most students As or Fs, but between these two extremes teachers have considerable leeway to assign grades on any basis they wish.

A fourth problem is that grades have little value as either incentives or feedback because they are often given infrequently, far removed from student performance, and poorly tied to student behaviors. Finally, the evidence indicates that grades are nearly useless in developing important qualities, for example, inventiveness, leadership, workmanship, good citizenship, personal maturity, and family happiness.

A **multigrade system** may involve different grades for different aspects of learning. Grades may focus on **product criteria** (a summative evaluation of student achievement that focuses on what students know and are able to do), **process criteria** (the processes students use to learn, including effort and work habits), or **progress criteria** (improvement scoring, learning gain). Although a combination of the three may be used to determine grades, usually the more process and progress criteria are taken into account, the more subjective and biased grades may become. Grades have also been proposed for (a) how the student's achievement compares with other students at the same grade level or with the standards set by the district, state, or country or (b) the degree of the student's effort.

STANDARDIZING YOUR SCORING SYSTEM

At the end of each grading period, you need to standardize your scoring system, combine the data on each student, and determine the total number of points earned by each student during the course. When you assign grades you usually combine the results from a variety of types of assessments. A student, for example, may have scores for tests, compositions, and projects. At the end of the grading period, add together all the scores for each type of performance and compare the actual number of points earned with the total possible number of points.

These different performances may be of different importance and, therefore, may be given different weights. The tests, for example, may count for 50 percent of the grade, the compositions may count for 25 percent, and the project may count for 25 percent. If all the assessments are converted to numerical scores, then the scores can be systematically combined. There are two steps in doing so: (a) Equalize the ranges of scores for the different performances and (b) multiply by the desired weight of each type of performance (Gronlund, 1998). Consider the following example.

Performance	Percent of Grade	Desired Weight	Range of Scores	Multiplier to Equate Ranges	Weight to Apply to Performances
Tests	50	2	40 to 200	1	2 × 1 = 2
Compositions	25	1	60 to 120	3	1 × 3 = 3
Project	25	1	10 to 50	4	1 × 4 = 4

Students	Raw Scores			Weighted Scores			Composite Score
				a (× 2)	b (× 3)	c (× 4)	$a(w) + b(w) + c(w)$ where w = weight
	a	b	c	where a, b, c = three different raw scores			
Frank	185	105	45	185 × 2 = 370	105 × 3 = 315	45 × 4 = 180	370 + 315 + 180 = 865
Helen	142	101	40	142 × 2 = 284	101 × 3 = 303	40 × 4 = 160	284 + 303 + 160 = 747
Roger	100	110	43	100 × 2 = 200	110 × 3 = 330	43 × 4 = 172	200 + 330 + 172 = 702

To interpret the data in these charts, follow the steps below:

1. At the end of the grading period, add together all the scores for each type of performance. Decide what percentage of the grade each performance will have. (See column 2 in the first chart.)

2. Decide how much weight each type of performance should have in the final grade. Weight the different assignments according to their accuracy in demonstrating what students have actually learned during the course. (See column 3 in the first chart.)

3. Determine the range of scores for each performance. (See column 4 in the first chart.)

4. Calculate the weight of each range so that they are equalized. (See column 5 in the first chart.)

5. Multiply the desired weight by the weight needed to equalize ranges to determine the weight given to each total score. (See column 6 in the first chart.)

6. Multiply the raw score for each performance by the total weight to determine the composite score for each student's performance for the grading period. (See column 7 in the second chart.)

7. Add together the composite scores to determine the final score. (See column 8 in the second chart.)

8. Look for extremely low scores on an assignment that may bias the results. Remember that the final grade should reflect what the student has actually learned and mastered. Use your judgment in discarding any extremely low scores that may have unfair influence on the final grade. Then recalculate the weighted score for that type of performance.

HOW TO GRADE

The power of grades to impact students' future life creates a responsibility for giving grades in a fair and impartial way. A procedure for doing so follows.

1. **Decide what the grade will represent.**
   a. Decide on the primary purpose of the grade. Usually, the purpose of grading is to indicate how much each student learned during the course; that is, the grade reflects achievement and achievement only.
   b. Decide for whom the grade is intended. Usually, the grade is primarily intended for the student.
   c. Decide on the results you are hoping to achieve with the grade. Usually, the hoped-for result is to enhance students' learning.

2. **Decide what student performances will be included in the grade.** A number of different performances should be used. Too frequently grades are based only on test scores. The validity of grades increases when other performances such as compositions, projects, laboratory work, and presentations are included.

3. **Describe to students, at the beginning of the instructional unit, what the grading procedures will be.** This includes what performances are included in the final grade and how much weight is given to each performance. Students should know at the beginning of the course how many points earn an A and how each assignment is weighted. Grades should never surprise students. Students should know how they are doing throughout a course and know how their grades are computed. Students should receive a handout describing what each letter grade represents.

4. **Estimate what percentage of students should receive each grade.** After grades have been awarded, you compare the actual number of students who received each grade with your ideal estimate.

5. **Set criteria for making categorical judgments about student performances in cooperative and individualistic contexts.** Seek help from the curriculum coordinator, subject matter specialists, teacher committees, the school administration, and from parents and students.

6. **Rank the students from best to worst in a competitive context.** The number of competitive learning situations should be limited to avoid their destructive effects. For a discussion of the conditions under which competition may be used constructively, see Johnson, Johnson, and Holubec (1998).

7. **Standardize the scoring system and determine the total number of points earned by each student during the course.**

8. **Personalize the evaluation.** Include notes on incidents and behaviors, with dates, summaries of conferences with parents and other teachers, and long-term growth information. Grades should not stand alone. Comprehensive, written narrative and checklist evaluations should be added to provide more information to students.

9. **Avoid practices that result in grades that misrepresent the student's level of achievement.** Grades should question the question, "What is the level of the student's achievement?" Grades misrepresent students' achievement when they are determined by averaging or when zeros have been assigned to missing or late work (Guskey, 1994; Guskey & Bailey, 2001).

   a. Averaging fails to provide an accurate description of what students have learned. If a student gets a B on a comprehensive final exam, for example, but receives a C as a final grade once all the test scores have been averaged, the C is confusing because clearly the student has learned the assigned material at a B level. Yet many teachers would give the student a C by averaging his or her scores over the entire course.

   b. When a student receives a score of zero for work that is late, missed, or neglected, his or her chances for a grade of A are usually eliminated because a single extreme score skews the average. If a student receives four As and one 0, for example, the resulting average would be a grade of B for the course. The grade of B misrepresents the student's actual mastery of the material covered in the course. The zero is usually assigned to punish students for not displaying appropriate responsibility.

Some districts have eliminated traditional letter grades at the primary level or even through the eighth grade and replaced them with checklists and narratives. Even in some high schools and colleges, traditional letter grades are being replaced with portfolios and other alternative assessment procedures. In addition, many special education students' needs and abilities are not addressed by traditional testing and grading procedures. Alternatives to these procedures are listed in Box 15.2.

CHECKLISTS AND NARRATIVES

Because of the limitations of a single-mark system of grading, some schools have adopted more complex and complete summative evaluation procedures, such as checklists and narratives.

Checklists

Checklists are aimed at providing a detailed analysis of the student's strengths and weaknesses. The advantages of checklists include (a) providing a clear description of achievement and (b) being useful for diagnosing what students do and do not know and for prescribing what students should study next. The disadvantages of checklists include (a) being often too complicated to understand and (b) seldom communicating appropriate progress students are making in relation to expectations for their levels.

■ ■ ■ ■ ■ ▬▬▬▬▬▬▬▬▬▬▬▬▬▬▬▬▬▬▬▬▬▬

BOX 15.2
CRITERIA FOR TESTING AND GRADING SPECIAL EDUCATION STUDENTS

TESTS
- Give tests orally, with questions and answers.
- Teacher, other student, or resource teacher reads regular test to student.
- Give regular test but allow using open book, class notes, or both.
- Modify modality of test, from written to oral (or vice versa as necessary), and from essay to multiple-choice questions.
- Redo test if it is not passed.
- Lower criterion for passing.
- Have cooperative group give test orally to student.

HOMEWORK AND IN-CLASS ASSIGNMENTS
- Have classmate or aide record reading assignments or read aloud to students.
- Have classmate read the assignment to students and help write answers.
- Give regular assignments with lower criteria for passing.
- Shorten the regular assignment (e.g., assign half the questions).
- Grade assignments as "complete" rather than with a letter grade.
- Modify the set of questions students answer.
- Have students give oral answers to teacher or classmate.
- Redo assignment if it is incorrect.
- Give credit for appropriate actions not normally graded, such as taking notes.
- Give extra credit for projects that student or teacher suggests.
- Have cooperative group supervise and assist student to complete the assignment.

Narratives

A narrative is a detailed, personal report written by the teacher containing all that is known about the student. The advantages of narratives are (a) providing a clear description of progress and achievement and (b) being useful for diagnosing what students do and do not know and prescribing what they should learn next. The disadvantages include (a) being time consuming for teachers to prepare, (b) not communicating appropriate student progress, and (c) containing standardized comments.

Narratives allow teachers the greatest latitude in personal judgment. Many teachers know their students, understand various dimensions of students' work, and have clear ideas about the progress students are making. Teacher judgments may yield accurate descriptions of what students have learned.

GIVING STUDENTS GRADES IN COOPERATIVE LEARNING

The way grades are given depends on the type of interdependence the instructor creates among students (Johnson, Johnson, & Holubec, 1998a). Norm-referenced grading systems place students in competition with each other. Criterion-referenced grading systems require students to work either individually or cooperatively. A number of suggestions for giving grades in cooperative learning situations are described.

1. **Individual score plus bonus points based on all members reaching criterion.** Group members study together and ensure that all have mastered the assigned material. Each then takes a test individually and is awarded that score. If all group members achieve over a preset criterion of excellence, each receives a bonus. An example follows.

Criteria	Bonus	Members	Scores	Bonus	Total
100	15 points	Bill	100	10	110
90–99	10 points	Juanita	95	10	105
80–89	5 points	Sally	90	10	100

2. **Individual score plus bonus points based on lowest score.** The group members prepare each other to take an exam. Members then receive bonus points on the basis of the lowest individual score in their group. This procedure emphasizes encouraging, supporting, and assisting the low achievers in the group. The criterion for bonus points can be adjusted for each learning group, depending on the past performance of their lowest member. Consider the following example.

Criteria	Bonus	Members	Scores	Bonus	Total
90–100	6 points	Bill	93	2	95
80–89	4 points	Juanita	85	2	87
70–79	2 points	Sally	78	2	80

3. **Individual score plus group average.** Group members prepare each other to take an exam. Each takes the examination and receives his or her individual score. The scores of the group members are then averaged. The average is added to each member's score. An example follows.

Student	Individual Score	Group Average	Final Score
Bill	66	79	145
Juanita	89	79	168

| Sally | 75 | 79 | 154 |
| Benjamin | 86 | 79 | 165 |

4. **Individual score plus bonus based on improvement scores.** Members of a co-operative group prepare each other to take an exam. Each takes the exam individually and receives his or her individual grade. In addition, bonus points are awarded on the basis of whether members' percentage on the current test is higher than the average percentage on all past tests (i.e., their usual level of performance). Their percentage correct on past tests serves as the base score that they try to better. Every two tests or scores, the base score is updated. If a student scores within 4 points (above or below) his or her base score, all members of the group receive 1 bonus point. If they score 5 to 9 points above their base score, each group member receives 2 bonus points. Finally, if they score 10 points or above their base score, or score 100 percent correct, each member receives 3 bonus points.

5. **Totaling members' individual scores.** The individual scores of members are added together and all members receive the total. For example, if group members scored 90, 85, 95, and 90, each member would receive the score of 360.

6. **Averaging of members' individual scores.** The individual scores of members are added together and divided by the number of group members. Each member then receives the group average as their mark. For example, if the scores of members were 90, 95, 85, and 90, each group member would receive the score of 90.

7. **Group score on a single product.** The group works to produce a single report, essay, presentation, worksheet, or exam. The product is evaluated and all members receive the score awarded. When this method is used with worksheets, sets of problems, and examinations, group members are required to reach consensus on each question and be able to explain it to others. The discussion within the group enhances the learning considerably.

8. **Randomly selecting one member's paper to score.** Group members all complete the work individually and then check each other's papers and certify that they are perfectly correct. Because each paper is certified by the whole group to be correct, it makes little difference which paper is graded. The instructor picks one at random, grades it, and all group members receive the score.

9. **Randomly selecting one member's exam to score.** Group members prepare for an examination and certify that each member has mastered the assigned material. All members then take the examination individually. Because all members have certified that each has mastered the material being studied, it makes little difference which exam is scored. The instructor randomly picks one, scores it, and all group members receive that score.

10. **All members receive lowest member score.** Group members prepare each other to take the exam. Each takes the examination individually. All group members then receive the lowest score in the group. For example, if group members score 89, 88, 82, and 79, all members would receive 79 as their score. This procedure emphasizes encouraging, supporting, and assisting the low-achieving members of the group and often produces dramatic increases in performance by low-achieving students.

11. **Average of academic scores plus collaborative skills performance score.** Group members work together to master the assigned material. They take an examination individually and their scores are averaged. Concurrently, their

work is observed and the frequency of performance of specified collaborative skills (such as leadership or trust-building actions) is recorded. The group is given a collaborative skills performance score, which is added to their academic average to determine their overall mark.

12. **Dual academic and nonacademic rewards.** Group members prepare each other for a test, take it individually, and receive an individual grade. On the basis of their group average they are awarded free time, popcorn, extra recess time, or some other valued reward.

SUMMARY

Teachers need to assess student learning and progress frequently, but they do not need to evaluate or give grades. Assessing involves checking on how students are doing, what they have learned, and what problems or difficulties they have experienced. **Grades** are symbols that represent a value judgment concerning the relative quality of a student's achievement during a specified period of instruction. Grades are necessary to inform students and other interested audiences about students' level of achievement, evaluate the success of an instructional program, provide students access to certain educational opportunities, and reward students who excel.

Grading systems may involve a single grade or multigrades. It is vital that grades are awarded fairly as they can have considerable influence on students' futures. Being fair includes using a wide variety of assignments to measure achievement. Grades may be supplemented with checklists and narratives to provide a more complex and complete summative evaluation of student achievement. Having students work in cooperative groups adds further opportunity to measure aspects of students' learning and assign grades in a variety of ways.

GRADING AND COMMUNICATING
STUDENT LEARNING

Class: _____ Grade: _____ Date: _____

Answer each of the questions below as honestly as you can.

1. What are your reasons for giving grades?

   a. _____

   b. _____

   c. _____

2. For whom is the information intended? _____

3. What are the desired results?

   a. _____

   b. _____

4. For your class, indicate (a) what percentage of students should ideally receive each grade and (b) what percentage of students receive each grade:

Grades	Your Class	Ideally
A		
B		
C		
D		
F		

5. List assignments you structured in the following ways.

   a. Cooperatively (criteria referenced): _____

   _____

   b. Individually (criteria referenced): _____

   _____

c. Competitively (norm referenced): _____

_____

6. Standardize the scoring systems and use the chart below to determine the total number of points earned by each student during the course.

Performance	Percentage Points	Weight	Total
Tests, quizzes			
Compositions			
Oral presentations			
Projects, experiments			
Portfolio			
On-task, reasoning			
Social skills, helping others			
Positive attitudes			
Learning log, journal			
Quality chart			
Homework, extra credit			
Attendance, participation			
Grand Total			

7. What are the criteria on which the final grade will be based (never assign final grades on a norm-referenced basis)?

Grade	Points
A	
B	

C	
D	
F	

8. How will you personalize the grade for each student?

   a. _____

   _____

   b. _____

   _____

   c. _____

   _____

9. What do you like most about assigning grades and using report cards?

   a. _____

   b. _____

   c. _____

10. What do you like least about assigning grades and using report cards?

   a. _____

   b. _____

   c. _____

CHAPTER SIXTEEN

INVOLVING STUDENTS IN ASSESSMENT

WHY INVOLVE STUDENTS?

Involving students in the creation of the criteria and rubrics needed to assess students' current work may significantly improve the quality of your assessment in a number of ways (Johnson & F. Johnson, 2000). One of the most important impacts of involvement is understanding the assessment criteria and rubrics. Involving students in this process tends to increase their understanding of the criteria and rubrics as well as what is expected of them in the learning situation. Because the criteria and rubrics represent students' own thinking, students have the ability to understand them.

Unless students take the assessment seriously and strive to provide valid and reliable performances, the assessment is not worth doing. Involving students tends to increase their sense of ownership for the procedures, criteria, and rubrics. Individuals tend be open to and interested in using assessment procedures, criteria, and rubrics when they feel a sense of ownership whereas they tend to be closed to and reject assessment procedures, criteria, and rubrics when they are imposed on them by others. For many students, teacher-conducted assessments are threatening. Defensiveness by the students can result in resistance to and distortion of feedback concerning the quality of their performances. Student defensiveness can be reduced by increasing their ownership of the assessment criteria and rubrics.

Involving students tends to increase students' commitment to implement the assessment procedures in a high-quality way. Compared with teachers explaining assessment procedures or having student committees help plan the assessment, direct involvement of all students in planning the assessment results in stronger commitment to implement the procedures. Individuals tend to be committed to procedures they have helped plan whereas they tend to reject, subvert, and resist procedures imposed on them by others.

Involving students can increase the quality of the criteria and rubrics. In general, the more students participate, the more resources are available and, consequently, the higher is the quality of the resulting criteria and rubrics. Students may be especially valuable for planning valid and reliable criteria and rubrics because they have the unique perspective of having been assessed many, many times.

Finally, involving students can increase their positive attitudes toward the assessment. Involving students in planning assessments tends to result in public commitment to complete assignments at a high level of quality and in the awareness that classmates are making the same commitment. What tends to result is greater motivation to learn and more positive attitudes toward learning and assessment.

Once the students help create the criteria and rubrics, they may be involved in using them to assess their own and their classmates' work. There are several advantages to such involvement (Johnson, Johnson, & Holubec, 1998a).

First, the assessment of classmates' work is a powerful teaching tool. Students may learn more from assessing their classmates' work than from the feedback they receive on their own work. By determining the quality of a classmate's topic sentences, for example, the student may learn more about how to write a good topic sentence than he or she does from receiving feedback about his or her own topic sentences. Just as true as the saying "Whoever explains, learns" may be the expression "Whoever assesses, learns." In addition, participating in assessments directs students' attention toward the intended outcomes of instruction. It requires students' to learn at the levels of understanding, application, and interpretation (as opposed to the level of knowledge simply), thereby increasing their retention and transfer of what is being taught. Having students use the criteria and rubrics to assess classmates' work increases the likelihood that students learn, retain, and transfer what is being taught.

Second, involving students can increase the frequency and quality of self-assessments. Assessing the work of classmates helps students gain insight into the quality of their own work, the degree of skill they have in various areas, and any misconceptions they have that need correction. Self-assessments tend to provide students with short-term goals, clarify the steps to be taken to complete assignments, and provide feedback concerning their learning progress.

Third, involving students in conducting assessments makes assessments more manageable. The limits on teachers' time restrict the frequency with which teacher assessments can take place. When students conduct peer assessments, the frequency with which assessments can take place increases dramatically. A teacher, for example, may only have time to assess students' writing once a month whereas students can assess each other's writing every day. Two ways in which students may be involved in the assessment process are helping create the criteria and rubrics used to assess students' work and communicating to their parents and other interested stakeholders the results of their efforts to learn.

HOW TO INVOLVE STUDENTS IN CREATING CRITERIA AND RUBRICS

The first step in involving students in creating the criteria and rubrics is to define the assessment procedure (Johnson, Johnson, & Holubec, 1998a). The procedure could be quizzes or examinations, standardized tests, written compositions, oral presentations, projects or experiments, surveys, historical projects, or learning logs and journals.

The second step is involving students in developing a set of criteria to use in evaluating the performance produced by students. A **criterion** is a predetermined standard used to assess a performance. Involving students in creating the criteria and rubrics for assessing students' efforts does not mean turning over total control to students. You, the teacher, have a responsibility for ensuring that criteria critical for instructional objectives are included. Because you have a clear idea of what some of the criteria should be, however, does not mean that you have to set all or even most of the criteria. You may want to reach an agreement with students whereby you set one-third or one-half of the criteria and they decide on the rest. The steps for involving students in setting criteria are to have students (a) brainstorm a potential list of criteria and (b) rank the criteria from most important to least important. Involve the whole class in deciding what criteria should be used in assessing students' efforts. You, of course, should ensure that criteria critical for instructional objectives are included.

The third step is to construct a rubric for each criterion. A **rubric** is a list of indicators of different levels of a criterion being used to assess a performance. A rubric is usually a scale ranking from *poor* to *good*. Rubrics are needed to assess the quality and quantity of each student's performance for each criterion. Students should construct a rubric for each criterion. Begin with the criterion ranked most important by listing indicators of very poor, poor, fair, good, and very good levels of performance. Once the rubrics are developed, they must be field tested and refined before they are adopted. Field testing consists of two steps: (a) having assessors analyze exemplary and very poor student performances to ensure each rubric accurately measures the students' strengths and weaknesses and (b) applying each rubric to a set of sample performances to ensure it works. Once the rubrics have been field tested, they may be adopted.

The fourth step is to train assessors so that they are cooriented, consistent, and reliable in their use of the criteria and rubrics. Assessors have to be able to apply the same rubric in the same way at different times. Different assessors have to be able to apply the same rubric in the same way. One procedure for training is to have assessors (a) score a student performance together as a group, discussing how the performance ranks on the rubric for each criterion, (b) score a set of student performances separately, with each group member scoring the performances on his or her own and then comparing the scoring to see whether team members are using the rubrics in the same way, and (c) have at least two group members score each performance and discuss any differences in their scoring until they agree.

The fifth step is to use the results of the assessment to plan how to improve the instructional program. The sixth step is to improve continuously the criteria, the rubrics, and the assessors' skills in using the rubrics to assess the quality and quantity of student learning. Continuous improvement is needed to ensure the subjective definition of criteria and rubrics do not drift or change. **Scoring criteria drift** exists when, after assessing numerous performances, the assessor's definition of the criteria (and rubrics) changes or is modified. As the assessor gains more and more experience a new idiosyncratic rubric is created. Ongoing training is needed to recalibrate periodically assessors' use of the scoring rubrics: just because assessors achieve a high level of interrater reliability at one time does not mean it will continue forever. Criteria and rubrics can sometimes be improved by enriching them with insight and information from other classes and schools.

In addition to retraining assessors periodically, criteria and rubrics need to change as the academic year progresses. What is expected of students in September is different from what is expected in January. As students master more and more knowledge and skills, the criteria and rubrics used to assess the quality of their work needs to become more demanding and reflect higher standards. Activity 16.1 guides you throught these six steps in involving students in the assessment process.

STUDENT-LED CONFERENCES

The purpose of the postevaluation conference is to review the student's progress in achieving his or her learning goals (Bailey & Guskey, 2001). In the postevaluation conference the student explains his or her level of achievement (what the student learned and failed to learn) to interested parties (cooperative learning group, teacher, parents), which naturally leads to the next goal-setting conference. Student-led conferences with parents are one example of a postevaluation conference.

Student-led conferences involve three groups of individuals: parents, students, and teachers. They are a modification of the traditional teacher–parent conference. Instead of the teacher explaining to the parent what the student has been studying and how well the student is learning, the teacher (a) helps the student prepare a portfolio and a presentation, (b) helps the student explain to his or her parent what has been learned, and (c) assesses how well the conference went. There are three phases to student-led conferences.

ACTIVITY **16.1** ■ CREATING RUBRICS TO ASSESS STUDENT LEARNING

Step 1. Define the assessment procedure. Indicate on the checklist below the procedures the team will use to assess students' learning.

_____	Quizzes, tests, examinations	_____	Homework, extra credit
_____	Compositions	_____	Other:
_____	Presentations	_____	Other:
_____	Projects, experiments, surveys, historical research		

Step 2. Develop a set of criteria to use in evaluating students performance. A checklist of steps for doing so follows.

_____ **a.** Brainstorm a potential list of criteria

_____ **b.** Rank order the criteria from most important to least important.

Step 3. Construct rubrics. Rubrics are needed to assess the quality and quantity of each student's performance for each criterion. A checklist for constructing a rubric for each criterion follows.

_____ **a.** Begin with the criterion ranked most important.

_____ **b.** List indicators of very poor, poor, fair, good, and very good levels of performance.

_____ **c.** Field test the rubric by applying it to examples of exemplary and very poor student performances to ensure the rubric accurately measures students' strengths and weaknesses.

_____ **d.** Field test the rubric by applying the rubric to a set of sample performances.

Step 4. Train students to use the criteria and rubrics. Make sure they are co-oriented, consistent, and reliable in their use of the criteria and rubrics. Assessors have to be able to apply the same rubric in the same way at different times. Different assessors have to be able to apply the same rubric in the same way. A checklist for one training procedure follows.

_____ **a.** Score a student performance together as a group, discussing how the performance should be assessed on each criterion.

_____ **b.** Score a set of student performances separately, with each team member scoring the performances on his or her own. Then compare the scoring to see whether team members are using the rubrics in the same way.

_____ **c.** Score all student performances with at least two team members scoring each performance. Any differences in the scoring are then discussed until two or more team members agree on the scoring of each student performance.

(continued)

ACTIVITY 16.1   *Continued*

Step 5. Plan how to improve the instructional program. Use the assessment results as the basis for your plans. List your suggestions below.

a. _____

b. _____

c. _____

Step 6. Continually improve in using the rubrics to assess the quality and quantity of student learning. Improve the criteria, the rubrics, and the assessors' skills in using rubrics.

_____   **a.** Beware scoring criteria drift.

_____   **b.** Periodically recalibrate team members' use of the scoring rubrics.

_____   **c.** Search for exemplary criteria and rubrics other classes and schools are using.

_____   **b.** Use these examples as benchmarks to improve your classes' assessment practices.

Phase I: Preparing for the Conference

There are five procedures for students to do before a conference.

1. Make an invitation for parents to attend the conference with the date, time, and place specified.
2. Create a portfolio.
3. Practice the introduction to the conference.
4. Role play the conference to practice their presentations.
5. Set up the room for the conference.

The cooperative learning group prepares each member for the conference by helping him or her compile a portfolio. The portfolio includes the student's (a) best work in the various subject areas, (b) progress reaching his or her learning goals, and (c) efforts to help groupmates reach their goals. Once the portfolio is constructed, the group helps the student prepare effective presentation aids and practice and refine the conference presentation. In preparing and practicing the presentation, students become well rehearsed in presenting their work and the rubrics used to evaluate it. They master the language needed to communicate their learning goals and academic efforts, and learn how to describe their progress.

Phase II: Conducting the Conference

Each student, with the teacher serving as coleader and coach, presents his or her work to his or her parents and discusses the next steps he or she will take to improve academically. Placing students in charge of the conference makes each student individually accountable, encourages students to take pride in their work, and encourages student–parent communication about school performance. A procedure for conducting the conference follows.

1. The student picks up the portfolio, goes to the table designated for the conference, and sits down with his or her parents.
2. The student introduces the portfolio to his or her parents, explains what the portfolio is, and gives an overview of what it contains. A portfolio organizer and table of contents helps this part of the presentation.
3. The student describes each section of the portfolio, explaining the rationale for why each work sample was included and why it represents a significant indicator of learning. A student, for example, might show writing samples from September, October, and November to show how his or her skills have been improving.
4. The teacher moves from conference to conference, monitoring the presentations and giving assistance when it is needed. When the teacher arrives, the student introduces the teacher to his or her parents.
5. The student concludes the presentation with a summary of what has been accomplished and what is yet to be done.
6. The student asks his or her parents to write any comments or suggestions they have for the student and to complete a reaction form to the conference. If the parents wish to have a conference only with the teacher, they may sign up to do so.
7. The student returns the portfolio to its place and reflects on how well the conference went.

Phase III: Assessing the Quality of the Conference

An assessment of the student's progress is made by (a) the student, (b) the cooperative learning group, (c) the teacher, and (d) the parents.

SUMMARY

Few actions are more important to conducting a high-quality assessment than involving students. Although students can be involved in each step of the assessment process, two steps in the process to ensure student involvement are particularly important: students developing the criteria and rubrics for assessing their work and students communicating the results of their efforts to learn to parents and other interested stakeholders.

ASSESSMENT RUBRIC

Student: _____   Class: _____   Date: _____

Project: _____

Write the indicators for each of the five levels of performance for each criterion.

Criteria	Indicators				
	Very Poor	Poor	Fair	Good	Very Good
Criterion 1					
1.					
2.					
3.					
Criterion 2					
1.					
2.					
3.					
Criterion 3					
1.					
2.					
3.					
Criterion 4					
1.					
2.					
3.					

Criterion 5					
1.					
2.					
3.					

Comments:

PORTFOLIO ORGANIZER

Name: _____   Class: _____   Date: _____

Reading	Writing
Science	**Math**
Social Studies	**Physical Education**

I believe I do the following well:

1. _____

2. _____

3. _____

Your comments and suggestions:

■ ■ ■ ■ ■ ■ ■ ■ ■

CHAPTER SEVENTEEN

REFLECTIONS

CONDUCTING ASSESSMENTS

In the time of change, learners inherit the earth, while the learned find themselves beautifully equipped to deal with a world that no longer exists.

—Eric Hoffer

There is far more to assessment than giving students tests. It is vital to assess what students know, understand, and retain over time (academic learning). It is equally important to assess (a) the quality and level of their reasoning processes and (b) their skills and competencies (such as oral and written communication skills and skills in using technology). In today's complex and ever-changing world, a broad view of education is needed rather than a narrow focus on the memorization of facts. More than ever, schools need to focus on teaching students appropriate work habits (such as completing work on time and striving for quality work and continuous improvement) and attitudes (such as a love of learning, a desire to read good literature, and a commitment to democracy).

In achieving these complex and long-term responsibilities of the school, teachers need to conduct three types of assessments: diagnostic, formative, and summative. These assessments need to focus on both the process and the outcomes of learning and instruction. Assessments need to take place in more authentic settings as well as in the classroom. The number of stakeholders in education have increased as the world economy and the interdependence among nations have increased. And the stakes of many of the assessments have increased, as students' futures are more and more determined by what they have learned and how many years of formal education they have completed. The standards and testing movement has increased the stakes for student achievement for students, teachers, administrators, and parents. As the seriousness of educators' responsibilities increase, so does the need to use a wider variety of assessment procedures.

Making Assessments Meaningful and Manageable

To conduct an assessment, you collect information about the quality or quantity of change in students, groups, classes, schools, teachers, or administrators. Your assessment is effective if it achieves its goals while it maintains effective working relationships between you and the individuals you are assessing and increases their motivation to participate in future assessments. If one of more of these conditions is not achieved, then your assessment is not effective.

Two of your central issues in conducting assessments are making the assessment meaningful and ensuring the assessment is manageable. When assessments are perceived to be meaningless, student and teacher motivation to participate in them decrease and may become nonexistent. An assessment tends to be seen as meaningless when its purpose seems trivial; the procedures, criteria, and rubrics seem ambiguous or impossible to understand; and the results have no relevance to future efforts to learn. Meaningless assessments are viewed as a waste of time and as deserving little commitment of energy and other resources. It is possible that the state department officials, administrators, or teachers may consider an assessment meaningful whereas students do not. All participants need to believe the assessment is meaningful. The persons whose performance is being measured need to believe the assessment is meaningful, otherwise they will be unmotivated to participate and the results will be both invalid and unreliable. In schools, it is usually students who are assessed; therefore, students especially, need to believe the assessment is meaningful.

When conducting an assessment of students, you ensure that they (a) perceive the assessment as having a significant purposes; (b) clearly understand the procedures, criteria, and rubrics being used; and (c) perceive the results as providing a clear direction for future learning. To ensure that students perceive the assessment's purpose as being significant, you involve students in setting the goals, structure the goals so they are interdependent with the goals of significant others, structure the assessment and lesson so that joint efforts of group members are required, and highlight the relevance of the assessment to students' immediate lives. To ensure that the assessment procedures, criteria, and rubrics are clearly understood, you explain them and you involve students in creating them. To ensure the results are useful, you structure the assessment and lesson so that the results are used in planning the lesson and setting the learning goals.

If teachers feel overwhelmed by the demands of the assessment or are actually unable to commit the resources needed, then either the assessment will not be conducted or it will be conducted in a way that compromises its validity and reliability. If an assessment requires considerable time and effort but yields information that is seen as trivial, teachers will be less motivated to manage it. In the United States teachers' time and energy are in such high demand that little is left for assessment. Many of the most valuable and useful assessment procedures cannot be used unless student help is organized and utilized. You increase the manageability of an assessment when you mobilize the resources needed to conduct the assessment and ensure that the information you obtain is valuable enough to justify the resources expended.

When conducting an assessment of students, therefore, you expand the pool of available resources by utilizing student help in (a) setting the goals (thereby inducing student commitment to achieve the goals), (b) planning the assessment procedures and the criteria and rubrics to be used to assess their work, (c) collecting and analyzing the data, and (d) recording the results and communicating them to interested stakeholders. In general, the more meaningful students perceive the assessment to be, and the more students are involved in managing the assessment, the more effective and useful the assessment is (see Table 17.1).

Involving Students in Assessment

The key to meaning and manageability is student involvement. One teacher working by him- or herself can no longer manage the entire assessment system. The most natural sources of help for teachers are students and colleagues. Students provide the most help because they are available at all times. The more you involve students in setting the learning goals, planning the procedures and constructing the criteria and rubrics, conducting the assessments, analyzing the results to determine the direction and nature of future learning efforts, recording the results, and communicating the

TABLE 17.1 Meaningful and Manageable Assessment

LESS MEANINGFUL ASSESSMENT	MORE MEANINGFUL ASSESSMENT	LESS MANAGEABLE ASSESSMENT	MORE MANAGEABLE ASSESSMENT
Trivial Purpose	*Significant Purpose*	*Teacher-Only Resource*	*Teacher Resources Plus Student Help*
Goals imposed	Students help set goals	Imposed learning goals	Setting goals students are committed to achieve
Isolated goals	Interdependent goals	Imposed procedures	Deciding on procedures
Work alone	Joint efforts required	Teacher only	Collecting and analyzing data
Unrelated to students' lives	Relevant to students' lives	Teacher only	Recording and communicating results
Ambiguous Procedures	*Clear Procedures, Standards, Rubrics*		
Unexplained	Explained		
Imposed as is	Students help create them		
Unrelated to Future Efforts	*Provide Direction for Future Efforts*		
No useful information	Reveal gaps in learning		
No useful information	Reveal next learning goals		

results to interested stakeholders, the greater is the meaning attached to the assessment and the more manageable assessments become.

Students need to be involved in assessments for many reasons, not the least of which is that teachers' time is so limited that, without student help, very little assessment would actually take place. Involving students allows you to accomplish the following tasks:

1. Provide students with powerful learning experiences that increase their achievement. Assessing the accuracy, quantity, and quality of one's own and classmates' work tends to make the assessment process an important and potent learning experience.
2. Conduct more frequent assessments. Whereas teachers, for example, do not have the time to assess the quality of student writing and presenting every day, students can write and present every day and receive feedback from classmates.
3. Assess a wider variety of outcomes (see Activity 17.1). With student help it is possible to assess cognitive reasoning, skills and competencies, attitudes, and work habits as well as achievement.
4. Use more modalities in assessing students' work. Besides reading and writing, students can observe each other presenting, performing cognitive and social skills, or engaging in creative endeavors.
5. Provide more sources of information. Self- and peer assessments add important supplementary information to teacher assessments.
6. Reduce the bias inherent in making reading and writing prerequisites for engaging in a performance. Students who cannot read can listen to classmates' summaries and explanations, and students who cannot write can explain what they have learned orally.

ACTIVITY **17.1** ■ YOUR ASSESSMENT PLAN

Given below are generic assessment targets and procedures. In planning your assessment program, check the targets that you want to assess and then check the procedures you want to use. Match the procedures with the targets so it is clear how you will assess each target.

TARGETS TO BE ASSESSED	PROCEDURES USED TO ASSESS
_____ Academic learning	_____ Goal-setting conferences
_____ Reasoning process/strategies	_____ Standardized tests
_____ Skills and competencies	_____ Teacher-made tests
_____ Attitudes	_____ Written compositions
_____ Work habits	_____ Oral presentations
	_____ Projects
	_____ Portfolios
	_____ Observations
	_____ Questionnaires
	_____ Interviews
	_____ Learning logs and journals
	_____ Student management teams

7. Reduce the possibility of teacher bias. Even the most fair and well-meaning teacher has biases that affect assessments. Some teachers are biased toward neatness; others are biased toward complexity of reasoning. The more students are involved in the assessment process, the more peer assessments balance teacher biases.

8. Create social support systems for remediation and enrichment activities. The limits on teachers' time prevent teachers from monitoring all the time each student's efforts to learn and requires that only a sample be assessed. In small cooperative groups, classmates can continuously monitor each other's activities. In addition, some students are more susceptible to peer influence than teacher influence. Students can keep track of each other's level of mastery, hold each other accountable for learning, and encourage remediation efforts and extending one's competencies.

9. Assess group as well as individual outcomes. Numerous assignments involving creative and scientific projects can only be assessed at the group level. Unless students work together, such assignments cannot be given.

10. Make assessment procedures congruent with instructional practices. Because cooperative learning promotes higher achievement than does competitive, or individualistic, learning, most teachers use it. Utilizing cooperative groups for assessment purposes enables teachers to enhance instruction and assessment at the same time.

Need for Cooperative Learning

If students are to be involved in assessment, you have your choice of structuring that involvement in a competitive, individualistic, or cooperative way. You can create competitive involvement by ranking students on the basis of their involvement from best to worst. You can create individualistic involvement by having students work alone to attain a criteria of excellence for involvement. You can create cooperative involvement by having students work in small groups to help set and achieve the assessment goals. Of these three choices, cooperative involvement provides the most commitment and the most effort in the assessment process. Competitive and individualistic students are not very helpful in creating a high-quality and continuously improving assessment system. To provide quality assessment, students have to be committed to classmates' learning as well as their own. Such commitment only comes from clear, positive interdependence and individual accountability, promotive interaction, appropriate social skills, and group processing (the basic elements of cooperation).

Cooperative learning groups provide the setting, context, and environment in which assessment becomes part of the instructional process, and students learn almost as much from assessing the quality of their own and their classmates' work as they do from participating in instructional activities.

1. Cooperative learning allows assessment to be integrated into the learning process. Continuous assessment requires continuous monitoring and support, which can best be done within cooperative learning groups.
2. The new assessment practices are so labor intensive that students who are sincerely committed to each other's learning and success may need to be involved.
3. Cooperative learning groups allow more modalities to be used in the learning and assessment process while focusing on more diverse outcomes.
4. Cooperative learning groups allow groupmates, in addition to the teacher and curriculum materials, to be sources of information.
5. Involving groupmates in assessment reduces possible biases resulting from the teacher being the sole source of feedback and from the heavy reliance on reading and writing as assessment modalities.
6. Cooperative learning groups provide each student help in analyzing assessment data, interpreting the results, and implementing improvement plans.

It is difficult to imagine a class in which cooperative learning groups do not help make the assessment system more manageable or how a comprehensive assessment program can be managed without cooperative learning groups.

CONFERENCING WITH STUDENTS

Without clear learning and instructional goals, assessment cannot take place. The goals are created and reemphasized in three types of conferences with each student: (1) a goal-setting conference is conducted to establish a contract containing the student's learning goals, (2) progress assessment conferences are conducted to review the student's progress in achieving his or her goals, and (3) a postevaluation conference is conducted in which the student's accomplishments are explained to interested parties.

Assessment begins with a goal-setting conference in which the student's learning goals and responsibilities for helping other students learn are established. The goal-setting conference may be between the teacher and the student (T/S), the teacher and the cooperative learning group (T/G), the cooperative learning group and the student (G/S), and a cooperative learning group and another group (G/G). In all cases, the emphasis is on helping students set and take ownership for learning goals that meet the START criteria (specific, trackable, achievable, relevant, transferable). The goal-setting conference contains four steps: (1) diagnosis of current level of expertise, (2) setting START goals, (3) organizing support systems and resources to help each student achieve his or her goals successfully, and (4) constructing a plan for utilizing the resources to achieve the goals and formalizing the plan into a learning contract.

Progress assessment conferences provide wonderful opportunities for teachers to hear how students are thinking about their work. Some schools recommend that a student be interviewed at least once per month. An elementary school teacher would then have one progress assessment conference per day whereas a secondary school teacher may need to have four or five conferences per day. Group interviews provide another option.

The hard truth is that most teachers do not have the time to conference with each individual student, whether in a goal-setting conference, a progress assessment conference, or a postevaluation conference. This does not mean that such conferences cannot happen. Teachers can engineer and supervise such conferences through appropriate use of cooperative learning groups. Groups can regularly have progress assessment conferences with each member while the teacher listens in or pulls aside one individual student for a conference. Finally, postevaluation conferences can be held with the teacher, student, and parents. These conferences are especially interesting and fruitful when the student leads them.

ASSESSMENT PROCEDURES

Once students have formulated and agreed to their learning goals, a variety of assessment procedures can be used. The assessment procedures include tests, compositions, presentations, projects, portfolios, observations, interviews, questionnaires, and learning logs and journals.

Tests and Examinations

Both standardized and teacher-made tests may be used to assess student learning. Standardized tests are often high-stake events for which students need to be carefully prepared. Teacher-made tests are often a routine part of an instructional program to assess quickly and efficiently a broad sampling of students' knowledge. They may be multiple choice, true–false, matching, short answers, interpretative, or essay. Although many assessment procedures are effective, testing remains a mainstay in what teachers do. Cooperative learning groups may be tested using the GIG (group preparation–individual test–group test) procedure, group discussion, and Teams–Games–Tournament procedures.

Compositions and Presentations

Every educated person should be able to present what they know in written and oral form. These are difficult competencies, and students need to write and present every day to become skilled writers and presenters. This presents an assessment problem because someone has to read each composition, listen to each presentation, and provide helpful feedback. Using cooperative learning groups to assess members' performances accomplishes four goals at the same time. It allows students to engage in the performance frequently, receive immediate and detailed feedback on their efforts, observe closely the performances of others to see what is good or lacking in others' performances, and provide the labor needed to allow students to engage in a performance frequently.

Two of the most common performances assessed are compositions and presentations. In composition pairs, students are assigned to pairs; discuss and outline each other's composition in their pairs; research their topic alone; write the first paragraph of each composition in pairs; write the rest of the composition alone; edit each other's composition; rewrite the composition alone; re-edit each other's compositions; sign off on their partner's composition, verifying that it is ready to be handed in; and then process the quality of the partnership. The procedure for presentations is very similar.

Individual and Group Projects

A standard part of most every course is allowing students to be creative and inventive in integrating diverse knowledge and skills. This is especially important in assessing multiple intelligences and the ability to engage in complex procedures such as scientific investigation. Projects allow students to use multiple modes of learning. The use of cooperative learning groups allows projects to be considerably more complex and elaborate than any one student could do alone.

Portfolios

Students become far more sophisticated and educated when they can organize their work into a portfolio that represents the quality of their learning in a course or school year. There is no substitute for having students collect and organize their work samples and write a rationale connecting the work samples into a complete and holistic picture of the student's achievement, growth, and development. The resulting portfolio may feature the student's "best works" or the "process" the student is using to learn. Like all other complex and challenging tasks, students need considerable help in constructing their portfolios and in presenting them to teachers, parents, and other interested stakeholders. Portfolios, therefore, may be more manageable when they are constructed within cooperative learning groups. The group can help each member select appropriate work samples and write a coherent and clear rationale. The portfolio may also include the group's assessment of the student's learning and growth. An interesting extension of portfolios is to have the student, the teacher, and the student's cooperative learning group all independently decide on what represents the student's best work, and why. They then have a conference to compare their assessments and resolve any differences.

Observing

There is a limit to the information gained by having students turn in completed tests, compositions, projects, and portfolios. Answers on a test and completed homework assignments tell teachers whether students can arrive at a correct answer. They cannot, however, inform teachers as to the quality of the reasoning strategies students are using, students' commitment to classmates' success and well-being, or the extent to which students' can work effectively with others. Teachers must find a way to make students' covert reasoning processes overt, demonstrate behaviorally their attitudes and work habits, and show how skillfully they can work with others. Observing students in action thus becomes one of the most important assessment procedures.

Using observation as an assessment tool requires that you understand the basis of observing, know how to prepare for observing, know how to observe, and know how to summarize the data for use by students and other stakeholders. Preparing for observing involves deciding what actions to observe, who will observe, what the sampling plan will be, constructing an observation form, and training observers to use the form. Observations may be formal or informal, structured or unstructured. In summarizing observations, the data may be displayed in bar or run charts, feedback is then given to the students or other interested parties, and the recipients reflect on the feedback and set improvement goals.

One of the primary goals of observation procedures is to assess the use of social skills. The assessment of social skills consists of several steps. First, you review the assumptions underlying the teaching of social skills. Social skills must be learned. Every cooperative lesson is a lesson in social skills as well as academics. You must understand what social skills to teach and how to teach them. When teaching social skills, be specific, start small, and emphasize overlearning.

Second, you teach students each social skill. You show the need for the skill; define it with a T-chart; set up practice situations in which students can use the skill; ensure that students receive feedback on their use of the skill, reflecting on how to improve; and ensure that students persevere in practicing the skill until it becomes automatic. Third, as part of teaching students social skills, you structure cooperative learning situations so students can use the social skills and you can observe them doing so. Fourth, you intervene in the cooperative learning groups to ensure that members are using the social skills appropriately and to reinforce them for doing so.

Fifth, you facilitate students' self-diagnosis of their level of mastery of the targeted social skills. Students can complete checklists or questionnaires to do so. Sixth, you assign students to increase their social competence by having them set improvement goals. Seventh, you assess students' knowledge of social skills. Finally, you report on the level of students' social skills to interested stakeholders, such as students, parents, and potential employers.

Interviewing

Closely related to observing students in action is interviewing students. Like observing, interviews can make the covert overt through asking students more and more detailed questions about their reasoning processes and strategies. The strength of the interview is that it is personal and flexible. The personal nature of interviews allows you to build a more positive, supportive, and trusting relationship with each student. The flexibility of interviews allows you to interview either one student or a small group of students before, during, and after a lesson and to use the interview for both assessment and teaching purposes. Socrates is an example of a teacher who used interviewing as his major instructional strategy.

Attitude Questionnaires

All learning has affective components, and in many ways the attitudes students develop may be more important than their level of academic learning. Getting an A in math class, for example, does a student little good if he or she has learned to hate math and never wants to take a math class again. Obviously, loving math and wanting to take math courses throughout one's educational career is far more important than the level of achievement in any one math class. Attitudes largely determine whether students continue to study the subject area, become uninterested, or want to avoid it in the future.

In assessing student attitudes, you (a) decide which attitudes to measure, (b) construct a questionnaire, (c) select a standardized measure if it is appropriate, (d) administer the measures near the beginning and end of each instructional unit, semester, or year, (e) analyze and organize the data for feedback to interested stakeholders, (f) give the feedback in a timely and orderly way, and (g) use the results to make decisions about improving the instructional program. In constructing a questionnaire, each question needs to be well worded and requires either an open-ended (fill-in-the-blank or free response) or closed-ended (dichotomous, multiple-choice, ranking, or scale) response. The questions are then arranged in an appropriate sequence and given an attractive format. A standardized questionnaire, such as the Classroom Life instrument may be used to measure a broader range of student attitudes.

Learning Logs and Journals

Students often do not spend enough time reflecting on what they are learning and how it relates in a personal way to their lives. Learning logs and journals help students document and reflect on their learning experiences. Logs tend to emphasize short entries concerning the subject matter being studied. Logs are especially useful in conjunction with informal cooperative learning. Journals tend to emphasize more narrative entries concerning personal observations, feelings, and opinions in response to readings, events, and experiences. These entries often connect what is being studied in one class with other classes or with life outside the classroom. Journals are especially useful for having students apply what they are learning to their action theories.

Traditionally, assessment procedures have been quite limited. Teachers often notice the light in a student's eye, changes in voice inflections, the "aha" of discovery, the creative insight resulting from collaborating with others, the persistence and struggle of a student determined to understand complex material, the serendipitous use of skills and concepts beyond the context in which they were learned, and reports from parents and other teachers on the changes in a student resulting from a course of study. What has been lacking is a systematic way of collecting and reporting such evidence.

Times have changed. The diverse assessment procedures discussed in this book are quite developed and may be used effectively as part of any instructional program. Each has its strengths and its weaknesses. Each can be integrated into ongoing instructional programs and managed when they are used as part of cooperative learning. Together, they allow cooperative learning groups to engage in total quality learning.

TOTAL QUALITY LEARNING

Total quality learning begins with assigning students to teams and assigning them the task of continuously improving the quality of the processes of learning and assessment. Continuous improvement is the ongoing search for changes that increase the quality of the processes of learning, instructing, and assessing. Each time students write a composition, for example, they should find at least one way to improve their writing skills. The changes do not have to be dramatic. Small, incremental changes are fine.

To improve continuously the processes of learning and assessment, students need to engage in eight steps. First, they must form teams. Quality learning is not possible without cooperative learning groups. Second, team members analyze the assignment and select a learning process for improvement. Third, members define the process to improve, usually by drawing a flow chart or cause-and-effect diagram. Fourth, team members engage in the process. Fifth, students gather data about the process, display the data, and analyze it. Tools to help them do so include observation forms, Pareto charts, run charts, scatter diagrams, and histograms. Sixth, on the basis of the analysis, team members make a plan to improve the process. Seventh, students implement the plan by engaging in the learning process in a modified and improved way. Finally, the team institutionalizes the changes that do in fact improve the quality of the learning process.

One way to enhance the use of total quality learning is through the use of student management teams. A student management team consists of three or four students plus the instructor who assume responsibility for the success of the class by focusing on how to improve either the instructor's teaching or the content of the course. The group members monitor the course through their own experience and the comments of classmates. There are four stages of using student management teams: forming the team by recruiting and choosing members, building a cooperative team by structuring the five basic elements, improving the instruction and content of the course, and reaping the long-term gains from the process by carrying on the improvements to the next course.

TEACHING TEAMS AND ASSESSMENT

The days are gone when a teacher, working in isolation from colleagues, could instruct, assess, and report results by him- or herself. The practices have become so labor intensive and complex that one teacher cannot expect to do them alone. Realistically, colleagial teaching teams are needed to coordinate and continuously improve the instruction, assessment, and reporting process. Teachers need to begin their instruction, assessment, and reporting efforts with forming a colleagial teaching team. This allows them to capitalize on the many ways teams enhance productivity. The team focuses its efforts on continuously improving both student learning and the quality of instruction. The team as a whole conducts the assessment and reporting process by developing rubrics, applying the rubrics effectively, and reporting results to interested audiences. The team then establishes a continuous improvement process focusing on maximizing the quality of instruction for each member. While engaging in the continuous improvement process, the team also engages in continuous retraining, aimed at improving the effectiveness of their use of the assessment procedures. The use of colleagial teaching teams provides the framework for developing school-wide criteria and standards to be used in assessment.

GIVING GRADES

Teachers need to assess student learning and progress frequently, but only occasionally do they need to evaluate or give grades. Assessing involves checking on how students are doing, what they have learned, and what problems or difficulties they have experienced. Grades are symbols that represent a value judgment concerning the relative quality of a student's achievement during a specified period of instruction. Grades give students and other interested audiences information about (a) students' levels of achievement and (b) the success of the instructional program. Grades provide students access to certain educational opportunities, and reward students who excel. Grading systems may involve a single grade or multigrades. It is vital that grades are awarded fairly as they can have considerable influence on students' futures. Being fair includes using a wide variety of assignments to measure achievement. Grades may be supplemented with checklists and narratives to give a more complex and complete summative evaluation of student achievement. Having students work in cooperative groups adds further opportunity to measure aspects of students' learning and assign grades in a variety of ways.

LOOKING FORWARD

There is an old story about 12 men in a lifeboat. One of the men announces that he has decided to bore a series of holes in the bottom of the boat. "You can't do that," the other 11 men cry. "Why not?" the man answers. "I've divided the boat into 12 equal parts. Each of us has part of the boat. We can do anything to our part of the boat we want to. I've decided to drill holes in the bottom of my part. You do anything you want with your part. It's your right!" Although many people see the world in these terms, assessment does not work that way. Assessment is a community responsibility involving everyone in the classroom and school.

At the end of this book you may be at a new beginning. Years of experience are needed to gain real expertise in (a) integrating the assessment procedures into instruction and (b) capitalizing on the strengths of cooperative learning groups to help you do so. Involving students in the assessment process eventually results in more sophisticated students who can help you continuously improve the assessment process. For too long adults have had the sole proprietorship of assessment. The highest level of Bloom's Taxonomy (1976) is generating, holding, and applying a set of internal and external criteria. It is time that much of the responsibility for assessment is shared with students. Working jointly with students creates a learning community in which students' involvement in the assessment process enhances all aspects of learning and instruction.

Academic tournament: Objective test conducted in a game format whereby students study in cooperative learning groups, compete in tournament triads (consisting of students from three different cooperative learning groups) to determine who has learned the material the best, and take their scores back to their cooperative learning group and compute a total group score. The cooperative learning group with the highest score is recognized.

Achievement test: Test measuring knowledge and skills learned in school.

Action theory: Theory as to what actions are needed to achieve a desired consequence in a given situation.

Aptitude test: Test measuring potential maximum achievement of students.

Assessment: The collecting of information about the quality or quantity of a change in a student, group, teacher, or administrator.

Attitude: Learned disposition to respond in a favorable or unfavorable manner to a particular person, object, or idea.

Authentic assessment: Requiring students to demonstrate desired procedures and skills in "real-life" contexts.

Basic Standards Test: Measures skills in reading, writing, and math that students should have learned by a certain grade.

Benchmarking: Establishing criteria based on best-known practices.

Category system: The observer lists a set of categories so that every observed behavior can be recorded into one, and only one, of a series of mutually exclusive categories.

Cause-and-effect diagram: A visual diagram of the relationship between some effect and all its possible causes.

Closed-ended question: Calls for student to indicate the alternative answer closest to his or her internal response.

Colleagial teaching teams: Two to five faculty members whose purpose is to increase teachers' instructional expertise and success by working together to implement with fidelity and flexibility instructional assessment and reporting procedures as well as solve any implementation problems that may arise.

Competition: A social situation in which the goals of the separate participants are so linked that there is a negative correlation among their goal attainments; when one student achieves his or her goal, all others with whom he or she is competitively linked fail to achieve their goals.

Completion item: Students are required to supply a brief answer consisting of a name, word, phrase, or symbol.

Continuous improvement: Ongoing search by everyone involved for incremental changes to increase the quality of learning, instructing, and administrating processes.

Cooperation: Working together to accomplish shared goals and maximize one's own and others' success. Individuals perceiving that they can reach their goals if and only if the other group members also do so.

Cooperative base group: A long-term, heterogeneous cooperative learning group with stable membership.

Cooperative learning: Students working together to accomplish shared learning goals and maximize their own and their groupmates' achievement.

Criterion: A predetermined standard.

Criteria-referenced procedure: Assigns a value or grade to a student's performance according to preset criteria defining excellence on learning tasks or skills.

Deutsch, Morton: Social psychologist who theorized about cooperative, competitive, and individualistic goal structures.

Diagnostic assessment: The collection of information about a student's entry-level characteristics before an instructional unit, course, semester, or year.

Discrimination: When a norm-referenced measure is used, each item has to discriminate among students as high, medium, or low on the skill or knowledge being measured.

Distributive justice: Rewards may be distributed according to *equity* (the person who contributes the most or scores the highest receives the greatest reward), *equality* (every person receives the same reward), and *need* (those who have the greatest need receive the greatest reward).

Essay tests: Students are required to write paragraphs or themes as responses to a question.

Evaluation: Judging the merit, value, or desirability of a measured performance.

Event sampling: The observer records a given event or category of events each time it naturally occurs.

Exhaustive categories: Every instance of observed behavior can be classified into one of the available categories.

Expertise: A person's proficiency, adroitness, competence, and skill.

Feedback: Information that allows individuals to compare their actual performance with standards of performance.

Fermenting skills: Skills needed to reconceptualize the material being studied, resolve cognitive conflict, search for more information, and communicate the rationale behind one's conclusions.

Filter question: Question used to exclude a respondent from a particular sequence of questions if the questions are not relevant to him or her.

Flow chart: Visual representation showing all the steps of a process or procedure and how they relate to each other.

Focused interview: Arranges questions like a funnel so that the initial questions are broad and general and subsequent questions require the student to give more and more precise and specific answers.

Formal cooperative learning group: A learning group that may last for several minutes to several class sessions to complete a specific task or assignment (such as solving a set of problems, completing a unit, writing a theme or report, conducting an experiment, or reading and comprehending a story, play, chapter, or book.

Formative assessments: The periodic collection of information to provide students feedback concerning their progress toward achieving their learning goals.

Forming skills: Management skills directed toward organizing the group and establishing minimum norms for appropriate behavior.

Formulating skills: Skills directed toward providing the mental processes needed to build deeper-level understanding of the material being studied, to stimulate the use of higher-quality reasoning strategies, and to maximize mastery and retention of the assigned material.

Frequency distribution: A listing of the number of people who obtain each score or fall into each range of scores on a test.

Functioning skills: Skills directed toward managing the group's efforts to complete their tasks and maintain effective working relationships among members.

Funnel sequence: Begins with broad question and then progressively narrows down the scope of the questions until very specific questions are asked at the end.

GIG test procedure: A procedure for giving tests where students prepare for the test in cooperative learning groups, take the test individually, and then retake the test in their cooperative learning groups to clarify the answer to each question and provide immediate remediation for anything the student does not know.

Goal: A desired place toward which people are working; a state of affairs that people value.

Goal-setting conference: Conference in which each student sets personal learning goals and publicly commits him- or herself to achieve them.

Grades: Symbols (letters, numbers, words) that represent a value judgment concerning the relative quality of a student's achievement during a specified period of instruction.

Grade-equivalent scores: The average of the scores of all students in the norming sample at that grade level.

Group discussion test: Students meet in their cooperative base group and discuss the content of the assigned readings to verify that all members can meet a set of criteria in their understanding of the material covered.

Group portfolio: An organized collection accumulated over time of group work samples and individual work samples of each member.

Group processing: Reflecting on a group session to (a) describe what member actions were helpful and unhelpful and (b) make decisions about what actions to continue or change.

High-performance cooperative learning group: A group that meets all the criteria for being a cooperative group and outperforms all reasonable expectations, given its membership.

High-performance organizational structure: Quality of students' learning is determined by continuously improving the process of learning.

Histogram: Shows how continuous measurement data are clustered and dispersed.

Individual accountability: The measurement of whether each group member has achieved the group's goal. Assessing the quality and quantity of each member's contributions and giving the results to all group members.

Individualistic goal structure: No correlation among group members' goal attainments; when group members perceive that obtaining their goal is unrelated to the goal achievement of other members. Individuals working by themselves to accomplish goals unrelated to and independent from the goals of others.

Informal cooperative learning group: A temporary, ad hoc group that lasts for only one discussion or one class period. Its purposes are to focus student attention on the material to be learned, create an expectation set and mood conducive to learning, help organize in advance the material to be covered in a class session, ensure that students cognitively process the material being taught, and provide closure to an instructional session.

Instruction: Structuring situations in ways that help students change, through learning.

Interpretive items: Students are required to study a graph, diagram, map, or descriptive paragraph, and interpret what it means.

Interview: A situation in which both the interviewer and the respondent are present when the questions are asked and answered.

Kaizen: A societywide covenant of mutual help in the process of getting better and better, day after day.

Learning: A change within a student that is brought about by instruction.

Learning goal: A desired future state of demonstrating competence or mastery in the subject area being studied, such as conceptual understanding of math processes, facility in the proper use of a language, or mastering the procedures of inquiry.

Learning journal: Self-report procedure in which students record narrative, personal entries concerning aspects of the subject matter being studied that has personal value and relevance. Entries may be personal observations, feelings, or opinions in response to readings, events, and experiences.

Learning log: A self-report procedure in which students record short entries concerning the subject matter being studied.

Likert scale: A question with a response scale of anywhere from 3 to 9 points.

Mass-production organizational structure: Quality of students' learning is determined by inspecting the final outcome to see if it is adequate or needs improvement.

Matching item: List of concepts and responses; students match one response with each concept.

Mean: The sum of all scores divided by the number of individuals.

Median: The midpoint in the set of scores arranged in order from highest to lowest.

Motivation: A combination of the perceived likelihood of success and the perceived incentive for success. The greater is the likelihood of success and the more important it is to succeed, the higher is the motivation.

Multigrade system: Contains different grades for different aspects of learning. Grades may focus on *product criteria, process criteria,* and *progress criteria.*

Multiple-choice items: Direct question or incomplete statement (called the stem) followed by two or more possible answers (called responses), only one of which is to be selected.

Mutually exclusive categories: Categories that are precisely distinguishable and independent from each other.

Normal curve equivalent (NCE) score: Standard score with a range from 1 to 99, a mean of 50, and a standard deviation of about 21.

Norm-referenced procedure: Assigns a value or grade to a score based on a comparison to other scores.

Norm-referenced tests: Designed to test a student's performance as it compares to the performances of other students.

Objective tests: Tests whose items are easily scored and analyzed, given to large numbers of students, take very little time to administer and score, and are free of bias in scoring and in requiring unrelated skills, such as writing.

Objectivity: The agreement of (a) experts on the correct answer to a test item and (b) different scorers on what score should be assigned to a test paper or questionnaire.

Observation: Recording and describing behavior as it occurs.

Observation checklist: A record-keeping device for teachers to keep track of the degree to which each student has demonstrated a targeted behavior, action, skill, or procedure.

Observation form: Used to tally and count the number of times a behavior, action, or event is observed in a specified time period.

Open-ended question: Calls for students to answer by writing a statement that may vary in length.

Oral examination: Students are interviewed about what they have learned.

Pareto chart: A form of vertical bar chart that helps teams separate the vital few problems and causes from the trivial many. It takes its name from the Italian economist Vilfredo Frederico Damaso Pareto (1848–1923).

Pareto principle (80/20 rule):   80 percent of the trouble comes from 20 percent of the problems.

Percentile rank: The percentage of the class with scores below that obtained by the student (ranges from 0 to 100).

Performance assessment: Students are required to engage in a set of actions to demonstrate their level of skill in enacting a procedure or creating a product.

Portfolio: An organized collection of evidence accumulated over time on a student's or group's academic progress, achievements, skills, and attitudes. Two common types are best works portfolios and process portfolios.

Positive interdependence: The perception that you are linked with others in a way so that you cannot succeed unless they do (and vice versa); that is, their work benefits you and your work benefits them.

Postevaluation conference: Conference in which the level of student achievement is explained by the student to interested parties.

Practicality: The cost per copy, the time it takes to administer, the ease of scoring, and other factors teachers have to take into account before deciding to use a particular measure.

Procedural learning: Learning conceptually what the skill is, when it should be used, how to engage in the skill, and practicing the skill while eliminating errors until an automated level of mastery is attained.

Process: All the tasks, organized in a sequence, that contribute to the accomplishment of one particular outcome.

Process criteria: An evaluation of students that focuses on the processes students use to learn including effort and work habit.

Product criteria: A summative evaluation of student achievement that focuses on what students know and are able to do.

Progress assessment conference: A conference in which the student's progress toward achieving his or her goals is reviewed.

Progress criteria: A summative evaluation of student achievement that focuses on improvement scoring or gains in learning.

Project: An assignment aimed at having students produce something themselves on a topic related to the curriculum rather than just "reproduce" knowledge.

Protocol: Agreed on guidelines that structure and guide teachers' conversations regarding assessment and students.

Pseudo group: A group whose members have been assigned to work together but they have no interest in doing so. The structure promotes competition at close quarters.

Psychological health: Ability to build and maintain cooperative, interdependent relationships with other people.

Quality chart: Shows the extent to which the quality or quantity of performance is increasing or decreasing over time.

Reliability: When a student's performance remains the same on repeated measurements.

Reliable assessment: Occurs when a student's performance remains the same on repeated measures.

Rubric: Indicators of different levels of a criterion being used to assess a performance.

Run chart: Used to monitor a process over time to see whether the long-range average is changing.

Sampling plan: A course of action specifying in what order you observe each learning group for what amount of time.

Scatter diagram: Displays the relationship between two actions, conditions, or causes.

Scoring criteria drift: When, after assessing numerous performances, the assessor's definition of the criteria (and rubrics) changes or is modified; new idiosyncratic rubrics are created as the assessor gains more and more experience.

Self-assessment: Reflection on how well a person performed academically and how often and how well a person performed the targeted social or cognitive skills.

Semantic differential: A series of rating scales of bipolar adjective pairs referring to the concept for which a person wants to obtain student attitudes.

Short-answer item: Requires students to supply a brief answer consisting of a name, word, or phrase, or symbol.

Short-essay item: Requires students to recall, explain, and apply (in their own words) specific information they have learned.

Sign system: Listing beforehand a limited number of specific kinds of behavior of interest, and recording only those behaviors that fall into one of the categories.

Small group interview: Verbal questions are asked of a group of respondents who give verbal responses. Often used to assess whether all group members have mastered and understood assigned material.

Social competence: Extent to which a person can use interpersonal and small group skills to ensure that the consequences of his or her actions match his or her intentions.

Social skills: The interpersonal and small group skills needed to interact effectively with other people.

Socratic interviewing: Procedure for using an interview to lead students to deeper and deeper insights about what they know.

Standard deviation: Average of the differences of all students' scores from the mean score.

Standard score: Indication of how far each student is above or below the mean in a way that allows comparison of scores from different tests, regardless of the size of the class or the number of items on the test. Found by subtracting the mean from the student's raw score and dividing by the standard deviation.

Standardized tests: Tests prepared for nationwide use to provide accurate and meaningful information on students' levels of performance relative to others at their age or grade; information on students' levels of performance relative to others at their age or grade levels.

Stanine score: Standard score with mean of 5 and a standard deviation of 2.

Structured coding system: Requires observers to categorize each group behavior into an objectively definable category.

Student management team: Three or four students plus the instructor assume responsibility for the success of the course by focusing on how to improve either the instructor's teaching or the content of the course.

Student performance: Set of actions demonstrating level of skill in enacting a procedure or creating a product.

Summative assessment: The collection of information at the end of an instructional unit to judge the final quality and quantity of student achievement and/or the success of the instructional program.

T-chart: Procedure to teach social skills by specifying the nonverbal actions and verbal phrases that operationalize the skill.

Teacher-made tests: Written or oral assessments of student achievement that are (a) not commercially produced or standardized and (b) designed specifically for the teacher's students.

Test blueprint: An analysis of a test to ensure that it covers a representative, accurate sample of what is covered in the learning unit.

Test norms: Records of the performances of groups of individuals who have previously taken the test.

Time sampling: The observer records the occurrence or nonoccurrence of selected behavior(s) within specified, uniform time limits.

Traditional learning group: A group whose members agree to work together, but see little benefit from doing so. The structure promotes individualistic work with talking.

Transfer: Person taking what he or she learned in one setting and using it in another setting.

True–false item: A fact, statement, definition, or principle followed by two responses: true or false.

Unstructured observations: Recording in a notebook or index cards significant, specific events involving students.

Valid assessment: An assessment that assesses what it was designed to assess, all of what it was designed to assess, and nothing but what it was designed to assess.

Validity: Validity means that the test actually measures what it was designed to measure, all of what it was designed to measure, and nothing but what it was designed to measure.

Z-scores: Standard score with a mean of 0 and standard deviation of 1.

REFERENCES

Afflerbach, P., & Sammons, R. (1991). *Report cards in literacy evaluation: Teachers' training, practices, and values.* Paper presented at the National Reading Conference, Palm Springs, CA.

Astin, A. (1985). Involvement: The cornerstone of excellence. *Change,* July/August, 35–39.

Austin, S., & McCann, R. (1992). *Here's another arbitrary grade for your collection: A statewide study of grading policies.* Paper presented at the American Educational Research Association, San Francisco.

Bailey, J., & Guskey, T. (2001). *Implementing student-led conferences.* Thousand Oaks, CA: Corwin Press.

Baron, J. (1994, April). *Using multi-dimensionality to capture verisimilitude: Criterion-referenced performance-based assessments and the ooze factor.* Paper presented at the annual meeting of the American Educational Research Association, New Orleans, LA.

Bennett, R., Gottesman, R., Rock, D., & Cerullo, F. (1993). Influence of behavior perceptions and gender on teachers' judgments of students' academic skill. *Journal of Educational Psychology, 85,* 347–356.

Bloom, B. (1976). *Human characteristics and school learning.* New York: McGraw-Hill.

Brookhart, S. (1993). Teachers' grading practices: Meaning and values. *Journal of Educational Measurement, 30*(2), 123–142.

Canady, R., & Hotchkiss, P. (1989). It's a good score! Just a bad grade. *Phi Delta Kappan, 71,* 68–71.

Cangelosi, J. (1990). Grading and reporting student achievement. In *Designing tests for evaluating student achievement* (pp. 196–213). New York: Longman.

Chastain, K. (1990). Characteristics of graded and ungraded compositions. *Modern Language Journal, 74*(1), 10–14.

Connecticut State Board of Education. (1991). *Common Core of Learning Assessment.* Hartford, CT: Author.

Connecticut State Board of Education. (1992/1994). *Connecticut Academic Performance Test.* Hartford, CT: Author.

Davis, A., & Felknor, C. (1994). The demise of performance based graduation in Littleton. *Educational Leadership, 51*(6), 64–65.

Deutsch, M. (1949). A theory of cooperation and competition. *Human Relations, 2,* 129–152.

Deutsch, M. (1962). Cooperation and trust: Some theoretical notes. In M. R. Jones (Ed.), *Nebraska symposium on motivation* (pp. 275–319). Lincoln: University of Nebraska Press.

Deutsch, M. (1985). *Distributive justice.* New Haven, CT: Yale University Press.

Deutsch, M. (1979). Education and distributive justice: Some reflections on grading systems. *American Psychologist, 34,* 391–401.

DeVries, D. & Edwards, K. (1974). Student teams and learning games: Their effects on cross-race and cross-sex interaction. *Journal of Educational Psychology, 66,* 741–749.

Ebel, R. (1979). *Essentials of educational measurement* (3rd ed.). Englewood Cliffs, NJ: Prentice-Hall.

Feldmesser, R. (1971). *The positive functions of grades.* Paper presented at the American Educational Research Association Convention, New York.

Frary, R., Cross, L., & Weber, J. (1993). Testing and grading practices for instruction and measurement. Educational Measurement: *Issues and Practices, 12*(3), 23–30.

Frisbie, D., & Waltman, K. (1992). Developing a personal grading plan. *Educational Measurement: Issues and Practices, 11*(3), 35–42.

Guskey, T. (1994). Making the grade: What benefits students? *Educational Leadership, 52*(2), 14–20.

Guskey, T., & Bailey, J. (2001). *Developing grading and reporting systems for student learning.* Thousand Oaks, CA: Corwin Press.

Gronlund, N. (1998). *Assessment of student achievement* (6th ed.). New York: Macmillan.

Hills, J. (1991). Apathy concerning grading and testing. *Phi Delta Kappan, 72*(2), 540–545.

Johnson, D. W. (1970). *Social psychology of education.* New York: Holt, Rhinehart, & Winston.

Johnson, D. W. (1991). *Human relations and your career* (3rd ed.). Englewood Cliffs, NJ: Prentice Hall.

Johnson, D. W. (2000). *Reaching out: Interpersonal effectiveness and self-actualization* (7th ed.). Englewood Cliffs, NJ: Prentice Hall.

Johnson, D. W., & Johnson, F. (2000). *Joining together: Group theory and group skills* (7th ed.). Englewood Cliffs, NJ: Prentice Hall.

Johnson, D. W., & Johnson, R. (1983). Social interdependence and perceived academic and personal support in the classroom. *Journal of Social Psychology, 120,* 77–82.

Johnson, D. W., & Johnson, R. (1985). Impact of classroom organization and instructional methods on the effectiveness of mainstreaming. In C. Meisel (Ed.), *Mainstreamed handicapped children: Outcomes, controversies, and new directions* (pp. 215–250). Mahwah, NJ: Lawrence Erlbaum.

Johnson, D. W., & Johnson, R. (1989). *Cooperation and competition: Theory and research.* Edina, MN: Interaction Book Company.

Johnson, D. W., & Johnson, R. (1991a). Cooperative learning and classroom and school climate. In B. Fraser & H. Walberg (Eds.), *Educational environments: Evaluation, antecedents and consequences.* New York: Pergamon.

Johnson, D. W., & Johnson, R. (1991b). What cooperative learning has to offer the gifted. *Cooperative Learning, 11*(3), 24–27.

Johnson, D. W., & Johnson, R. (1994). *Leading the cooperative school* (2nd ed.). Edina, MN: Interaction Book Company.

Johnson, D. W., & Johnson, R. (1995a). *Teaching students to be peacemakers.* Edina, MN: Interaction Book Company.

Johnson, D. W., & Johnson R. (1995b). *My mediation notebook.* Edina, MN: Interaction Book Company.

Johnson, D. W., & Johnson, R. (1995c). *Creative controversy: Intellectual challenge in the classroom.* Edina, MN: Interaction Book Company.

Johnson, D. W., & Johnson, R. (1999). *Learning together and alone: Cooperative, competitive, and individualistic learning* (5th ed.). Boston: Allyn & Bacon.

Johnson, D. W., Johnson, R., & Anderson, D. (1983). Social interdependence and classroom climate. *Journal of Psychology, 114,* 135–142.

Johnson, D. W., Johnson, R., & Holubec, E. (1993). *Circles of learning: Cooperation in the classroom* (4th ed.). Edina, MN: Interaction Book Company.

Johnson, D. W., Johnson, R., & Holubec, E. (1998a). *Cooperation in the classroom* (6th ed.). Edina, MN: Interaction Book Company.

Johnson, D. W., Johnson, R., & Holubec, E. (1998b). *Advanced cooperative learning* (3rd ed.). Edina, MN: Interaction Book Company.

Johnson, D. W., Johnson, R., & Holubec, E. (1995). *The nuts and bolts of cooperative learning.* Edina, MN: Interaction Book Company.

Johnson, D. W., Johnson, R., & Smith, K. (1998). *Active learning: Cooperation in the college classroom.* (2nd ed.). Edina, MN: Interaction Book Company.

Miles, M. (Ed.). (1964). *Innovation in education.* New York: Teachers College Press.

Middleton, W. (1933). Some general trends in grading procedure. *Education, 54*(1), 5–10.

Nava, F., & Loyd, B. (1992). *An investigation of achievement and nonachievement criteria in elementary and secondary school grading.* Paper presented at the American Educational Research Association, San Francisco.

O'Donnell, A., & Woolfolk, A. (1991). *Elementary and secondary teachers' beliefs about testing and grading.* Paper presented at the American Psychological Association Convention, San Francisco.

Ornstein, A. (1994). Grading practices and policies: An overview and some suggestions. *NASSP Bulletin, 78,* 55–64.

Osgood, C., Suci, C., & Tannenbaum, P. (1957). *The measurement of meaning.* Urbana: University of Illinois Press.

Page, E. (1958). Teacher comments and student performance: A seventy-four classroom experiment in school motivation. *Journal of Educational Psychology, 49,* 173–181.

Peters, T., & Waterman, R. (1982). *In search of excellence.* New York: Harper & Row.

Schwartz, R. (1996). Student management teams. *ASEE Prism,* January, 19–23.

Selby, D., & Murphy, S. (1992). Graded or degraded: Perceptions of letter-grading for mainstreamed learning disabled students. *British Columbia Journal of Special Education, 16*(1), 92–104.

Shavelson, R., Gao, X., & Baxter, G. (1991). *Design theory and psychometrics for complex performance assessment: Transfer and generalizability.* Los Angeles: University of California, Center for Research on Evaluation, Standards, and Student Testing.

Starch, D., & Elliott, E. (1912). Reliability of the grading of high school work in English. *School Review, 20,* 442–459.

Starch, D., & Elliott, E. (1913). Reliability of the grading of high school work in mathematics. *School Review, 21,* 254–259.

Stiggins, R. (1994). Communicating with report card grades. In R. Stiggins (Ed.), *Student-centered classrooom assessment* (pp. 363–396). New York: Macmillan.

Stiggins, R. (1988, January). Revitalizing classroom assessment: The highest instructional priority. *Phi Delta Kappan,* 363–368.

Stiggins, R., & Duke, D. (1991). *District grading policies and their potential impact on at-risk students.* Paper presented at the American Educational Research Association, Chicago.

Stiggins, R., Frisbie, D., & Griswold, P. (1989). Inside high school grading practices: Building a research agenda. *Educational Measurement: Issues and Practice, 8*(2), 5–14.

Swain, M., & Swaim, S. (1999). Teacher time. *Amercian Educator, 23*(3), 1–6.

Sweedler-Brown, C. (1992). The effect of training on the appearance bias of holistic essay graders. *Journal of Research and Development in Education, 26*(1), 24–29.

Watson, G., & Johnson, D. W. (1972). *Social psychology: Issues and insights* (2nd ed.). Philadelphia: Lippincott.

White, N., Blythe, T., & Gardner, H. (1992). Multiple intelligences theory: Creating the thoughtful classroom. In A. Costa, J. Bellanca, & R. Fogarty (Eds.), *If minds matter: A foreword to the future,* Volume II (pp. 127–134). Palatine, IL: IRI/Skylight Publishing.

INDEX